The Peckham Set
1896 - 2000

A Story of Poverty, Privilege, Pioneering and Partnership

The Peckham Settlement, 2000

By

Jennifer Stephens BEd, MSc.

Published by Stephens Press

Published 2002 by Stephens Press
Bickton
Fordingbridge
Hampshire
SP6 2HA

ISBN 0-9542598-0-7

Printed and bound in Great Britain by RPM Reprographics
2-3 Spur Road, Quarry Lane Industrial Estate, Chichester, West Sussex, PO19 8PR

KENSINGTON PALACE
W8 4PU

It is with pleasure that I write a foreword to this history of Peckham Settlement.

My Grandmother, Queen Mary, was especially interested in the Peckham area of London. She visited the Pitt Street Mission and the Union of Girls' Schools for Social Service, as The Peckham Settlement was then called, in Peckham Road, before opening the present building in Staffordshire Street in 1931. Following my Grandmother's example, I became its Patron in 1947, one of my first Patronages.

The Union of Girls' Schools for Social Service was one of the first settlements to encourage schoolgirls to work in practical ways to alleviate poverty and the social ills of the inner city. I remember going to the Settlement in 1948, where I spoke with the people who used its facilities and some of the girls whose schools supported its work. The Lord Bishop of Southwark, The Right Reverend Mervyn Stockwood, whose Diocese included the Parishes in Peckham, also kept me acquainted with the work at the Settlement.

During many years of Patronage, I have followed the Settlement's progress with great interest, and have been present on many occasions, both to meet those closely involved and to celebrate landmarks in its history. The Settlement represents a fine example of pioneering and dedicated voluntary work. The way in which it has adapted to the modern world and contributed to the very different and complex problems that need to be solved is to be admired and applauded. It was a particular joy to return to the Settlement in February 1999, where I was presented with a beautifully inscribed dish to commemorate my 50 years of Patronage.

I am very pleased to be associated with The Peckham Settlement. I hope that future generations will maintain these same high standards of social service and continue this most valuable work for the people of Peckham.

January 2001 Margaret

Contents

FOREWORD 1

ILLUSTRATIONS 5

CHRONOLOGY OF EVENTS 9

INTRODUCTION 13

CHAPTER 1 15

THE SETTLEMENT MOVEMENT

CHAPTER 2 17

THE BIRTH OF THE PECKHAM SETTLEMENT

CHAPTER 3 21

THE WORK AND ACTIVITIES OF THE SETTLEMENT

Community Development *24*

Activities Concerning Housing *25*

Activities Concerning Unemployment *26*

Activities Concerning Poverty *28*

Activities Concerning Education *31*

Activities Concerning Health *42*

Activities Concerning Social Needs *45*

Social Activities *50*

The Friends *54*

The Present *56*

CHAPTER 4 58

THE RELIGIOUS INFLUENCE

Formal Church Services *59*

The Mission Work *64*

CHAPTER 5 .... **68**

THE NEIGHBOURHOOD AND THE SETTLEMENT BUILDINGS

The Neighbourhood *71*

The Settlement Building *75*

The Interior Rooms *77*

CHAPTER 6 .... **84**

THE ROLE OF THE SUPPORTING SCHOOLS

How the Schools and OGAs Supported the Settlement *85*

Training and Education *92*

The Old Girls' Associations *97*

The Changing Nature of Social Service Support by the Schools *98*

The Schools' Inheritance *106*

CHAPTER 7 .... **110**

INCOME AND EXPENDITURE

From Inception to World War Two *110*

The Heyday of the UGSS, 1946-1972 .... *114*

The Expansive Era of 1972 to 1985 .... *121*

The Years of Difficulty *125*

The Present, 1997 to 2000 .... *129*

CHAPTER 8 .... **131**

THE VISITS OF THE PATRON, HRH THE PRINCESS MARGARET

DRAMATIS PERSONAE 1896 TO 2000 .... **138**

REFERENCES **139**

PHOTOGRAPHS AND ILLUSTRATIONS **144**

APPENDIX: ACRONYMS **146**

ACKNOWLEDGEMENTS **147**

BOOK AND DOCUMENT LIST **149**

INDEX **152**

Illustrations

1	*The Peckham Settlement, 2000*	*1*
2	*The Reverend Harry Veasey, 1896*	*18*
3	*Canon Harry Veasey, 1946*	*18*
4	*Jane Francis Dove, 1896*	*18*
5	*UGSM Church Hall & Clergy House, Kempshead Road, circa 1900*	*19*
6	*UGSM Church Hall & Clergy House, Kempshead Road, circa 1940*	*19*
7	*UGS Settlement, Peckham Road, 1906 – 1930*	*20*
8	*Club Rooms & Gardens, Peckham Road*	*20*
9	*The Wildlife Area, 1985*	*22*
10	*Furniture Making using Barrels, circa 1975*	*26*
11	*A Helping Hand at the Job Club, 1990*	*27*
12	*Princess Margaret visiting the Friary Open Learning Centre, 1999*	*28*
13	*Mary Pittard, 1968*	*29*
14	*Mary Pittard, 1975*	*29*
15	*Mary Pittard, 1986*	*30*
16	*The Mums' Library, circa 1950*	*31*
17	*Summer Play Scheme, Richmond Park, 1971 and Peckham Rye 1972*	*32*
18	*Peckham Summer Youth Projects, 1992*	*33*
19	*Mother & Toddler Clubs, 1973 and 1982*	*34*
20	*Lady Astor Opening the Nursery School, 1935*	*34*
21	*The Nursery School, circa 1938*	*35*
22	*The Nursery School at Glyndebourne, 1944*	*35*
23	*The Nursery School in the Settlement Garden, 1956*	*37*
24	*Children in the Nursery School, 1965*	*39*
25	*Princess Margaret's visit to the Nursery School, 1982*	*40*
26	*The Fence dividing the Two Nursery Schools*	*41*
27	*The All Nations Nursery School, 2000*	*42*
28	*The Nursery Play Area, 2000*	*42*
29	*The Old People's Foot Clinic, 1950s*	*43*
30	*The Old People's Dinner Club, late 1940s and 1956*	*43*
31	*Meals on Wheels, late 1950s*	*44*
32	*At Ramsgate, 1965*	*45*
33	*Visiting, 1975*	*46*
34	*The Youth Club, 1955*	*48*
35	*The Youth Club, 1982*	*48*
36	*The Mums' Club, 1950s*	*50*
37	*The Mums' Club Outing, 1967*	*51*
38	*The Youth Club Band, 1956*	*51*
39	*Cinderella, 1960*	*52*
40	*The Make-Do-and-Mend Club, 1950s*	*52*

41 *Jane Johnson Sings at the Friday Club, 1967* *53*
42 *The Wednesday Club, 1966* *53*
43 *The Squirrels, 1950s* *53*
44 *The Acorns, 1950s* *53*
45 *The Pensioners' Pop-In, 1985* *54*
46 *Miss Cousins Receives the Stage from the Peckham Road Fire Station, 1958* *55*
47 *The Friends Hand Over the Blue Van, 1970* *55*
48 *Reverend Harry Veasey* *58*
49 *Wing Commander Baker Reading the Lesson at the Annual Service* *61*
50 *School Girls Attending the Annual Service, Southwark Cathedral, 1960s* *61*
51 *The Parish Church of St John's 1966* *62*
52 *The Right Reverend Mervyn Stockwood, The Right Reverend Michael Marshall, Lady Howe and the Pearly King and Queen of Peckham at the 80th Birthday Event, 1976* *63*
53 *The Cover for the Order of Service for the 90th Birthday Celebrations, 1986* *63*
54 *Archbishop of Canterbury at the Settlement, 1986* *64*
55 *The Chapel, 1965* *65*
56 *The Right Reverend Bertram Simpson, 1970* *66*
57 *The Reverend Geoffrey Heal, Vicar of St John's Church, 1964* *67*
58 *Peckham Settlement, 2000* *68*
59 *Peckham Settlement showing the Old Wesleyan Chapel, 2000* *68*
60 *Queen Mary Passing Mr Heard's Sweet Shop on Her Way to Open the Settlement, 1931* *69*
61 *Queen Mary Receiving Purses at the Opening of the Settlement, 1931* *69*
62 *UGS Settlement, 1935* *70*
63 *The Goldsmith Road Houses, 2000* *70*
64 *The Pickle Factory, circa 1950* *71*
65 *Demolition of the Pickle Factory. The Wildlife Garden is seen in the Background, 1996* *72*
66 *The Environs of the Settlement, circa 1975* *73*
67 *The New Housing in Staffordshire Street. The Travellers' Site is in the Background, 2000* *74*
68 *The Entrance to the Settlement in Goldsmith Road, 1997* *76*
69 *The Stage in the Hall 1960* *78*
70 *The Hall Showing the Polished Dance Floor, 2000* *79*
71 *The Spiral Staircase, 2000* *79*
72 *Painting the Mural, 1999* *81*
73 *The Finished Mural, 1999* *81*
74 *The New Improved Play Area, 2000* *82*
75 *The Old Wesleyan School Building is Exposed after the Demolition of Surrounding Buildings, 1996* *82*
76 *Paddy Cribb, the Chairman of the Executive Council Presents Leaving Certificates to George and Ann Smith, Caretaker and Cleaner of the Settlement Building for Many Years, 1997* *83*
77 *Jumble Sales in the 1940s and 1970s* *88*
78 *Mission Day at Wycombe Abbey, 1904* *89*
79 *The Pensioners Visit to Sydenham High School, 1999* *89*
80 *The Friday Club Visit to Bellerby's College, 1999* *89*
81 *The Thursday Club Prepare to Visit Wycombe Abbey, 1999* *90*
82 *A 'Mish' Kid at Wycombe Abbey, 1920s* *90*

83 *Jennie Fisher Lighting Candles at the Old People's Christmas Party, 1966* **93**
84 *Eve Keatley (on the left of the picture) Helping at the Old People's Christmas Party, 1966* **93**
85 *The Urban Studies Centre at the Settlement, 1977* **96**
86 *Students on an Urban Trail, 1982* **96**
87 *Elsie Bowerman, 1947* **101**
88 *Grace Griffiths (standing) at the Christmas Party, 1966* **102**
89 *Joan Kirby OBE Talking to Princess Margaret, 1999* **102**
90 *Mary Rose Bateman (centre) with Girls Who Took Part in the Windsor Great Park Sponsored Walk, 1986* ... **104**
91 *Members from Supporting Schools at Princess Margaret's Visit to the Settlement, 1999 Lady Howe, Gill Fletcher-Watson, Reverend Richard Warden (all from Wycombe Abbey) and Jennifer Stephens (James Allen's Girls' School)* **109**
92 *Miss Joyce Baxter, Warden of the Settlement, 1955-1957* **114**
93 *The Cover of the UGS Record, Spring, 1949* **115**
94 *Wing Commander C.H. Baker, Warden of the Settlement, 1964 - 1972* **118**
95 *The UGS Review No. 1 Autumn, 1965* **119**
96 *A Group of Settlement Residents Meet with John Lane, Director of the Settlement 1972 - 1977 (far right), and Geoffrey Heal* **120**
97 *The Winner Takes Possession of the Mini-Car, 1976* **121**
98 *Dr Martin Pickstone, Director of the Settlement, 1977 - 1985* **123**
99 *Mr E. F. T. (Paddy) Cribb, Chairman of the Executive Committee since 1981* **125**
100 *Mrs Kitty Leek, Director of the Settlement, 1986 - 1997* **125**
101 *Mr David Kitchen, MBE, the Present Director of the Settlement with a Child in the Nursery.* **129**
102 *David Kitchen, Florrie Whale, Michael Franks and Derek Lowman serving out Christmas Dinner at the Settlement, 1998* **130**
103 *Princess Margaret 1947* **131**
104 *Princess Margaret at the Settlement 1948* **131**
105 *Princess Margaret 1956* **132**
106 *Princess Margaret at the Royal Festival Hall, May 9th 1956* **132**
107 *Princess Margaret Visits the Settlement, 1960* **134**
108 *Princess Margaret Visits the Settlement, 1972* **135**
109 *Princess Margaret Meets Members of the Youth Club, 1982* **135**
110 *Princess Margaret at the Settlement, 1999, with Paddy Cribb, Chairman of the Executive Board, Baroness Howe, President and David Kitchen, Director* **136**
111 *Princess Margaret Presents Florrie Whale with a Crystal Bowl, 1999* **137**

Chronology of Events

1895 First discussion on setting up a Settlement for young ladies.

1896 UGSM [United Girls' Schools Mission] set up in St. Mark's Parish, Camberwell in a building on the corner of Calmington Road and Longcroft Road, Camberwell.

1897 First Mission room opened in Kempshead Road. First Annual Service held on March 4th.

1898 First outing for Mission inhabitants to Wycombe Abbey.

1902 Clubrooms and Mission Hall opened in Kempshead Road by HRH the Princess Christian. Rev Harry Veasey appointed vicar of St Mark's Church. ICAA [Invalid Children's Aid Association] financed by Wycombe Abbey.

1906 Move to 19 Peckham Road. Georgina Gooch appointed first warden. Henrietta McArthur died.

1907 Georgina Gooch died. 17 Peckham Road added to Mission site. Miss de Burgho- Hodge became Warden.

1908 Second Mission district of St Andrew's added. Miss Dove addressed Ruri-Decanal Conference. Princess Christian opened the Lads' Club and the Men's House in Kempshead Road. The Melanesian Mission in the South Seas opened.

1910 Bishop Edward Stuart Talbot left Southwark.

1911 Dr Burge, Bishop of Southwark became Warden.

1913 Settlement in Quesnal, British Columbia, Canada, opened. First UGS Infant Welfare Clinic opened.

1914 Outbreak of First World War. UGSM had 160 supporting Schools and 65 Old Girls' Associations.

1915 The Quesnal Settlement closed.

1918 The 21st anniversary of the Settlement celebrated.

1920 The Constitution was revised to include Old Girls on Executive Council.

1922 Miss R E Green became Warden.

1923 The first holiday play scheme started in the gardens of 19 Peckham Road.

1924 Name changed to UGSSS [The Union of Girls' Schools for Social Service]. 15 Peckham Road added. First Social Service weekend conference held. Free legal advice centre opened. Third mission district of St. Chrysostom's added.

1926 First issue of UGS Record. The Prime Minister, Stanley Baldwin, addressed the Annual General Meeting.

1927 Miss Frances Dove resigned from the Settlement Council.

1928 Miss Dove became Dame of the British Empire. Peckham Road site sold to LCC [London County Council].

1929 Stafford Street site purchased from Wesleyan Day School.

1930	The Settlement moved to Stafford Street. Miss Elsie Bowerman became Honorary Treasurer. Dr Gertrude Willoughby became Warden.
1931	HM The Queen Mary opened the Stafford Street site on March 18th. Lady May Abel Smith became President.
1932	First Gooch Scholarship awarded to student.
1933	Mrs Townsend donated 5 houses in Goldsmith Road to the Settlement.
1934	Rev C R Bailey died.
1935	The Nursery School opened 2nd September and was officially opened on December 10th by Lady Astor.
1937	Stafford Street renamed Staffordshire Street from 1st July.
1939	Outbreak of Second World War.
1940	Miss Ellis became Warden. Communal kitchens opened to serve daily and Christmas midday meals to Old Aged Pensioners. Settlement used as bomb shelter for the immediate area. The Nursery School evacuated to Glyndebourne.
1941	A wartime day nursery opened on October 8th. UGS Infant Welfare Clinic closed.
1942	Dame Frances Dove, one of the founders of the Settlement and Head of Wycombe Abbey died on 23rd June at the age of 94.
1945	The Dinner Club formed [beginning of Meals on Wheels]. Community Club for men and women over 20 years formed.
1946	Miss Gordon Jones became Warden. Canon and Mrs Veasey celebrated their 50th anniversary in Camberwell. UGSSS celebrated 50th Jubilee. Canon Veasey awarded MBE. The Nursery School returned from Glyndebourne.
1947	HRH the Princess Margaret became Patron of the UGSSS Settlement.
1948	HRH the Princess Margaret visited the Settlement. Mission prayer revived.
1950	The Foot Clinic opened.
1951	Canon Harry Veasey died in August.
1954	Miss Jessica Broomhall became Warden. ICAA moved to Lewisham.
1955	Miss Joyce Baxter became Warden. The Chapel was dedicated. Memorials dedicated to Canon Veasey in Southwark Cathedral on April 30th and in St Mark's Church on June 4th
1956	60th Diamond Jubilee celebrations took place at The Royal Festival Hall on May 9th.
1957	Miss Elsie Bowerman became temporary Warden. Miss Margaret Cousins became Warden. Lady May Abel Smith opened the Rest Room on October 23rd.
1959	Friends of the Settlement formed.
1960	HRH the Princess Margaret visited the Settlement on November 8th. First AGM of The Friends. Canon George Potter of St. Chrysostom's Church died on February 15th.
1961	The Foot Clinic and the Settlement Kitchens [Meals on Wheels] taken over by Camberwell Borough Council.
1962	The Acorn flats occupied. A two-shift system began in the Nursery School.
1964	Dulcie Groves appointed Warden. Borough of Camberwell integrated with the Greater London Borough of Southwark.

1965	First permanent male warden appointed, Wing Commander (Ben) Baker. First UGS Review printed. Entrance changed from Staffordshire Street to Goldsmith Road. Playing in the Park Scheme started. Triple S Scheme started.
1966	Consecration of St John's Church on 11th June. Association of Friends of the Settlement inaugurated. Camberwell Settlements Enquiry held.
1967	Elsie Bowerman became President.
1968	Headstart Scheme began.
1971	The Dove-Bowerman Trust established. 75th Birthday Bazaar took place at James Allen's Girls' School.
1972	HRH The Princess Margaret visited the Settlement. Lady Howe became President. Rev John Lane appointed Director. The Advice Centre opened. The Urban Studies Centre opened.
1973	Elsie Bowerman died. Peckham Mirror replaced UGS Review. Name changed from UGS to Peckham Settlement. ILEA took over Nell Gwyn Nursery School.
1974	Last Annual Service at Southwark Cathedral. Peckham Youth Project opened.
1975	First Annual Service at St John's. Reception at Greenwich.
1976	80th Birthday Service at Southwark Cathedral. Reception at The Guildhall.
1978	Dr Martin Pickstone appointed Director. Private view at the History Gallery at the Tower of London.
1979	HRH The Princess Margaret attended the Reception at London Zoo. Grace Griffiths died.
1980	Reception at The Museum of London.
1981	Reception at The Victoria and Albert Museum. Peckham Newsletter started. All Nations Nursery opened. PDCCA [Peckham and Dulwich Caribbean Community Association] began activities at Peckham Settlement. Mr E F T (Paddy) Cribb became Chairman of the Executive Committee.
1982	HRH The Princess Margaret visited the Settlement. Marks and Spencer's Fashion Show at the Guildhall, London.
1983	Christine Richards began work as first Turning Point Apprentice.
1984	Concert at Lambeth Palace. Separate Board of Governors for The All Nations Nursery [day nursery]. Leon Brittan addressed a large audience on "The role and contribution of Settlements today" at The Royal Commonwealth Society.
1985	Reception at Guy's Hospital. Latch Key Project initiated. BASSAC [British Association of Social Service Action Centres] centenary. Urban Studies Centre moved to Willowbrook. Peckham Project disbanded. Greater London Council abolished.
1986	Mrs Kitty Leek appointed Director. Reception at Jeffrey Archer's penthouse. 90th birthday celebration service at St John's Church at which The Archbishop of Canterbury preached. Street party opened by the Mayor of Southwark. Sponsored walk in Windsor Great Park. Schools Liaison Committee disbanded.
1987	Job Club opened. Advice Centre opened. The Wednesday Club closed. Mary Pittard died and second-hand shop closed. Reception for Settlement staff held at Lady Howe's home.

1988 The Latch Key Project formalised. John Patten, MP, gave a talk on "Business in the Community" at the Settlement.

1989 Service held at St. John's for the Edinburgh Settlement after the gas explosion disaster.

1992 The Constitution revised, with a Mission statement and Aims. First Peckham Police and Youth Project Summer Holiday Scheme. Gooch Memorial Fund wound up.

1994 Nell Gwyn Nursery School moved to Rye Annex, Meeting House Lane. John Lane awarded OBE. Pitt Street Settlement and the Camberwell Society for the Relief of those in Need Trust closed.

1995 Jane Johnson died. David Kitchen awarded the MBE.

1996 Centenary of the Settlement. Centenary Service held at St John's to which the Archbishop of Canterbury came.

1997 Present Director, David Kitchen, appointed. Kitty Leek and George Smith awarded Southwark Civic Award for services to the Community. Assets of Pitt Street transferred to Peckham Settlement.

1998 The Plough Redemption Foundation Trust took over the Latch Key Project and the Summer Play Schemes. Management restructure of Peckham Settlement.

1999 HRH The Princess Margaret visited the Settlement to commemorate her 50 years of patronage. Lady Howe awarded the CBE. The Settlement affiliated to East Peckham Consortium.

2000 Capital Cares had two action days at the Settlement. Open Door Housing Trust began. Hour Bank Volunteers launched. Asylum Seekers project began. Travellers Action Group began. Legal Advice sessions began. Four people ran the London Marathon in support of the Settlement.

Introduction

It is quite extraordinary how much of an influence the Peckham Settlement has had in so many people's lives. It is also amazing that so many people have kept a connection with the Settlement, some for a number of years, or having broken that connection, returned to bond again with a rare spirit which exudes from that rather unattractive building in Staffordshire Street in the heart of South London. The Peckham Settlement has in its time fostered criticism, frustration, anger and complaint but it has far surpassed these nasties with an abiding love of humanity which is exhibited in devoted service, a pioneering zeal, enduring friendships and a host of fond and nostalgic memories.

Or perhaps this is not all so surprising. Despite the turmoils of funding, the vagaries of the building, the difficulties of staffing and other institutional dilemmas, an ethos emanates from the Peckham Settlement which is obviously deeply ingrained in everyone who comes across it. This is, of course, why it has been in existence over one hundred years. There is always a need to reassess and re-evaluate things past, but I have no doubt that the Peckham Settlement will enter the new millennium with renewed vigour and energy and will remain to serve that area of South London for many more years.

I was a schoolgirl of the 1950s when I worked as a volunteer there. I can still remember the smell of the building, a powerful evocative sense, and the very strong desire to put all the children into a hot bath and scrub them clean. I was asked to help make a film with another school-friend about the work of the Settlement. This was shown later at the Festival Hall for the Diamond Jubilee celebrations in 1956. Little did I think that forty years on, this episode would return to make another impact on my life. During the intervening years, I had made a career in teaching, raised a family, retired and was working with children who had special needs, in fact a very typical life story of so many of the schoolgirls who came to Peckham. Out of the blue came a letter from the South London Film Society inviting me to join in their celebrations of fifty years of film making. The society was going to show my film. I attended this function, cringed at the sight of a fifteen-year-old with plaits, panama, thick shoes and socks and at the very non-politically correct text of the film. Here I met Derek Lowman and after talking to him, the urge to visit my schoolgirl haunts was too strong to ignore. Some months later I met David Kitchen, who had just taken the post of director at the Settlement. I visited Peckham again and luxuriated in memories. The smell and the spiral staircase transported me back all those years. Before I knew it, I had offered to write this history.

Then followed one of the most rewarding times of my life. I have read copious amounts of material, in spidery handwriting, in very bad typing, and in glossy print. I have visited schools, libraries and been invited into homes. I have met the most marvellous mixture of people from fifteen to ninety-five, all of whom have given so much material for this history. I have corresponded with many more people both here and abroad, who have willingly recorded their reminiscences by letter, telephone and electronic mail. A full list of acknowledgements is in the Appendices, but here I would like to thank everyone who spared their valuable time to contribute and without whom this history would never have been written. The detective work has been absorbing, and although many records have been lost or mislaid, there has been enough to piece together this fascinating story.

The history of the first fifty years of Peckham Settlement, 1896-1945, has already been written by various authors and has been widely distributed. Both John Lane, one-time director, and George Nicholson, a part-time education officer employed in the Urban Studies Centre, have recorded some of the historical events of the Settlement. I acknowledge their contributions to this history. Mrs Alison Heath, the archivist at Wycombe Abbey, has spent much time and money finding material concerning the early years of the Settlement. As this material has not been referred to in other histories, I have included some of this as it makes fascinating reading. Helen Braund, one time head teacher at Bournemouth School for Girls, tracked through the school's magazines for relevant details. I thank her very much for the tremendous amount of work she did. Many thanks go to Eve Keatley who gave time to comment on the script. I am deeply indebted to John Beasley, a local South London historian, who has come to my rescue several times with his abundant knowledge of Peckham, and performed the mammoth and meticulous task of proof reading. Sincere gratitude goes to David Kitchen and the other staff at Peckham who have patiently borne my questions, tolerated the ferreting in boxes and papers and drinking their coffee. Without my husband's support and technical help this history would never have gone to press. He has endured the last years of preoccupation, monopoly of the computer, the copious pieces of paper, books and telephone calls. Thank you.

Histories are never finished and maybe more material will come to light with the publication of this book. Typically, information has been gleaned from annual reports, some directors and executive committee reports, the UGSM and UGSS school sheets, school magazines, a miscellany of publicity pamphlets, newspaper accounts and personal reminiscences. The lack of continuity and sometimes differing information is reflected and influenced by the material available. At times this history has threatened to turn into a social treatise, but I have tried to keep this very much as a record with personal viewpoints. Reminiscences are not the most scientific method of collecting factual material, as details, dates and names become lost in the mists of time, but they give a personalised and warm feeling to an historical report. After all, the Peckham Settlement is about people and this should be reflected in its history.

Jennifer G Stephens
January 2001

Chapter 1

The Settlement Movement

by Derek Lowman
Member of the Executive Committee, Peckham Settlement

The Peckham Settlement is one of a number of settlements in several countries throughout the world. It is part of a movement which began in 1884, and although the term 'settlement' may now seem inappropriate it was originally quite clear and relevant.

During the nineteenth century, when industrialisation was replacing agriculture as the mainstay of the economy, London and other cities such as Manchester, Birmingham and Liverpool expanded rapidly. Workers and their families were crowded into inadequate housing with poor sanitary arrangements, no compulsory education until 1880, no pensions or unemployment pay and non-existent public welfare services except for the Board of Guardians administering the Poor Law. Some Members of Parliament were concerned and things improved to some extent after the passing of the Reform, the Factory, the Ten Hours and the Public Health Acts. It was in the very early stages of the Government's attempts to improve living conditions for the poor, to force factory and mine owners to make circumstances better for their workers and to include more people in the democratic process.

The relief of distress and the alleviation of poverty was, then, the province of individuals and charitable bodies. The well-off and people from the country would send money and gifts for distribution to the deserving poor and it would often fall to the lot of the clergy and missioners who lived in an area to deal with the administration of these donations. There were, too, some volunteers who worked for these charitable institutions involved in the distribution. It was not always a satisfactory way of coping with the very real needs of the people and it gradually became obvious that some sort of organisation of charitable giving was essential. There were too many instances of those with the best stories and guile exploiting the generosity of the givers, and others who were in real need missing out. To combat this state of affairs, the Charity Organisation Society (COS) began in mid-century to keep a central register of recipients of charitable gifts. The missioners, the clergy and the volunteers who visited the needy saw for themselves the condition of the poor. They realised the vast majority were neither indolent nor feckless but victims of the dramatic changes going on around them.

An experiment in the provision of better well managed housing helped to prove the point. Octavia Hill bought houses and provided volunteers and some paid rent collectors who did not just collect rents. They were urged to treat the tenants as people with standards and aspirations for themselves and their families, and to make sure the houses were kept in good order and repair. Octavia Hill's methods provided the basis of Housing Management Theory which exists today.

With the coming of more organised charitable activity and the increasing presence of middle and upper class volunteers and workers in poor areas, the wealthy and the comfortable middle classes became more conscious of the needs of the inner cities. They began to see that giving money wasn't everything and that more needed to be done in providing education, opportunities for leisure pursuits, better working and living conditions and in promoting health and welfare.

One of the clergy who was involved in the problems of his area was Canon Samuel Barnett, the vicar of St Jude's Church in Whitechapel. He realized that his role was not only to help the members of his congregation, but also to include others of different and non-Christian faiths. He had a large multi-ethnic population in his parish of people arriving from the nearby docks. He saw that first-hand knowledge of the local conditions was essential if anything was to be done. He recognised that if working people were given better educational opportunities and a chance to develop their individual potential, it would create a much happier and more equitable society. His solution was to match the problems to the resources needed to overcome them.

Barnett was well placed to do something about this and was supported by his wife Henrietta (later Dame Henrietta) who was an heiress and who later founded the Hampstead Garden Suburb with Octavia Hill and others.

Samuel Barnett gave a speech at St John's College, Oxford and put forward a proposition that if some graduates and undergraduates could come and live in the East End for a time, they would not only see the awful conditions for themselves, but would begin to understand the problems, help with the educational and leisure activities, and *"consider the advancement of plans to promote their* (the poor) *welfare" [1].* They would also benefit themselves by facing up to the realities of life. They could perhaps bring to the notice of those in power the need for more changes and maybe influence some innovations themselves when they assumed the place of leadership in the country. He proposed, *"there should be settlements of university men in poor areas of great towns" [2].* It is from this phrase that we get the name of 'Settlement'. He stressed also that it should not be another Mission even if activated by Christian motives. It would welcome everyone of all faiths and nationalities and not concern itself with proselytising. His vicarage became the first Settlement, Toynbee Hall, in 1884. Two of the most well-known people later involved with it were Clement Attlee, the post-war Labour Prime Minister and Lord Beveridge, the architect of the Welfare State.

Other settlements were established quickly both in this country, in America and in other parts of the world. Some of the Settlements did however still see themselves as Missions, but adopted the idea of residents working with and for people of every faith and nationality.

It may not seem to us nowadays to be much of a move away from 'patronising and do-gooding' but for that period it was a tremendous step forward. Times have changed and so have settlements. Now, few have residents, most have paid staff, and they are now more wide ranging 'social action centres' or 'community centres', but their basic aims remain the same. These are to help the communities in which they are situated to develop potential in every way both individually and collectively. *"The Settlement movement paved the way for the future evolution of community development, youth work, advice and information" [3].*

Chapter 2

The Birth Of The Peckham Settlement

Henrietta McArthur was reputed to be the first person to have had the idea *"simmering in her head in quite early days... ... of the value of girls' clubs in these crowded streets," [Manchester Guardian] [4]* or a young ladies' mission amongst the poor of London. The Bishop of Rochester, Randall Thomas Davidson, had long been urging the parish missions to move across the Thames to South London. He had seen the East End Missions do very valuable work and realised that South London needed such support also. The All Saints Mission was opened in Walworth in 1885. Pembroke House followed in 1886. The Time and Talents Mission began in 1887 *"in which girls of leisure and education can use their time and talents in the Service of others"[5].* Mrs Abel Smith was their president and the Bishop of Kingston, Rev F Hawkes was the Chairman. Other Settlements or Missions were: - Lady Margaret Hall Settlement in Kennington (1897); Docklands Mission in Rotherhithe of which Princess Margaret became President in 1977 (1888-1991); Charterhouse in Tabard Street (1885 to present); Cambridge House, which later amalgamated with Talbot House (1889 to present); and Pitt Street (1908-1994) which all opened within fifteen years to serve the area of South East London. By 1951 there were 31 residential settlements in London and 11 in the Provinces.

A letter to Miss McArthur in May 1895 suggested *"My earnest wish to enlist on behalf of our poor South Londoners some of the force of sympathy, generosity and helpfulness, which is apt... ...to be wasted for lack of any suitable and easy opportunity of exercising it... ... South London has the biggest areas of unbroken poverty to be found anywhere in England......best of all perhaps it would be if some special district of poverty and ignorance could be helped by the starting of a Mission supported by the Girls' Schools Guild on the lines of the missions supported by Colleges and Boys' public Schools. You know how much interest these Missions awaken and sustain and how they deal with every side and part of life - sacred and secular" [Bishop Randall of Rochester] [6].* This seems to have coincided with the thoughts of Rev and Mrs C R Bailey, the two people credited with the initial formation of the Peckham Settlement. Mrs Bailey wrote *"It all began in a fireside talk one winter's evening in 1894. My husband ......had just returned from visiting one of the prosperous Public School Missions (boys only)......and asked why were girls' schools left out. What a settlement from the schools could do in South London! ......There should be a small settlement first in its own parish and extending its work in South London, then gradually reaching out its tentacles throughout the world" [UGS Record, Spring 1964][7].* The search for a Mission site was mooted on May 14th 1896 by John Dyke, the Rural Dean of Camberwell, and the Rev R Appleton, the vicar of St George's Church, Camberwell, in a letter to the Lord Bishop.

The diocese of Rochester was later divided and Bishop Talbot was chosen to be Bishop of Southwark in 1905. He became the first Warden and oversaw the Settlement and the parish of St. Mark's. His wife became the president of the Settlement in 1902. South London loved Bishop Talbot dearly. *"He was over six feet, standing with his hand on the shoulder of his charming wife, telling the assembled company of a large cheque which he had just received for the work. He told us that he had decided to focus the work of the mission on a district of Camberwell and give it in charge of a young clergyman, Harry Veasey. Mrs Bailey called him 'a spark of fire' which shone just as brightly fifty years later" [Miss Alsop, School Mistress.] [8].* The Rev Harry Veasey was a fervent missionary.

2 The Reverend Harry Veasey, 1896

3 Canon Harry Veasey, 1946

With his wife he lived in Camberwell, brought up his family and worked tirelessly for the poor of the area for over fifty years. The population in Peckham was already quite mixed. There were large numbers of Scots and Irish, and in 1918, substantial numbers of Belgians, Czechs and other Europeans came to Peckham, bringing different cultures and religions. The parish churches in that area were providing much of the support and the missionary zeal was evident.

In the history of Peckham Settlement written by Harry Veasey, there is a different version of events. *"It begins with an Old Girl – the wife of Rev C R Bailey, the then organizing secretary of the South London Church Fund. She wondered how it was that though the boys of England's public schools and colleges had their Missions, there was nothing of the sort from the Girls' side ... ... So the Baileys, after consulting Bishop Davidson... ... called together the Heads of a few suburban girls' schools... ... who decided that girls' schools also should have a Mission of their own, depending entirely upon their united contributions and exertions" [9].* The head teachers of the three London schools of Surbiton, Clapham, and Wimbledon, Miss Morrison of Graham Street and Miss Oldham of Streatham Hill combined with Miss Dove of Wycombe Abbey, Miss Williamson of Princess Helena College, Miss Douglas of Godolphin School in Salisbury and Miss Miller of St Bernard's in Bexhill on Sea. The force of these ladies was stimulus enough to unite twelve schools.

4 Jane Francis Dove, 1896

With the added enthusiasm and missionary fervour from the Reverend Harry and Mrs Veasey, the first Missioners, they settled on an area which was entirely suitable for the ministry of schoolgirls, St Mark's Parish (Coburg Road) in Camberwell. The United Girls' Schools Mission, (or the Ugly Girls' Schools Mission as it became affectionately known) was born in 1896.

On March 7th 1897, a Mission Room was opened at 33 Kempshead Road to serve a district of six and a half acres and 7000 people.

5 UGSM Church Hall & Clergy House, Kempshead Road, circa 1900

6 UGSM Church Hall & Clergy House, Kempshead Road, circa 1940

An additional house was purchased in Calmington Road (on the edge of what is now Burgess Park Lake). In 1906, 19 Peckham Road was bought, in 1907, number 17, and then in 1924, number 15 was added to what was now the UGSSS or Union of Girls' Schools for Social Service, the name it kept for the next forty odd years.

"The Settlement... ... was to be scientific in attitude, to give the best possible training for those who took up special work as a career, but also to provide a place where Old Girls could come for short periods to see how life was lived in South London, and to learn from contact and discussion with practical and experienced people. At the same time it was to be a social service centre for the people living in its neighbourhood"[10].

7 UGS Settlement, Peckham Road, 1906 – 1930

The Settlements in South London had a network of support. The Bishops of Southwark, Woolwich and Kingston were chairmen or heads of more than one Mission. Their wives were Presidents or Honorary Secretaries. Members of the Royal family were closely involved with most of the Settlements as presidents or patrons. Queen Mary is recorded to have taken a special interest in Pitt Street, where she had presented the founder, Charles Lisle Watson, a statuette of St. Michael. Princess Christian went to at least three separate openings of missions including Peckham. Aristocratic ladies, especially those involved with the new emergent women's franchise movement, played a very large role in the beginnings of these Settlements, for example Lady Astor and Lady Abel Smith. Miss Shove was treasurer of no fewer than three missions, including the Talbot and Peckham. The ladies who worked in the Settlements often transferred from one Mission to another. Girls' public schools, such as Benenden, Downe House and Roedean, often supported more than one Mission. There was certainly a sense of unified purpose and vision associated with the early social action centres, and there were enough interested and influential people to ensure the value and success of the early settlements.

8 Club Rooms & Gardens, Peckham Road

Chapter 3

The Work And Activities Of The Settlement

The work and activities of the Settlement have been, and still are, many and varied. The sheer number of projects, clubs, initiatives, training enterprises, and provision of the basic needs of life for the people of Peckham is to be viewed with deep admiration. When the Settlement opened in 1896, it was to combat 'the social problems of great towns' brought about by the move of people from rural England to the urban setting to seek work. Work was not easy to come by and the crowding of areas such as Peckham was overwhelming. This exodus created ills in which *"bad housing, poverty, bad health conditions, and spiritual destitution" [Bishop of Kingston] [11]* were described as rife. The problems were recorded as *"Housing- 7000 adults and children in six and a half acres of three storey tenements. Poverty - No unemployment pay, no old age pensions, no sickness or maternity benefits, no provident collecting or jumble sales. Health - no district nurse, no school clinics... ...no hospital savings association, no ante-natal clinics or dental aids. There were no clubs or organised play hours for children, or amenities for either the men or young people, the public houses were the only places to go for social and bodily refreshment. There was also a religious problem – soul life was almost non-existent. Lying and stealing abounded" [attributed to Harry Veasey] [12].* To its credit the Settlement did establish a solution to many of the problems it had identified. Housing, unemployment, poverty, health, education, and social need are still the criteria which govern the Settlement's work today.

In tune with other settlements of the time, there were endeavours to promote social awareness and to attempt to alleviate some of these ills in six main ways. Firstly, the Settlement has acquired a reputation for responding to immediate requests and needs of the moment. A national need is often reflected in the locality. There is a tradition of local people coming to the Settlement, needing capable, unbiased information and help. Some of the issues to which the Settlement responded were:-

- the nursery school which opened 'because the child population was such that it was desperately needed' (1935)
- a day nursery which began in the Second World War because so many mothers were working whilst the fathers were fighting (1940)
- the delivery of coal, blankets and meals to the house-bound who would otherwise go without (from 1897 to around 1972)
- the provision of hot meals every day and on Christmas Day because the old people were lonely, too poor or did not have the facilities to cater for themselves (from 1940)
- the school holiday play schemes because the children had nowhere to go and would only roam the streets (from 1923)
- the controversial decision to concentrate on young, disaffected unemployed black people, who badly needed somewhere to meet each other (from 1973)
- the work with the tenants' associations in the local housing estates (from 1973)
- the job centre (from 1987)

Secondly, the Settlement activities have included all age groups. Many activities tend to concentrate on children, in compliance with Bishop Talbot's original dictum that the area chosen for the UGSM should be *"poor and crowded and where (as especially suitable for girls) the ministry of children predominated" [Bishop Talbot] [13],* but the Settlement has catered for the needs of all ages through the years.

Thirdly, the Settlement has been the pioneer of so many excellent ideas which were initiated, consolidated and then passed on to statutory authorities to develop into national institutions. As Harry Veasey said in 1945, "(We) *tested possibilities, made mistakes which are inevitable with new ventures but which a government cannot risk" [14].* In 1956, Lady Anne Ogilvie reiterated this sentiment at the Diamond Jubilee celebrations. *"There* (is) *still plenty of room for social experiment which groups of private citizens, with the freedom of action that public authorities in a democratic state could never have,*(are) *best fitted to carry out" [Times Report, 1956] [15].* John Lane endorsed the idea, "(The Settlement) *can organise things which might be unpopular, support groups which could be considered socially or politically undesirable" [16].* Some of these pioneering ideas were -

- The Provident Collecting Scheme which led to the National War Savings Scheme. (Pre 1906).
- An apprentices' committee which became the Juvenile Advisory Committee of the Labour Exchange (Pre 1906).
- The infant welfare clinics complete with a sunlight room, in one of which Miss Whitelaw worked when she retired as head teacher from Wycombe Abbey (1913). These clinics were to become the forerunner of the Infant Welfare Clinics of today
- The first hospital teachers were sent from the Settlement to teach the chronic sick children in the local Infirmary in Havil Street (1912-4).
- The Unemployment Insurance Scheme, begun by a sidesman in St Mark's Parish, which became a government national act in 1947.
- The first Meals on Wheels which began informally at the Settlement in 1937, and was put on a formal footing in the Second World War. This service continued until 1961, when the Borough of Camberwell took over the kitchens and the administration.
- The Head Start Scheme which was also pioneered in other parts of the country. This scheme was a summer camp for children aged four to five, who hadn't attended nursery school, to prepare them for the rigours of daily school life. The scheme was a month long, and in the first year 51 children attended (1969).
- The Settlement provided office space for the Southwark Wildlife Group. The Group, one of only a handful of conservation groups in London at the time, was instrumental in setting up a wildlife garden on derelict land in Goldsmith Road, at the instigation of Bob Smyth, a local councillor. The Settlement provided the front office of the London Wildlife Trust (1982).

9 The Wildlife Area, 1985

"We see this pioneering as an example of one of the chief functions of a voluntary body: to find a need and meet it until it becomes in due time a necessary part of social services" [UGS Record] [17].

A fourth strand has been the well-established tradition of initiating and supporting self help groups to work with people and to develop their skills.
Some of these groups have been -

- the Lads' club where they were taught boxing, football, wood carving, basket work, designing, Morris dancing (circa 1912)
- the girls' clubs which taught sewing, singing and drama, country dancing (circa 1901)
- the Mums' club which flourished during and after the second world war (1939)
- the British Caribbean Society which rented space from the Settlement (1974)
- the Open Door mental health outreach (1999).

Fifthly, the Settlement has become the local centre for national organisations. In its time the Settlement has been the headquarters of

- The Charity Organisation Society
- The Invalid Children's Aid Association [ICAA]
- The Children's Country Holiday Fund (pre 1914 and later in 1990s)
- School management and care committees of which there are several mentions in the local history of Peckham Park School (pre 1914 and later in the 1950s)
- The Soldiers' and Sailors' Families Association (1914-1918)
- The Soldiers' and Sailors' Help Society (1914-1918)
- The Prince of Wales Fund (1913)
- The Guiding and Scouting Movements (to about 1956)
- The Band of Hope (circa 1910-1936)
- The King's Messengers (1908-1911)
- The Camberwell Housing and the Camberwell Health Society (to about 1939)
- The Settlement had its own group of the Hospital Savings Association, begun in 1922, which had over 1000 members in 1947, before the Government took over the administration of hospitals in 1948.
- The Settlement has worked with the Women's Voluntary Service, Family Welfare, the Citizens Advice Bureau, St Mungo's Charity and the Duke of Edinburgh's Scheme.

Finally, the Settlement's work has been seen as a good training and educational base for social work. In fact one of the prime reasons for beginning the Settlement was the desire of the head teachers to provide a means of 'character education' for their charges, and *"a mission to them whilst at school and by them then and after as Old Girls [Harry Veasey] [18]; "to have a first hand knowledge of the social problems of the day, to kindle in them a desire and to offer them the opportunity of giving practical help… … and take a full share in solving problems they will find around them" [Executive Committee] [19].* The social service training conferences were highlights of the school and Settlement yearly calendar. By 1925, the Settlement was a recognised training and education centre for university social work, although students from London School of Economics had been using the Settlement since 1906. The Settlement has been a designated training place for the Turning Point Apprenticeship Scheme initiated from Goldsmiths College in New Cross, from 1983. The idea had come from two BASSAC members, and was initiated at Goldsmiths College in 1981. Students with no formal qualifications but with great commitment can become apprentices and complete a two-year full-time field-based training programme for community work. Young people come to the Settlement for work or community experience and placement still, and to gain first qualifications in childcare or community work.

Community Development

The Settlement has always responded to the local community's needs. In the early days, the needs were assessed and managed by a band of dedicated and religious people, most of whom were women and who worked voluntarily. The provision and support of poor people was mainly reactive. A need arose, a plan instigated and the need was generally satisfied. The management of this need was also decided mainly by the volunteers with little input from the receivers, but much of the Settlement's activity in response to local need did lead to national reform.

Around 1950 it was recognised that the volunteers should be more organised. Within South East London, there were at least seven Missions and probably many other organisations all working at the same problems and in many of the same ways. The professional social workers of the time were instrumental in organising these bands of volunteers towards planned ventures and targets. There was now a neighbourhood or social worker at the Settlement. One initiative of these times was the Triple S Scheme (Southwark Service Scheme) and which is described later. Field workers were funded by ILEA grants, the City Parochial Foundation and the Gulbenkian Foundation.

In 1966 the Settlement Development Working Party, arising out of the Camberwell Settlements Enquiry, illustrated the need for a designated post solely for community development. Change was inevitable and from this study came the phrase 'social action centres'. In 1970 the management committee agreed to the appointment of a full-time community worker to *"encourage local people to participate more fully in finding solutions to their problems in creating mutually supportive groups and in pressing... ...for better services and facilities" [John Lane, Director] [20].* The concept of community work now was the paid professionals guiding and working with bands of volunteers. Social change in Peckham was constantly dynamic and fluctuating. There was massive rebuilding, constant movement of population and a general discontent with the policies of the time, which seemed to deal only with the tip of the iceberg, rarely recognising the deeper emotional and counselling needs of the community. The Settlement community worker aimed at bridging this gap. When the activities became generally more universal and attuned to the greater social service scene, the immediate response to needs was more carefully planned and a long-term vision was put in place. *"Modern centres of social service... ... must not only give help but also encourage self-help" [ibid] [21].* The thorny problem of funding these projects was often geared to the latest government initiative or flavour of the time. Phrases such as 'the Settlement must be rooted in its community' or 'the Settlement must be increasingly community oriented' seemed to ignore the fact that the Settlement was serving the community even if the ways were not politically correct, large scale or modern. Although the volunteer was still important, the paid professional directed the enthusiasm.

Community Development was the name of the game now. In 1985, Christine Richards was one such worker. Her extensive brief was to assist the tenants' associations, to liaise with the local community groups, to assist people facing deportation in Peckham, to enable and empower self-help groups and to attend conferences, tribunals and other formal occasions where people's rights needed to be maintained. Her successor, Deirdre O' Reilly, worked on unemployment, the local women and new emerging groups. She set up a rape crisis line, supported the Southern Arab community groups and advised on health issues for Irish women. No longer was the recipient seen as helpless, poverty-stricken, and with little energy or wherewithal to fight his/her corner, but as a powerful self-realising force with a right to autonomy and with influence over the services provided. The community worker was an advocate and a support, a liaison between the community and the authorities. Despite this development, the areas of concern remain much the same as they had been in 1896.

Activities Concerning Housing

Housing deprivation of one sort or another has been a constant theme of the work in the Settlement. The people of Peckham come to the Settlement largely because of housing problems, which have included limited play space, unsanitary conditions, lack of services, poor maintenance and security issues. There was always a need to tackle the local authorities about vermin. Cockroaches, rats and ants topped the list of complaints for many years and were still discussed on a pensioners' outing in 1999. The staff could sympathise with these problems as the Settlement in its time has contended with plagues of mice, far too many pigeons and the eternal dry rot. The Settlement gave temporary accommodation to the first Acorn Place Tenants' Association in 1964 in recognition of building up a good community in the new high-rise flats. One of the recommendations of the Camberwell Settlements Committee of Enquiry in 1966 was that *"special attention should be given to housing issues which conspicuously affect the Camberwell area" [22]*. The cause of the riots in Peckham in 1985 was mostly attributed to housing disaffection. The hall in the Settlement has been used on more than one occasion to host a meeting between tenants and the local authority. Later the Southwark Resident Group was set up at the Settlement. Their aim was to *"unite all the Tenants' Associations into a common agenda to face the council" [John Lane] [23]*. Christine Richards helped to develop an outreach programme, principally with people from the local housing estates. Her task was to meet with and listen to the residents of the area around the Settlement and try to help with some of the many problems, to arrange and promote meetings with the local authority to address some of these issues, and to work with the tenants' associations situated in the estates, principally the Bells and the Oliver Goldsmith Estates. The main thrust here was to help the associations organise their meetings in a business-like way and to encourage the role of such an association, giving information on where to seek advice and to monitor closely the needs of that estate's population.

Homelessness was also an issue through the years. Rooms in the Settlement were often lent as temporary refuges or crash pads. The Settlement was given grant aid in the late 1970s to provide homes for the young black population. A community worker dealt with forty black homeless teenagers aged between fifteen and eighteen who needed short-term accommodation. In 1974 a house was given to the Karib organisation, a voluntary organisation set up by the sometime youth worker at the Settlement. Because Karib had no constitution at the time the house was 'given' to the Settlement as an administrative manoeuvre by Southwark Council until Karib was formally constituted. The house was to be home for fourteen young people and a youth worker. The Settlement was alerted some twenty years later that the house had never been used for its intended purpose and had actually been empty for sometime. An inquiry was held into the affair. The Settlement was exonerated from the responsibility of the council tax arrears and the house was handed back formally to Southwark Council.

Activities Concerning Unemployment

Although there were many factories and places which needed unskilled labour until the early 1970s, the factor of unemployment was and still is a serious problem for the Peckham area and the cause of much of the poverty found there. In the 1970s there was a growing problem of disaffected, unemployed and mainly black people who were living in large numbers in Peckham. Although Peckham has always been an area of multi-nationals, the black rights movement was becoming more powerful and this in turn affected the Settlement's activities. An unemployment club was set up in the basement under the name of The Peckham Project. Here young black men made furniture, using the empty barrels from the neighbouring factory and gaining useful carpentry skills.

In 1981, the Work and School Project [WASP] was conducted from the Settlement, for a short time by the Peckham Project. This gave part-time work experience for fifteen-year-olds who were considered at risk by the Education Services of the area. The youth were expected to work for about twenty hours a week and were paid a small sum. A consultant who reviewed the work of the Settlement in 1982 suggested that it should extend its services to help unemployment. In 1985, Peckham was selected as one of eight localities to experiment with the new Task Force, backed by one million pounds of government money for two years. Its principal aim was to help the long-term unemployed. When Kitty Leek began her tenure as Director of the Settlement in 1986, one of her priorities was the local unemployed.

10 Furniture Making using Barrels, circa 1975

The Job Club

In 1987 the very successful and innovative Job Club was set up. Peckham Settlement was one of the first voluntary organisations to establish such a centre and was leading the way in the community. The Job Club liaised closely with the local Job Centre and employers to encourage facilities and initiatives for local unemployed people, many of whom were deemed 'hard to place'. The aim of the club was to give people some quality training and self-esteem. If they had been unemployed for more than six months, they received advice and training in looking for work, compiling a CV, writing letters and attending interviews. Most people attended four mornings a week. The centre ran eight sessions of about two hours each week. The group produced its own training pack and took on twelve people during this time to do the training. The average stay for the client was three to six months, a great achievement in those days. The success rate of the club was admirable. In 1987 the Job Club was also working with groups of ex-offenders. In 1988 seventy people had found permanent full-time employment, and another twenty were undertaking courses of training or going into self-employment. In 1989 the club was given an extension of the grant for another two years. After a blip of staff changes and difficulties with the referral system, the results continued to show remarkable success. In 1990 one hundred people were placed in employment with the aid of this club and by 1991 there was a waiting list of people wanting to join.

Unfortunately, the club was stopped because it didn't reach its targets of placing people in work. Most of the members comprised those who were over 40 years of age or had been unemployed for more than two years - the very people for whom the whole scheme was set up, and for whom the target setting seemed inappropriate. Several years later, a gentleman stopped Kitty Leek in Lewisham High Street and said, *"Do you remember me? I went to your job club. You introduced me to a man in a suit and I've been in work ever since" [Paddy Cribb, Chairman of Executive Committee][24].* Testament to the success of the club, this gentleman had a criminal record and had been out of work for ten years before he came to the Settlement.

The work for unemployed people did not stop however. The Settlement tendered for and won the task of holding three one-day seminars for unemployed professionals and graduates offering intensive training sessions in job descriptions, CVs and interviews. In 1992 it was awarded a contract with the South Thames Training Enterprise Council (TEC) to run an ACCESS scheme. This scheme offered work experience to long-term unemployed people. Many placements were made and some 24 people went into employment or further education courses.

11 A Helping Hand at the Job Club, 1990

Through Business in the Community [BITC], an organisation which linked businesses to local voluntary agencies, the Settlement was involved in bussing people to work in factories in Crawley. The Settlement was also renting space to the Vietnamese Employment Bureau. As the age of technology took over, the Computer Insight group booked the hall to run in-house training programmes. Now the Friary Open Learning Centre contributes to the training of people for the workplace. In 1994 the Settlement was contributing to three strands of the unemployment issue - the Employment Action Service, a training access point and a weekly surgery for job advice. Unemployment is still a problem and recognised as such by the Settlement.

12 Princess Margaret visiting the Friary Open Learning Centre, 1999

Activities Concerning Poverty

Harry Veasey constantly described the poverty of the area and he was an ardent spokesman on the subject of Poor Law. The debilitating nature of the poverty was emphasised by Dr Willoughby, a Warden of the Settlement. In 1933 she reported the neighbourhood as having *"an air of poverty which... ...makes* [the whole area] *sordid and desolate" [25].*

The Shop

The main contribution to the relief of poverty is epitomised by the second-hand shop set up to meet the need for provident clothing. The shop was an important resource in its time and lasted for a good fifty years. Its long time proprietor was Mary Pittard. The first mention of the shop was in 1932 when Dr Willoughby was Warden, where second-hand clothes were sold very cheaply twice a week. Mary Pittard probably came to the Settlement soon after this. She ran the shop in the basement. Later the shop moved into the room which is now the Director's office. Here the residents could have ready access to her wares, but where they would have to bargain. Many of the residents in the area relied on this shop and there were often emergency calls for clothing. Long-time residents in Peckham remember her with gratitude and were very thankful to buy clothing, especially for the children, so cheaply. One resident remembers using the shop for all her children's requirements and many of her own. *"She takes endless trouble to suit her customers" [Annual Report] [26]; "We used to take the kids there to get dressed... ...we didn't have the money to go elsewhere. She'd say, 'I've put this away for you'. It cost 2/- a dress and a coat was about £1...... and you could always get shoes" [Doris Munday, Settlement User] [27]; "her importance was... ...brought into focus when she had a week's holiday. Three days running a man came to enquire anxiously about her return as he was in need of some working trousers" [Annual Report] [28].* In 1957 it was recorded that she sold new and second-hand clothing. It would appear that much of the new attire came as donations from the schools. Regular appeals for clothes appeared well into the 1970s, with Wellington boots or long men's underpants always urgently needed.

13 **Mary Pittard, 1968**

This service had extended into a travelling shop by 1958, which went round the neighbourhood with volunteer helpers taking goods to housebound people. Measurements for sizes would be taken and the volunteers would return to the shop to get the required clothes and take them back to the customers - a mail order supply with a difference. These volunteers also delivered food and coal.

Mary was given an honorarium of £10 in 1959 but otherwise she worked voluntarily. A description in 1962 said, *"the shop has been busier than ever providing garments for all age groups. Customers are limited to club members or if there is a special need. Charges are on a sliding scale from nil to a fair price. This fills a very real need, particularly for the old aged pensioners who are thus able to dress smartly and economically" [Annual Report] [29]; "One advantage is that...... she knows all the dealers by sight and will not let them buy from our stock for resale" [Theo Waite, Organising Secretary] [30].* The Moral Welfare workers, employed by the Church of England deaneries of Camberwell and Dulwich and which rented offices in the Settlement, often bought articles from the shop. The LCC Public Health Department asked Mary often for her help to provide clothing for needy cases in the 1960s. Elspeth Howe, the President of the Settlement, commented on the shop in her report to the Seniors of Wycombe Abbey in 1971. *"The second hand shop is a good source of money and any gifts of clothing which Seniors could send would be most welcome" [31].* Indeed the shop was making a substantial contribution to the Settlement funds. In 1968 *"more than 60 people have used our shop every week. The shop is open for 50 weeks of the year which means a total of 3000 customers. We are not always able to supply everybody's requirements immediately such as the old man with an extra large waist or the lady crippled with arthritis who needs a button through dress. But Mary Pittard keeps them in mind until they are suited. More young mothers than ever before now use the shop ...... the shop helps people in other ways too. Mary may perhaps learn of someone who has an odd table or chair to dispose of and then she discovers from her chats with her customers a need for these and so arranges the transaction. Or someone has a problem with which they are reluctant to seek help. In some cases Mrs Pittard will discreetly pass them on to one of our qualified staff" [UGS Review] [32].*

14 **Mary Pittard, 1975**

Her social awareness was such that Mary made a contribution to the publicity pamphlet in 1977. *"You don't get the neighbours now... ...Today you can be indoors all the time and never see a soul...*

...It's those flats. The whole circumstance and character of the place has changed because of them" [33]. Mary visited a 97-year-old lady every week and helped at the Wednesday club regularly for many years.

It was not all plain sailing and there is a lovely story told of Mary. *"The director ordered a Father Christmas outfit for the Settlement Parties. In the past we had always gone to Jones and Higgins for it. We used to borrow it for ten bob and have it back at a certain date. Well, this particular year he decided to borrow one, cost £70, from Harrods and it was delivered down here but that was unbeknown to Mary. When it was finished with, someone brought it out and laid it on the rack of second hand clothing downstairs. When they came to look for it Mary had sold it. 'Course there were ructions about that and* (the director) *had to pay back the charge for it but it was very funny" [George Smith, Settlement Worker] [34].* On another occasion Mary sold a very good leather handbag for fifty pence. She became a legend in her own lifetime. *"She was as old as the building" [Tania McPherson, Settlement Worker] [35]; "The shop has been here from time immemorial as has Mary Pittard who runs it" [Newsletter] [36].* It was widely broadcast when Mary broke her arm and the shop was closed for several days. Later in 1986, it was suggested that she and Jane Johnson were nominated for the honours list, but this proposal did not go further.

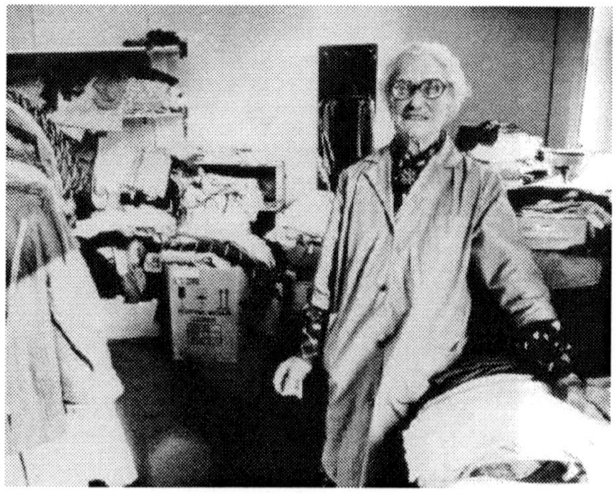

15 Mary Pittard, 1986

Mary was due to retire in 1988 and a discussion about her retirement present was a subject at one of the Executive Committee meetings but Mary died just before this. Her obituary read, *"Mary was a well-known person both in the area and in the Settlement. For many years she ran our shop where items of clothing and bric-a-brac were recycled for the benefit of the local people. Four days a week, come rain, hail or snow, Mary was open for business, the exception being Wednesdays when she was helping at the pensioner's club. Everyone was very proud of Mary. After all not many organisations can boast of a 92-year-old employee and so it was very sad news and a real sense of loss when we heard of her death in November 1987......it was the end of an era for the Settlement. Although everyone was aware that Mary's work went back to 1952 and possibly beyond, no one is clear of just how many and varied were the tasks she undertook. In recent years she was a volunteer helper with the Wednesday Club, where she did the washing up after lunch......It was agreed that the shop was very much Mary's and it therefore should end with her death" [Annual Report] [37].*

Care Committees

The school care committee had been the initiative of a local volunteer. The Settlement provided a secretary for the committee which was run from Peckham Park School and affiliated to the London

Child Care Organisation. The care committees were later taken over by the London County Council and became part of the education system. In 1933 the LCC had 6000 care committees. The care committee situated in the Settlement consisted of volunteers including the school head teacher and local personnel. Its brief was to assess the poorest families for free school meals, clothing and other welfare matters, to assist the doctor with family details and to help the family access information and available medical benefits. The committee members attended medicals, kept in touch with families and tried to make sure that the families kept hospital appointments for their children. The secretary did all the home visits and reported to the monthly meetings. Maureen Marshall was the voluntary secretary from 1961 to 1963 before she went on to university. She regarded the work as preventive as much as curative and believed it provided much support for families who would otherwise become a more serious social problem. The Settlement provided additional support with the shop, the nursery school, Christmas and harvest hampers and ensuring the needy children went on holiday through the Children's Country Holiday Fund.

Activities Concerning Education

Education, especially for young children, was always on the agenda of the Settlement. There had been a French book library for the 150 Belgium and Flemish refugees housed at the Settlement in 1940. In 1942, an infant reading group was begun because it was felt children needed space and quiet to appreciate books and was described as being very well used by the children. The reading room was still being patronised in 1961. The Mums' Club availed themselves of a comprehensive and free library during the 1950s. The Right to Read Campaign, launched by BAS in January 1973, was endorsed when John Lane became chairman of the council on education which ran the seminars at Goldsmiths College.

16 The Mums' Library, circa 1950

Play Schemes

The first organised holiday play scheme was held in the Settlement garden in 1923. At Staffordshire Street, a play centre was set up in 1959 in 'our little bit of back garden' for the holidays and open every Saturday morning. By 1965 more organised and bigger play schemes were taking place. One of these was the 'Playing in the Parks Scheme'. The Settlement combined with other organisations to provide facilities in Greenwich or Brockwell Parks. It was estimated that only one third of the children in Southwark had holidays away from home and so the play project was extended for four weeks in August to involve nearly 120 children from the Peckham area, and 40 helpers a week. In fact, 500 children took part using six school buses and the UGS minibus. There was a conscious effort to include the parents of these children and many joined in. At 10/- a week for a family this was quite affordable, but in special circumstances the fee was waived. The volunteer helpers had to be seventeen or over and preference was given to those with a special talent or interest which could be used in the programme.

17 Summer Play Scheme, Richmond Park, 1971 and Peckham Rye 1972

The programme was very varied and interesting, with visits to museums, zoos, lidos, farms, the seaside and the surrounding countryside which probably explained the popularity of this scheme. It was obvious from the reports that both the volunteers and the children had a marvellous time. In 1991 forty children attended the scheme daily. These schemes were extended to the Easter holidays and included an under fives' play scheme.

Eventually the community organisations liaised with the police, Southwark Council and the Settlement to pioneer the very successful Peckham Summer Youth Project. Two local policemen and Kitty Leek set up a public meeting at the Settlement to initiate a summer activity programme for the 11-16 year olds, the age group which caused most trouble for the neighbourhood purely because they were bored. *"One of the principal aims of the project was to give the young people something useful to do...... what we didn't anticipate was the tremendous rapport of the community and the police working together, and this is something we aim to build upon" [Kitty Leek, Director] [38]*. The Settlement gave much of the support for this venture. Kitty Leek trained the volunteers and took office in the organisation. The Settlement administered the financial affairs of the project. The project was an enormous success. The first year of 1992 involved 450 young people, some fifteen police officers and more than 30 volunteers.

Very good relationships were established with the police, the young people and the local people where previously respect had been little or non-existent. The following year the project's name was changed to Southwark Youth Project to enable the involvement of police officers borough wide and more sites were added. Paradoxically, improvement in employment issues led to the closure of the project in 1999 when it was no longer possible to recruit enough volunteers.

It was not the first time the police had liaised in a formal way with the Settlement. The local police have been closely connected with the Settlement right through the years, often calling upon the Wardens and the staff to help with tearaway children. In 1974 there was a concerted effort to bring black teen-agers together with the local police in a series of debates and meetings to combat racial tension between the 'black and the blue'.

18 Peckham Summer Youth Projects, 1992

<u>Latch Key Children</u>

The term 'latch key' was first identified during the war years of 1939 to 1945. A social experiment in Cheshire in 1941 had concentrated on keeping children, of mainly adolescent age, off the streets. The Settlement had viewed this development with interest. In 1959 the observation of small boys and girls playing in the streets with a front door key hanging round their necks led to the first holiday play scheme. Many of the activities were aimed at the latch-key child, especially in the 1960s. The Latch Key Project, begun in 1985, was funded for three years by BASSAC, and was initially an after-school club for children. Now a 'Before and After School Club' using the same title of Latchkey is now run by Femi Mafoh of the Plough Redemption Foundation Trust. It looks after children early in the morning before school, giving them breakfast and taking them to school, later collecting them and keeping them occupied until their parents can fetch them after work. This project has now been extended to five days a week.

<u>Pre-school Children</u>

The education of pre-school children is perhaps the biggest contribution of the Settlement to the needs of the area, and is the abiding link between the aims of the founders and the demands of the modern age. This activity has never ceased in the last hundred years and so deserves some extended mention.

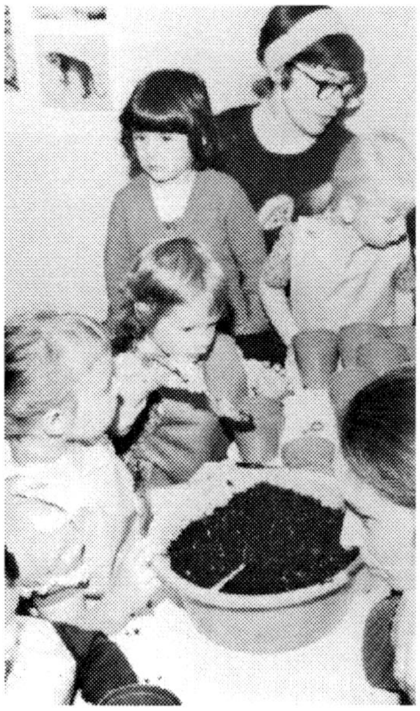

19 Mother & Toddler Clubs, 1973 and 1982

Nursery Education

Activities for pre-school children began as soon as the Settlement opened in 1896. A nursery school was first registered in 1927 with 36 children of two to five years old, but it was not until 1935 that education for pre-school children was set on a formal footing. It was reputed that this was the first nursery school in the borough. A Nursery School Committee was established to oversee the school and to monitor its function. Preference was given to children whose fathers were unemployed and whose mothers had to work. The authorities estimated it would cost £600 to provide pre-school education for forty children. The Settlement would have to provide £120 of this amount with the council paying the other £480. On September 2nd, five children enrolled. Miss Lambert was employed as the first superintendent at £175 a year. A cook/laundress was also employed at 25/- week and a girl helper at 10/- a week. The children paid eight pence a day for cocoa and biscuits, lunch and tea. The poorest children paid nothing. Lady Astor formally opened the nursery school for two to five year olds on December 10th 1935.

Lady Astor was an excellent patron of the school and frequently gave money to help it on its way. *"I am such a tremendous believer in nursery schools. I know the Government has put open-air schools on its programme. We are grateful for it, particularly when we realise that there are one and three quarter million children between 2 and 5 in this country. 4000 are in nursery schools, 155,000 are in infant departments of elementary schools and 50,000 are in day nurseries. This is about one and a half million children who are not provided for - nine out of ten children. I think that it is only a question of time before mothers are going to demand some sort of open-air school in every part of the country" [Report in The Times, 1935] [39].*

20 Lady Astor Opening the Nursery School, 1935

The main cost was supposed to be borne by the London County Council and the Board of Education, but the grants were very slow in coming. There was a continuous stream of letters between 1945 to 1951 from the Honorary Secretary of the Nursery School Committee to the Education Board concerning lack of payment or the supposedly incorrect calculation of grants. This always seemed to hinge on the way the number of attendees at the school was calculated. Twice the Honorary Secretary, Miss Isobel Turner, threatened to close the nursery school but fortunately this never materialised.

A report on the school in 1939 recounts "(the children) *are brought in about eight and go straight to their little pegs, each marked with a distinguishing animal, to change into their blue pinafores. They also clean their teeth and have their own special toothbrush. They play in the garden. They are provided with milk during the morning and have a large mid-day meal. After lunch each child rests in a collapsible cot and is encouraged to sleep as long as possible. They amuse themselves until tea which consists of bread, butter, milk and apples. There is just time for a game before mother comes to collect them at 6 o' clock" [A Cobb, Schoolgirl] [40]*. The health of the children influenced much of the timetable. The concept of open-air was enforced rigidly with the children playing in the garden for much of the day. *"The school is an excellent idea. The children fresh from the welfare clinics continue to thrive on good food and in fine surroundings instead of becoming a target for rickets and consumption" [ibid] [41]*, but there were recorded incidences of diphtheria in the early days.

During the Second World War, the nursery, with all its children and staff, was evacuated to Glyndebourne and the nursery space at the Settlement was used as an emergency dining area for the local residents.

21 The Nursery School, circa 1938

22 The Nursery School at Glyndebourne, 1944

Things were not too good in Glyndebourne. There was difficulty in keeping the children from each Settlement in their own groups, and a family atmosphere was hard to maintain. As time went on the older children no longer qualified for a nursery place and so had to be billeted out to families in the neighbourhood. *"Accommodation is proving rather uncomfortable and they are hoping to move in a few weeks time" [ibid] [42].* Miss Lambert was unhappy and asked to come back to the Settlement as the nursery school at Glyndebourne was becoming too large. A wartime day nursery had been set up for those children still in Peckham, keeping children from 7 am to 7 pm and Miss Lambert helped there instead. The nursery school returned after the war. Miss Lambert was now employed in her rightful place at £336 per annum and she had an assistant, Miss Chidwick, who received £252 per annum. The nursery school reopened on 22nd June 1945 as a voluntary nursery school. The wartime nursery appears to have closed down.

On the 50th birthday in 1946, the school gave an entertainment for the Friends of the Settlement *"dressed in red and green smocks who enlightened us as to how Peter plays with one hammer and what happens down at the farm" [43].* The nursery school were taken back to Glyndebourne for a fortnight's holiday in 1947. The organisation of this makes the mind boggle, as they took 'all the nursery children, furniture, cooking utensils and toys'. Great emphasis was still laid on health and the children were regularly weighed and examined. *"Dirty heads were far from uncommon and children were permanently excluded because of this condition" [Joan Serle, headmistress] [44].* Cod liver oil and orange juice supplemented the meals, and the children were expected to sleep for at least one and a half hours in the afternoon. The Board of Education inspection in 1949 suggested that the dinner should be at noon, that children should use knives and forks and that the milk allocation should be two thirds of a pint. It also noted that clothes should not be dried in the laundry and that routine use of chamber pots should be discontinued. There was no mention of educational activities. The nursery was described as *"a nice bright room decorated with pictures of Donald Duck and other nursery favourites. The children who attend the nursery are those whose mothers go out to work during the day" [Schoolgirl report] [45]; "the nursery school is full and is about to have a change of staff. The assistant who came for a year is to go to college and the superintendent is leaving at the end of term. The nursery is having special help from the Norland Institute who come as part of their training" [Theo Waite, Organising Secretary] [46].*

The nursery was failing to pay off its debt to the Settlement's general fund. There was a crisis as the London County Council and the Ministry of Education grants *"do not suffice to cover the full cost of management, especially as the salaries under the Burnham scale have risen" [Elsie Bowerman, Wycombe Abbey Senior] [47]* and Elsie sent appeals to the schools. *"The nursery school is still much needed as so many young mothers in the neighbourhood are obliged to go out to work" [ibid] [48].* In the Annual Report of 1951-52, response from these appeals were acknowledged as having saved the Nursery School from closure. By then the nursery school had 34 children and the grants from the LCC and the Ministry of Education were £1,032 and £368.10s.8d. respectively. The emphasis was still largely on a healthy way of life. *"The nursery has 35 children between two and five and gives them good food, fresh air and an afternoon rest" [Film Commentary] [49].* The annual registration detailed twice termly visits from the doctor and daily visits from the council school nursing sister. The school was also expected to take precautions against the spread of disease ensuring the children had separate beds, flannels, towels, blankets and that suspects would be moved to an isolation room if necessary.

23 The Nursery School in the Settlement Garden, 1956

There was a concerned debate in the Executive Committee in 1957 about certain families not deserving of a nursery place so fees were put up to 15/- a week and needy families could pay a reduced fee. A report in the Record says *"there are 38 on roll, with 9 new ones, with an average age of three and a half years... ... they were again 'sowing the seeds of good citizenship' in these children."* A mawkish description follows. *"Lonely little children who have no back garden, not even a yard. That is the problem of children in flats - where are they to play? I was most impressed and touched by a mother who came to enter her little girl aged four, 'She's lonely, she will go up to anyone in the street and talk to them. Will you take her?' The child asked if she could go and play with them. The others were climbing the frame, riding tricycles, wheelbarrows, rocking horse and on the helter skelter" [MLL (probably May Lee, Chairman of the Nursery School Committee] [50]; "The case of every child admitted is investigated most carefully. Some are very sad, children of one parent only, unmarried mothers, deserted wives, deserted husbands, widows and widowers. We need toys, for toys will wear out and break" [ibid] [51].*

The descriptive tone became slightly different in 1958, when the nursery had 40 children now and who were *"practically all problems. This term we seem to have a large proportion of very young ones who spent the first day or two crying in unison for their mothers... ... Nowadays we get so many children whose parents simply cannot manage them and they come to us as 'uncontrollable' at the age of three or thereabouts!! I think part of the trouble may be caused by the fact so many families now live in flats and the children have nowhere to play and have to be quiet for fear of the neighbours" [Theo Waite, Organising Secretary] [52].* By 1960 the school was described as *"thoroughly cosmopolitan and at the moment we have two Jamaicans, two Indians and one Turk on our register" [Annual Report] [53].* As more estates were being built, the aim was for the children *"to get out in the playground and enjoy the sunshine. The tinies are still in the majority and need great care and attention at first but soon settle in happily. There is no racial question here and the little West Indians mingle naturally with the other children sharing all their toys and games. Several of the children come from problem families and the regular life in school is of great benefit to them" [EB, probably Elsie Bowerman][54].*

Florrie Whale recalls working in the nursery. *"The head was Mrs Bellamy. The children arrived in the morning and stayed all day. I used to help around the teacher, sitting with the older ones to cut out pictures and make up picture albums, take them to the toilet, help to feed them... ...they were all put down to sleep in their little beds and we used to have to make sure they closed their eyes. I was actually in the nursery when Princess Margaret came to visit" [55].* Princess Margaret visited the nursery school on November 8th, 1960. She talked to thirty-seven *"toddlers of the nursery school (who) stood in a group and solemnly said their prayers but found it impossible to keep their eyes tightly shut. They couldn't resist peeping at the lady who was praying with them for the lady in the smoke blue velvet suit and feather hat was Princess Margaret" [Christine Parsons and Margaret Morland, Schoolgirls] [56].* When they had sung two songs for the Princess, they had their tea with blancmange and jelly as an extra treat.

May Lee, who was Chairman of the Nursery School Committee, reported *"41 children under 5 welcomed at 8.45 by the head mistress. In the playground there was a slide, roundabout, climbing frame and sand pit. They left at 4.15 pm. Life in a flat - 'There is no playground-the balcony is an incentive to climb- the neighbours complain if a train is wound up and allowed to run on the floor- mother becomes tense and taut- she can never relax. They* (the children) *have a good dinner- joint, fresh vegetables, pudding and custard prepared by the cook who has been with us 7 years......special cake, complete with candles on birthdays, bread and butter, jam, cake and free milk given for tea"* Educational activities were now mentioned. *"There are two trained nursery nurses who do simple teaching, singing, painting and toy making. Valuable foundations are laid when the children are taught at this early age to pray and give thanks. Suitable prayers and hymns and a Bible story are taken each morning, grace is said at meals and the day ends with goodbyes, a hymn and prayers" [57].* Numbers were such now that two shifts were needed and in 1963 thirty-four children attended in the morning and forty in the afternoon. The school was opened from 8.45 am to 4.30 pm five days a week for the usual school terms. Each group of children, aged from three, came for two and half hours. The assistants were all trained nursery nurses. The nursery school was reputed to *"provide a happy and secure environment in which children can work and play with materials which exercise their imagination and creative abilities as well as indulging in boisterous play when they can 'let off steam' without harming themselves or others. Sand and water are essential materials with which children can gain a first insight into capacity and number. There is a quiet room where there's a book corner and puzzles. Some......never have the opportunity at home to look at books or use puzzles" [UGS Review] [58].* Four years later the staff consisted of a head teacher, three assistants, eighty children and another fifty-five on the waiting list. With this increase in numbers there was a need to *"have someone on the door, when children go in and out, as security" [Executive Committee] [59].*

Mary Welsh was Chairman of the Nursery School Committee for five years. She and Bettie Skinner, one of the teachers on James Allen's Girls' School staff and a long time worker at the Settlement, worked hard to raise money for the nursery. The Princess Elizabeth Flag Day was an annual event of great importance as all the proceeds went to the nursery school and the schoolgirls took part in selling the flags. Even though Bettie Skinner hailed this 'as our great money raising effort', only £65 was collected in 1965. The nursery now had a second large room which was blue and white. They had a new Wendy house, a new sink unit, and a new garden shed, so 'no longer are the toys damaged by damp'. The supporting schools gave all these items.

24 Children in the Nursery School, 1965

In 1967, a very detailed document was sent to the education office, referring to the recently published Plowden Report, in a move to open two satellite nursery schools, one on the Acorn Estate and one in Queen's Road. There is no record of this happening although both were very badly needed.

It was obvious from reports in the early 1970s, that the nursery school was treated apart from the other activities in the Settlement. It had been taken over by the Inner London Education Authority who paid for the salaries, maintenance and equipment. No direct mention was made of the nursery school although publicity brochures did mention there were facilities for nursery-aged children. The business plan of 1978 included the nursery school with the old people's clubs and the PDCCA [Peckham and Dulwich Caribbean Community Association], all of whom paid some rent to the Settlement for use of premises. Then in 1981, the annual report stated that the educational needs of the very young were catered for and news of the nursery school started to reappear in the school bulletins. The new head teacher Jane Keefe was *"keen to dispel the notion of the school as an isolated unit cut off from the wider community" [Barbara Hill, Education Officer] [60]*. She and Mike Phillips (a community worker in the Settlement) were working on the idea *"of using part of the building's basement as a drop-in for nursery school mothers and mothers from the local estates" [ibid] [61]; "for the very young children when they can learn to mix with other children and through creative play gain a first appreciation of shape, colours, etc" [Appeals Brochure] [62]*. The Nell Gwyn Nursery (as it was now called) had 13 staff including a male part-time teacher.

25 Princess Margaret's visit to the Nursery School, 1982

From its earliest days the nursery school has attracted teacher trainees, nursery nurse trainees, NVQ students, social science students, both male and female, and schoolgirl volunteers. This continues to this day.

The Day Nursery

In 1980, a mother and toddler group run by Sharon McNeil, was meeting in the Settlement. This grew so popular that the opening hours were extended to give birth to the All Nations Day Nursery, a separate entity from the nursery school.

The name, suggested by Sharon, reflected the ethnic mix of the children. *"There are no Chinese children... ...they supply their own day care and no Asians because of their extended family... ...we have mostly West Indians, Nigerians, and White British" [Kate Lindsay, Nursery officer] [63].* It started with fourteen children and expanded quickly. Tania McPherson came to work as a volunteer helper at the new day nursery and later took qualifications as a nursery assistant. She and Sharon still work in the day nursery. *"This is what a settlement is all about. Two local women came to ask if they could have a room to run a crèche. They did and gave the children lunch. After a while it needed to be put on a proper footing. So the Settlement went out, raised the money, made the proper communications and hence the day nursery which has gone from strength to strength" [Kitty Leek, Director] [64].* The day nursery was formally opened by the Mayor of Southwark.

Tania remembers the visit of Princess Margaret in 1982. *"We were in (what is now) the computer room. I remember actually curtsying, we had to practise that - only seems like yesterday. She's actually quite small. She shook my hand and said, 'You must really enjoy working here with all these children'. I'll always remember because she's the first and only royal I've ever met" [65]* and where *"one of the children direct(ed) the Princess's attention to a large spider crawling out of the woodwork with a nudge and a quick 'ere Miss'" [Barbara Hill, Education Officer] [66].* By 1983 the nursery was in receipt of a Borough of Southwark grant and an earmarked £7,200 from BASSAC. A year later the Women's Committee Support Unit granted some financial aid too.

It was decided to convert the old residents' wing at a cost of £63,900 but this took nearly seven months to do, and the nursery occupied the Youth Club area for the duration of the building work. In 1990 the All Nations Nursery was open from 8.00 am to 6.00 pm, five days a week. In keeping with the sensitive race issues of the time, a lady from the local authority came to inspect the day nursery to ensure the ethnic mix reflected the local community. This caused a real dilemma. *"That means she was going to tell me to hold the next eight places for white children. The black parents get their names down first on the waiting list. If you are on the top of the list you get the next place. A lot of black parents are on their own as well so they need the nursery places" [Kitty Leek, Director] [67].*

26 The Fence dividing the Two Nursery Schools

The Mother and Toddler group had continued under the leadership of Carole Corless and was funded by Southwark and there was a drop-in centre for mothers, too. The Settlement was also involved in the Southwark Institute Educational Home Visiting Scheme.

There was some rivalry between the two nurseries. An argument over play space ended with the shared space being fenced off to provide two separate play areas. A separate board of governors for the All Nations Nursery was formed in 1984. A year later the mother and toddler groups moved to the Bells Garden Community Centre and the fence between the play areas was removed. The London Borough of Southwark then intimated that it wanted to move Nell Gwyn School to new premises. The nursery now had sixty children on roll but did not cater for working mothers. There was a debate about moving the school to the Rye Annexe in Meeting House Lane. The rent from the Nell Gwyn was an essential part of the core costs and should have been double the present rent asked, but the lease for the school did not expire until 1995. However, there was a new 'under eights' manager in Southwark Borough Council who gave the go ahead for the move. The nursery school moved out in January 1994. The Settlement was awarded £18,000 if it offered five additional places in its day nursery. The numbers there were now twenty-five with 300 children on the waiting list. A community work student on placement, who was assigned to the day nursery, reported *"I work in the All Nations Day Nursery every Friday, all day. There are not a lot of men working in a nursery. The first day I was flavour of the day and the children wanted to play with me and sit with them at lunch. One thing… …there were no guns, action men dolls or things that would separate the boys from the girls, which is good. If anyone needs to learn observational skills, the nursery is the place, your eyes have to be everywhere" [Trevor Swaby, Student] [68].*

The All Nations Nursery went through a bad patch in 1995 with staff leaving and being ill. It was still looking for an Officer in Charge. The nursery hours had been extended and parents were now paying £45 a week. Eventually in September 1995, Nicki Brown was appointed to be in charge of the nursery. When Kate Lindsay joined as deputy she recalls *"My first impressions… …it's bright and airy… …it's got lots of windows and light. The children were busy doing and there was lots going on. I liked the staff and the whole feel of the place" [69].*

Southwark Borough Council announced it was very satisfied with All Nations Nursery, and in 1997 it passed its DfEE Ofsted inspection with flying colours. *"The personal and social development is a strength of the nursery. Staff and children treat each other with respect and consideration...... The teaching is uniformly good, often excellent......partnership with parents is excellent." [Ofsted Inspection] [70].* Two years later, the nursery was recorded as making a substantial contribution to the community in Southwark's Community Survey of Consort and Friary Wards.

27 The All Nations Nursery School, 2000

28 The Nursery Play Area, 2000

Activities Concerning Health

The health of the residents in Peckham has always been a concern for the Settlement. Harry Veasey described the problems. *"Bronchitis, consumption and other lung diseases are specially prevalent amongst the men and women... ...children grow up weakly with far too large a population suffering from hip and spinal complaints, rickets and a terrible number of infants sicken before they are a year old" [71].* These diseases were of course closely allied to the poverty of the people and efforts to combat some of the worst problems and to educate people into healthy ways are well documented. The outings to the schools and the country were primarily initiated for the health of the residents and were actually called the 'Fresh Air Outings.' The work of the Infant Welfare Clinics was superlative in combating some of the children's ailments as well as introducing the idea of preventative measures and health education. It was claimed that the UGS had helped to reduce the Peckham infant mortality rate from 200 per 1000 in 1897 to less than 70 per 1000 in 1929.

The Foot Clinic

In 1950 a foot clinic was begun for old aged pensioners. At first this was held twice a month. It cost one shilling and sixpence a session, but proved so popular that by 1957 there were two sessions a week, the waiting time for an appointment was 'only 4 weeks' and there was a total of 534 treatments a year. Mr Heaton Ward was the voluntary chiropodist who supplied all his own equipment and gave at least 114 sessions free, *"an outstanding example of faithfulness and service" [Annual Report] [72]*, a phrase that could have been applied to so many who worked at the Settlement. Schoolgirls helped as receptionists and *"heard several histories of feet from their owners" [E Allen, Schoolgirl] [73]*. The clinic was taken over by the Borough in 1961.

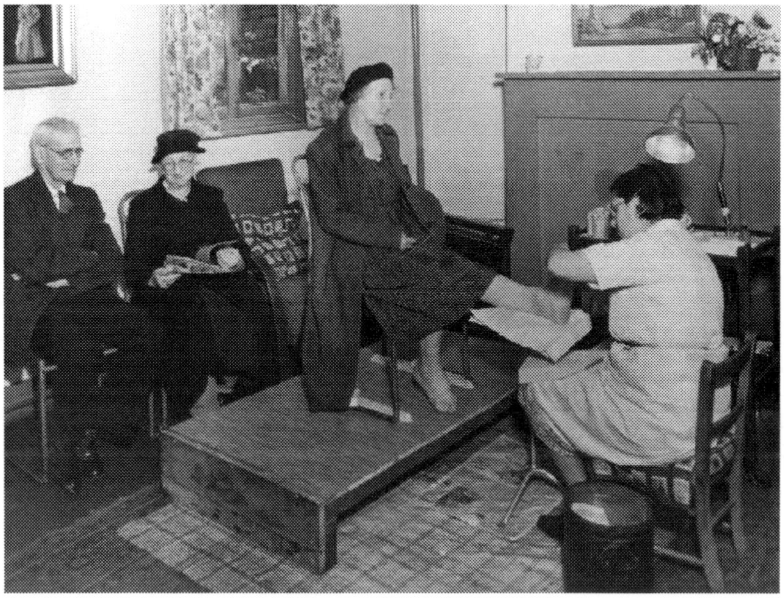

29 The Old People's Foot Clinic, 1950s

Meals on Wheels

Meals on Wheels was one of the services supplied by the Settlement, ensuring that the old people of the area could have a hot meal in the middle of the day. This had started in the Second World War when twenty to thirty tables were set up in the hall every day to feed about 150 people in 'a homely atmosphere so unlike a restaurant'. A blackboard in the porch announced a healthy meal of 'minced beef, carrots, potatoes and fig pudding' in 1941. It is recorded that 15,000 hot meals were sent out in 1945, an enormous undertaking. For six pence, the dining club members could eat steak and kidney pie, swede and potatoes, rice pudding and jam.

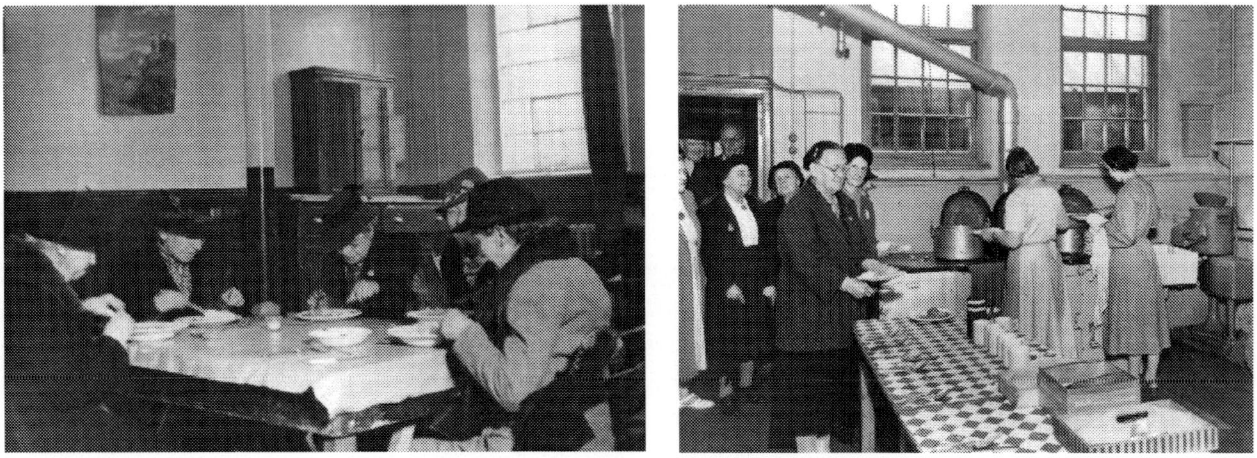

30 The Old People's Dinner Club, late 1940s and 1956

Escorting the van was one of the fondest memories for the schoolgirls and the other volunteers. *"The meals were prepared, placed in heat conservators, and stacked in a van……I accompanied the van driver and delivered and served the meals to people in their own homes. To be eligible for these meals the people had to have a doctor's certificate to say they needed them and cannot get their own" [ibid.] [74]; "the meals were cooked in the Settlement Kitchen and there were three routes to cover" [Jill Andrews, Student Worker] [75]; "Christmas Day* (was) *spent taking dinners out to housebound people in the vicinity and serving dinners at the Settlement to members of the old peoples' clubs" [Mary Welsh, Chairman of the Nursery School Committee] [76].* At least eighty people sat down to Christmas dinner in the 1950s.

31 Meals on Wheels, late 1950s

In 1957, 32,414 hot dinners were cooked at the Settlement, of which 19,569 were sent out to Camberwell and Deptford, using five borough vans with paid drivers and some paid escorts. Camberwell took over the responsibility for the financial organisation of Meals on Wheels in 1961 and rented the kitchens from the Settlement for a further few years.

Food was a perennial topic and great attention was given to correct feeding especially with the young babies. In 1963, a student commented, *"mothers sometimes asked for money to buy food; they could be fairly insistent if not intimidating. We were able to give them vouchers which could be exchanged for powdered milk or baby food. We were not allowed to give them tins of food which apparently just got sold for cash" [Susan Waggitt, Student Worker] [77].*

Country and Seaside Holidays

The Ramsgate holidays had started in 1961. Twenty-two old people went on the first holiday to a hotel where the proprietress *"didn't mind taking handicapped old people"* and *"where television was a fascination even when it was not on." [Settlement News, March 1961][78]. "They* (the guests) *came either from our clubs or were referred to us by the Camberwell King George VI Club for disabled people. We took over a small family run hotel in Ramsgate, took huge quantities of equipment with us such as wheelchairs, commodes and knitted blankets. We ran the holidays with two staff, a volunteer and two St John's Ambulance helpers. As far as I remember we went twice yearly and each time ran two holidays each of ten days" [Maureen Marshall, Student Worker] [79].*

By 1964 eighty-eight people had stayed at Ramsgate. The Friends of the Settlement helped prepare for this great event, dealing with the necessary packing and travel arrangements. *"A large box of toilet holdalls, filled with everything from soap to denture powder" [80].* Gifts came from the schools. *"One problem is nightwear……*(so we) *decided……to buy yards and yards of winceyette material and make dressing gowns, pyjamas and nightgowns to lend to those who might need them" [UGS Record] [81].* A St. John's Ambulance man always accompanied the coach and cars. George Hale was the friendly coach owner, who transported the old people from their homes to Ramsgate and back again. He made a special set of shallow steps so the old people could get in and out of the coach more easily. The first task in the mornings was to empty the commodes. *"Miss Grace Griffiths who was a voluntary worker* (and a Wycombe Abbey Senior) *was wonderful here and with rubber gloves and sprays she would announce 'Only number ones, dears, no number twos'" [Jennie Fisher, Social Worker] [82].* The value of fresh country air was enumerated in 1965 when it was recorded that holidays had been given to 109 people with physical disabilities, 10 old aged pensioners and 41 children.

32 At Ramsgate, 1965

The Children's Country Holiday Fund, working through the Settlement, was sending large numbers of children on holiday, until the 1960s. In 1957, 104 children went to the country from the Peckham area. The CCHF operates to this day and still uses the Settlement on occasions as a Headquarters.

Activities Concerning Social Needs

Visiting

The visiting of old and lonely people was considered to be a major task of the Settlement, until the 1980s. There were constant exhortations for volunteers and schoolgirls to give time for visits each week and to write letters. Miss Hetty Barnes was a lady who probably did very well for visitors as she is mentioned in many school magazines and was a star in the Diamond Jubilee film. She had daily meals-on-wheels and somebody from the Settlement put her to bed every Tuesday night. It is not mentioned how she managed on the other evenings. This lady died in 1961 and a memorial to her from the members of St Chrysostom's Church raised £27 9s 6d. Nearly fifty, mostly older, people were visited regularly in 1965. *"Most of the housebound are confined to their homes by the snow…… we are very worried for fear they might be marooned at home without food or fuel and everyone who can be spared was sent round visiting. We were glad we did this as we found a number ill in bed……and most of them were running short of coal" [Theo Waite, Organising Secretary] [83].* Visiting was sometimes a dangerous business. *"We have made a plan which everyone at the Settlement is supposed to learn by heart of the position of the occupied flats* (in the Goldsmith Mansions from which families were gradually being moved out) *and what to do if the whole place went up in smoke. There is so much combustible material......we have piles of blankets and torches at various strategic points so that we can sally forth and catch the babies if they have to be dropped out of the windows" [Newsletter] [84].* It is interesting that fears for personal security are never mentioned at this time. This issue reared its ugly head in the 1980s.

33 Visiting, 1975

Triple S Scheme

The appointment of Dulcie Groves as warden in 1964, the first qualified and professional community worker, heralded a more structured organisation of services from the volunteer section. In the late 1960s the Southwark Service Scheme, or Triple S as it became known, was an attempt to increase volunteer activity especially amongst the young, as there was a critical shortage of responsible adult volunteers. The Sembal Trust had given a grant for the purpose of setting up school visiting teams. The Social Service conference at the Settlement was entitled 'Opportunities for voluntary work in the community' to reinforce the message. Although the initial task force was a national idea, four Settlements in South London, Cambridge House, Blackfriars (one worker was David Kitchen, later to become Director of Peckham), Bede House and Peckham took this on board and developed their own service. Jennie Fisher had the task of organising bands of volunteers as working parties to do rescue jobs in Peckham, decorating houses, gardening, mending furniture, doing small repairs, hairdressing, helping pensioners move house, shopping, changing books at the library, escorting on outings, writing letters, or just talking or eating hotdogs. Her appointment was providential. *"A valuable part of her work has been to establish and strengthen our links with other voluntary and statutory social services at the local level and with the newly created Municipal Authorities" [Geoffrey Heal, Acting Warden] [85]* and there is ample evidence that she did just that. She is described as *"a breath of fresh air, full of life and practical, always cheerful who led a first rate team" [Eve Keatley, Organising Secretary] [86].* In 1966, Jennie Fisher reported in the UGS Review that sixty-six girls had visited forty-one people. 'Rewarding' and 'worthwhile' were the buzzwords in these reports, and there was obvious enjoyment and real friendliness from both sides. The girls remember this invaluable work vividly. There were two reports from them which ended with *"I was a little uncertain when I came here whether the Settlement was quite working… …now I am convinced that it is doing a wonderful job in the community of Peckham" [Lindsay Dowling, Schoolgirl] [87]; "because of their difficulty in getting about, the Settlement does them* (housebound people) *great service" [Anne McFadyen, Schoolgirl] [88].*

During the year 1967/8, five hundred young people volunteered for work at the Settlement and at least four hundred old people were visited regularly. Annie Courcier had taken over from Jennie Fisher by now. The whole venture was very successful because it fulfilled the short-term needs of the neighbourhood and in the long-term fostered community spirit. *"Friendliness is part of the answer. Behind the kindness has to be organisation to be sure people are not let down. Organisation and know-how are needed for putting people in touch with agencies who can help them. Skill as well as kindness is needed" [UGS Review] [89].* James Allen's School magazine quoted *"many girls still take great pleasure in weekly visits to the old and lonely people in the neighbourhood. Often a few visits suffice to establish a warm and friendly relationship and some of our present contacts have survived three years or more" [90].*

The settlements had proved there was a need for an efficient volunteer bureau. It was found, though, that the volunteers needed constant supervision and advice, and as many referrals came from the Council Welfare Department, some of the cases were not always suitable for a school workforce. A school-aged band represented a rapid turnover of personnel and this made continuity quite difficult. Also, this band of volunteers had worked with mainly old and disabled people and it was felt there was an equal if not greater need for volunteers to work with all age groups. Nevertheless, *"Triple S had been a resounding success – it's success… …raises further questions about the contribution of young voluntary community care and about community development as a method of social work" [Robin Guthrie] [91].*

<u>Other Social Needs</u>

In the early days of the Settlement it was obvious that the Mission just wanted to help the people who had little money for the basic needs of life. Over the years, this approach seemed to change or it may have just been the development of neighbourly feeling. The mission was now to help the misfits or unfortunates of society. This description of people who came to the Settlement is an example of much of this thinking. *"The sad, the lonely, the tired… …those with too much leisure and the ones with not enough, the ones who want to expend their energies and those with none left to expend, the anxious, the confused, the happy, the light-hearted, the assiduous and the vandals (all of whom are lovable and under twelve years of age)" [92].* This was reiterated in 1971 when it was emphasised the Settlement was a community 'village' centre with the task of creating a neighbourly feeling and where people could go especially *"the lonely, odd ones out in society" [Wycombe Abbey Gazette] [93].* The spirit of this age can be summed up perhaps in Elsie Bowerman's words in 1957. *"This is the answer to those who say that there is no need for social service now that we have a Welfare State. We have to work through existing agencies such as school care committees, Nursery schools, the Clubs and any other means… …to bring us into personal touch with our neighbours. Our concern, at a deeply personal level, is with old Mrs S. who is housebound, with the T. family being evicted tomorrow, and Mrs G. whose husband has just come out of prison... ...Personal involvement makes it painfully aware that the welfare state is not enough... ...this is an over-riding advantage of a local Settlement and this is the greatest contribution that can be brought between statutory and voluntary services" [94].*

Patty Paice began a club for children at risk, who came from broken homes or lived in poor surroundings. Patty organised art projects in the basement and outings to encourage these children, many with personality and other social problems, to meet and talk. In 1968 there were 62 children in small groups with a team of three adults to each group so that each child could have some attention, affection and care.

Youth Work

Work with the teenagers was a theme throughout the early years, in an effort to occupy them with activities which were worthwhile, interesting and fulfilling. A coffee bar was opened in 1963 for teenagers, principally to keep this population off the streets and give them something constructive to do. It soon had a steady regular membership of eighty. The club band played regularly and the club joined other Settlement activities, collected funds for the other clubs and participated in the local football and cricket matches. Helen Thompson, the club leader, organised holidays to Spain and Belgium and her work was much respected by the local police.

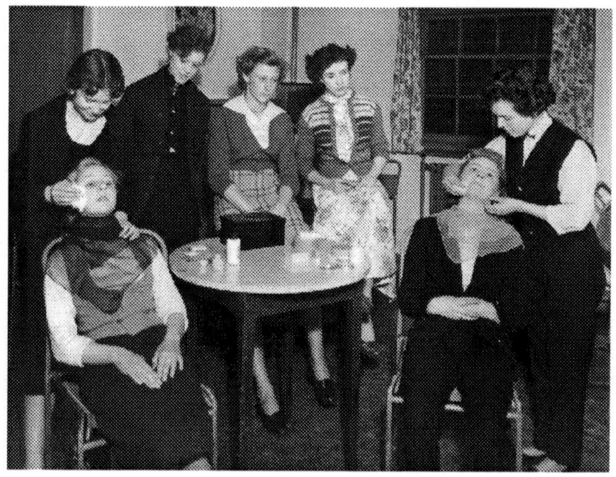

34 The Youth Club, 1955

35 The Youth Club, 1982

In 1980, the director wrote that the *"Peckham Settlement is almost unique amongst Settlements because much of the scope of its projects and activities is to help the West Indian Community" [95]*. In 1981 ILEA agreed that the building should provide social and recreational activities for young people until 2009. The GLC extended this date to 2015, and grants were paid for the provision of part-time youth workers. The youth club was racially mixed now, but disputes with the nursery school and other Settlement activities led to its closure and the youth work was taken over by the Peckham Youth Project. This project organised work with homeless youngsters, ran discussion groups for young black women in schools and set up a drop-in day centre for young black teenagers. It later extended its services to some artistic, dance and drama activities, again mainly for the black population.

The Friary Neighbourhood Youth Development Project used offices in the Settlement in 1994. It was affiliated to The Bird in the Bush Youth Club, the Acorn Youth Club and employed a part-time worker who ran a group for young travellers.

Two highly committed volunteers ran the Visions Youth Club in 1997. This club was for 13 to 17 year-old pupils, some of whom had been excluded from school. It was held three times a week in the basement of the Settlement, and supported by the police and officials from All Saints Church. In 1998 this much needed club ceased because there was no funding for it to carry on.

<u>The Advice Centre</u>

From the very early days, the Settlement has given free advice to the people in the community. Much of this advice is informal and given when requested. The day centre, the care committees, the welfare clinics and many of the early clubs all had advice sessions as a component part of their activities. In 1955 there was *"a steady stream of visitors with requests for help" [Annual Report] [96]*. On several occasions the giving of advice was set on a more formal footing. From 1924 to 1928 Miss Honor Davy, one of the first women barristers, ran a free legal aid and advice centre. In the Second World War, the Settlement was recognised as the Citizens' Advice Bureau of the area. Staff at the Settlement attended courses to learn how 'to become encyclopaedias'. The Poor Man's Lawyer advised on legal problems but the staff was inundated with housing, domestic, health and bombardment questions. When in 1946 all but five of the Borough's bureaux closed, the Settlement was one which continued the work. Legal matters, housing, the benefit system, and unemployment have always been the main issues for advice. The requests were far ranging from 'How do I get a bus pass?' to essential house repairs.

The first formal advice centre in the last fifty years appears to have been established in 1973, mainly as a response to the new flat dwellers, the problems with that housing and communication with the local authorities. This centre ran on Saturday mornings for two and a half hours for several years. In 1980 the day centre for the young West Indians offered counselling and educational advice. Specialised and practical advice was given, especially to teenaged mothers. This centre ran until 1982. In the early 80s, it became obvious that women in the area had special problems and the Safety Valve Group was started to counsel and advise women experiencing divorce, abuse and violence.

Then in 1985 a group of women asked Christine Richards, the community worker, for help with budgeting and debt problems. From this small beginning the very successful advice centre began and ran until 1996. The centre opened initially twice a week with three locally trained volunteers. Demand grew into seven 2-hour sessions each week which included two evenings and Saturday mornings. Travellers and single parents were among the groups given specialist advice. In 1988 an astounding 874 people had asked for advice either by letter, visits or telephone calls.

The main presenting problems were social security, housing, unemployment, debts, tax, immigration and justice. This was especially amazing as the other nearby settlements and organisations were also offering advice sessions. In 1989 a twenty-four-hour advice marathon raised £200. In 1990 the centre dealt with 566 enquiries of which 424 people returned for more help. 25% of these people were employed and 75 % were out of work, two-thirds were females, and seventy had some disability. The highest usage by age was 20-29 years. By nationality, 170 were white, 121 Caribbean, 106 UK black, 76 Irish, 41 African, 31 Asian, 11 European and 8 Turkish. The centre was manned by volunteers on the lines of the Citizens' Advice Bureau in a typical self-help programme run by the community worker.

An unexpected benefit of the advice project was the effect of the training and general confidence gained by the volunteers. As a result there was a regular moving on to employment and many people entered work in the 'people field', a prospect they would have never entertained as an option. This experience gave the Settlement the idea for work with the local unemployed as it had first-hand evidence that with support and relevant training, local people could undertake most jobs.

In 1992 the lynchpin of this enterprise, Christine Richards, left and the sessions had to be curtailed to one evening and one morning a week. The Freeman's Trust injected additional funds and the service managed to expand. Although the need had not diminished, the lack of trained volunteers did. In 1995 the advice centre was operating three times a week where the main issues were still housing, debt and unemployment but now advice was being sought on immigration, drugs, health problems and asylum seeking, too. This latter issue was not new. In 1940 the Settlement helped refugees with billets. A refugee club was started to help them with their particular problems and a plea for people who spoke foreign languages was sent out. By 1996 the centre was incurring debts and so closed. However, the informal giving of advice and help continued.

In the middle 90s, Peckham Settlement had become the Community Centre of the area. Public meetings were held at the Settlement from 1991 and rooms were rented out to various community organisations with their own funding. The centre became a surgery for prospective councillors initially. Subsequently, the local ward councillors met once a month and later in 1994, the local members of Parliament used the Settlement. Space was also rented to organisers of the Duke of Edinburgh Scheme, Face to Face, and the Southwark Youth Project.

Social Activities

The plethora of clubs for different ages abounded after the Second World War in the Settlement. In 1947 it was recorded that all the clubs had wonderful outings to the schools. The youth club, the Acorns and two other clubs went camping. The Settlement ran five separate children's clubs in 1956 from under five to fifteen years of age.

36 The Mums' Club, 1950s

The Mums' club was flourishing with a total of 80 regular members in the late 1950s, and was described as fairly self-sufficient by 1960. They organised visits to local factories such as Peak Freans, Cherry Blossom, Stork and Cadbury's, demonstrations, and talks by people such as RNLI, drama lessons and outings without the children. The mothers would do keep fit, gym, tap-dancing, handcrafts, cookery, singing, and first aid. Florrie Whale remembers *"one of the students took us for drama classes and we put on a play. We were quite good and we entered this play against other clubs. I played the part of the cook, and was made up with rather a lot of rouge on my face to look chubby but by the time it was time for us to go on, I was so hot with nerves......it looked like I was on the bottle... ...I forgot the proper lines and put my own in and everybody was screaming with laughter. Needless to say we didn't win but it was good fun" [97].*

37 The Mums' Club Outing, 1967

Peggy Wraight was the Wycombe Abbey Senior who inspired this activity, but she principally worked with the teenagers aged between fifteen and twenty. She helped organise cookery, interior decorating, beauty culture, drama, ballroom dancing and entered them into the Camberwell Youth Drama Festival and the Camberwell and District Annual Sports Shield. This club had trained instructors for boxing and physical training and opened four nights a week. Participants paid the princely subscription of sixpence a week. The club also had a good band in 1956 and *"put in much serious practice... ...and proved it to the surrounding neighbourhood" [E Allen, Schoolgirl] [98].*

38 The Youth Club Band, 1956

By 1968 the Youth Club had 125 members and deliberately set out to capture 'the misfits' of the area, by discretely organising projects and outings which might appeal to them.

The fun element was always present when the students and older people's clubs put on pantomimes. The Monday Club frequently gave concert parties, using the splendid new stage that the

Fire Brigade had donated and built. *"They were wonderful friends and gave lots of practical assistance, e.g. preparing stage scenery for shows" [Maureen Marshall, Student Worker] [99].* The Club toured other old people's clubs in the area to perform, and the pantomime of Cinderella in 1960 was particularly memorable. *"The slapstick scene involved a lot of flour and water, very messy in spite of the tarpaulin" [Susan Waggitt, Student Worker] [100].*

39 Cinderella, 1960

The Tuesday club used to have keep fit classes, where they would *"jump the horse, use the mat, skip to music, swing the baton, balance on forms" [Florrie Whale, Thursday Club] [101].* This club joined the League of Health and Beauty and for many years put on shows in other parts of London. The local police voluntarily ran gym classes for boys in the hall, and one resident remembers helping with a boys' music club. There was a cookery club for the boys too, but the lack of male leaders was a constant problem. Tuesday also saw the meeting of the Blind Club every month.

A very popular club was held on Wednesdays, the needlework club, where ladies were taught to make do and mend, *"because we were all poor. We used to buy second hand dresses, take the tops off and make dirndl skirts out of them...... to turn an old coat inside out and make it look like new... ...to make small things for our children" [ibid] [102].*

40 The Make-Do-and-Mend Club, 1950s

Jane Johnson ran a very successful club for some years for the pensioners with disabilities, who were brought to the Settlement in ambulances by volunteers for a singsong and tea. Auld Lang Syne was always sung at the end of each meeting because it was quite likely one of the club members would not be there the next week. Jane was utterly dedicated to these pensioners and had run this club from the late 70s. She was an Old Girl of Putney High School, had been helping as a volunteer from about 1957 and served on the Executive Committee. She would often pack at least six old ladies into her ancient Rover and take them on outings as well. She gave an unsecured loan to the Settlement and bought a piano. It was a sad day for the Settlement when she died in 1995.

41 Jane Johnson Sings at the Friday Club, 1967

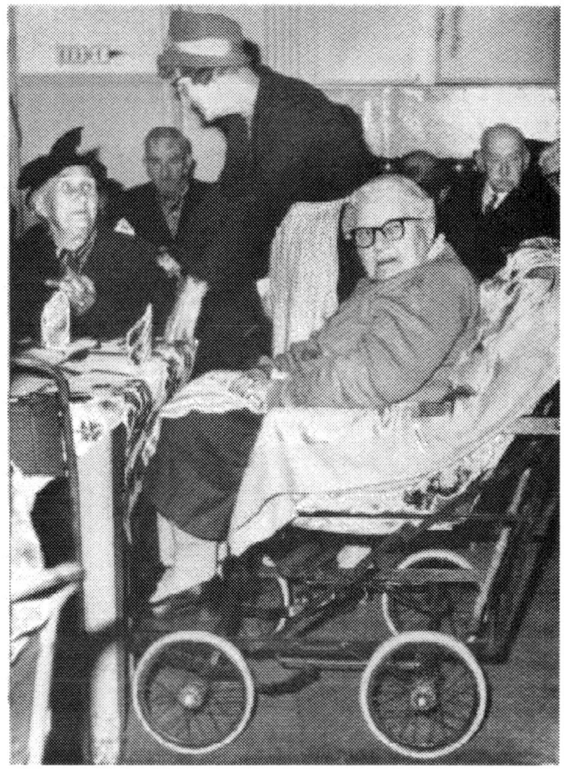

42 The Wednesday Club, 1966

The Squirrels club was on Fridays after school as was the youth club. Sue Wright, (a Wycombe Abbey Senior and from a family whose sister and mother both helped at the Settlement), remembers *"the youth club took place in the main hall or in the semi-basement. It was a boisterous rowdy affair and I felt ill equipped to manage. One time I……got locked in the downstairs area with a whole lot of young people and I remember feeling an awful fool" [103].*

43 The Squirrels, 1950s

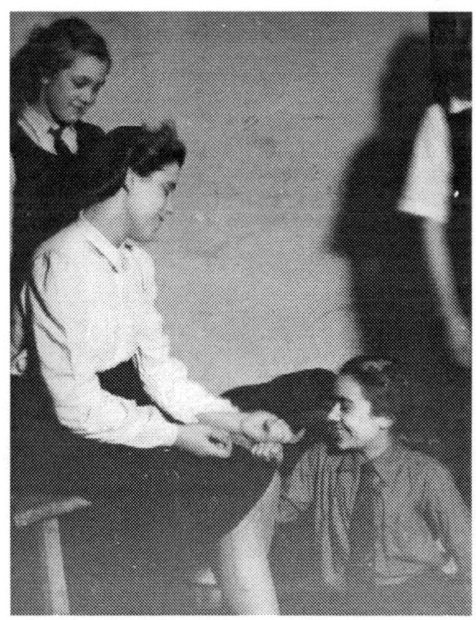

44 The Acorns, 1950s

The problems of young girls helping with the youth of Peckham are highlighted in another account of 1956. *"One afternoon we took the girls (the Acorns) to an art gallery. But they soon wanted to leave and preferred to play games at the Settlement" [E Allen, Schoolgirl] [104].*

Peggy Wraight reinstated the Sunday evening meetings which were debates, discussions and religious instruction. A Sunday club for pensioners was started in 1967, where many people with severe disabilities came for lunch and a chat. In the 1950s these clubs used to cost about 2/6 a year.

The youth club was still functioning in the 1970s but was now all black and was run by the Karib society rather than Settlement volunteers. There was the Dynamo football club. The packed and very popular disco club ran on Thursday and Sunday evenings for the 16+ groups. Pamela Roach (now training at the Friary Open Learning Centre) attended every evening until she moved away. *"I would never miss it if I could help" [105].* The Sojourner Truth Youth Association also operated from the Settlement. In 1982, there was a black girls' youth club, African dancing, silk screens projects, a video club, the youth club, and four clubs for pensioners. Organisations outside the Settlement began to come in to use the vacant premises. One such organisation was the Peckham Varieties, a theatre project group, which gave regular performances of drama, singing and dance. This organisation operated from 1983 until 1985. A Peckham Settlement Project, funded by City Parochial Foundation, was Crystal Prospect, an arts and entertainment group which included singing, steel band tuition, ballet, tap, and jazz dancing. In 1985, the New Theatre Programme held popular jazz workshops.

There were always clubs for senior citizens. At one stage there were no less than five groups but in later years this has become three, which are thriving. In 1982 the Settlement was funded for a voluntary worker to help with the pensioners, and two years later it applied for £300 to up grade the kitchen for the pensioners pop-in centre. There was also an attempt to start a group for the older black people but so few came this was disbanded. There was an effort to include the Vietnamese Elder Persons Group in the activities but there was concern over the 'foreign food' served, so this group did not come either. The pensioners' groups remain exclusively white, and the vast majority of them are ladies, although husbands join in on occasions.

45 The Pensioners' Pop-In, 1985

The Friends

This group was established informally in 1954, although a small set of Friends is reported to have been in existence in the 1920s and 1930s. Sixty of the Friends attended the Annual Service in 1955. It was formally established in 1958, with a ball, and held its first AGM in 1959. The group arranged its own social programme as well as fund-raising and helping the Settlement. At first it was a band of twelve local voluntary workers who were a faithful emergency corps providing practical help, visiting, assisting with Settlement activities and manning the travelling shop. The organisation was principally for those residents, Old Girls or other people who could not help at the Settlement regularly but still wanted to give time and money to the cause.

46 Miss Cousins Receives the Stage from the Peckham Road Fire Station, 1958

Fire Officer Adams (stationed at the nearby Fire Station) was Chairman of the Friends in 1959 and instrumental in the collection of money and erection of the stage. He also served on the Executive Committee for some years.

There were now 48 members who all paid a small subscription and volunteered for various tasks. Also that year an Association of Friends was inaugurated especially for those who lived at a distance from the Settlement. *"Although (The Friends) was meant originally for those living near at hand, so many others have asked to join that we have decided to have an Associate Section for non-active members, who by paying a higher subscription, will help with the expenses incurred by those who are actually doing the work. We think this may appeal to girls leaving school who want to keep in closer touch with the UGS than they can do through their own OGA" [Letter to St Swithun's School][106].* In 1960 it was suggested each Friend should adopt one of the housebound in the area. George, the friendly coach driver, mentioned on many occasions, became a Friend. The Friends raised £1,000 for the Settlement's van, which was used until 1971, and the organisation paid for the petrol and maintenance and carried out escort duty on the outings. This van was bright blue and a very familiar sight in the locality. *"In winter, we load the van with coal and blankets for the elderly people and in the summer we take it to the seaside full of material... ...for the Ramsgate holidays" [UGS Record, Spring 1963] [107].*

47 The Friends Hand Over the Blue Van, 1970

The Friends were meeting at least once a week now. By 1967 there were a substantial number of local people who raised funds and helped with the social activities. The Association of Friends numbered

120 who all paid 2/6d a year and received the UGS Newsletter. Constance Irons was the Secretary of the Friends in 1966 and reported on the group in the UGS Review. She died in 1974 having completed fifteen years as the Friends' Secretary and 70 years as a volunteer helper at the UGS. As so often happens when the stalwart goes, the link was broken.

There is very little reference to a support group after 1972 although twenty-one very influential Members of Parliament, businessmen and women, actors, broadcasters, Union leaders, authors, and members of the Church were listed as Friends and supporters of the Settlement in the early 80s. People were able to become members of the Peckham Settlement and donated £300 in 1996. In 1999 the new Director urged people to become a Member Friend of the Settlement by donating £10 for which they would receive a newsletter, the Annual Report and be invited to special events. The number of Friends is now growing especially amongst the residents of the community.

One of the most valuable assets to the Settlement is illustrated both by the Friends, the Old Girls and the Supporting Schools. This is the value of networking. The ability to ask for favours, donations and other gifts in kind from their own friends and acquaintances cannot be underestimated. This has ranged from using influence to ask particularly high profile people to acknowledge the Settlement, encouraging organisations to involve themselves with the Settlement and to giving large donations, grants or legacies. Much of this networking has emanated from Wycombe Abbey Seniors, and from some Executive Committee members. This silent but exceptional asset has given an impetus to the work of the Settlement and maybe even saved the Settlement from closure on one occasion.

The Present

An update in the Wycombe Abbey Gazette for 1996 gave the state of the Union. *"The two nursery schools enjoy an active programme, both inside their bright premises and outside in the garden. The lack of play areas, coupled with the number of children living in high-rise flats means that organised holiday schemes are of great importance. During the summer holidays the Settlement caters for six to eleven years olds giving them a programme of activities and trips out. There is also the Peckham Summer Project, providing activities for the eleven to nineteen year olds during the holidays. Local students, teachers and the police give their time to help with this scheme. The three pensioners' clubs meet three times a week and the advice service offers help at the Settlement three evenings a week. The Settlement has been working with the unemployed and has provided a Task Force outreach worker... ...the staff, though tiny in number, do a wonderful job in providing much needed services to this inner city community" [Gill Fletcher-Watson, Wycombe Abbey Senior] [108].*

When Princess Margaret visited the Settlement in 1999, on the occasion of her 50 years patronage, she saw the All Nations Nursery, the Latch Key Project, and the Friary Open Learning Centre which has been run by Babs Sohna for the last three years. Four religious organisations rent rooms, with nineteen other groups regularly using the premises. These included the Southwark Police and Community Consultative Group, the Sexual Abuse Support Association, the Agape Foundation which is a support service for East African refugees, a site art project, Help at Hand Hour Bank, Samaritan Outreach, Southwark Childminding Association, and a play group for children with special needs.

In the last two years there has been a revival of many familiar-sounding social services under different guises. Advice sessions began in 1998 funded by a £350 grant from St John's and St Andrew's churches. A solicitor from a local law firm comes every week, and attendance is increasing. Tenants' liaison meetings take place regularly. The Open Door Housing Trust, an organisation with seven workers who deal with people with mental health problems, rents offices. The HourBank time currency Project is also based at the Settlement. Volunteers hold a weekly café on the same day as Southwark Asylum Seekers Project hold their day centre in the Settlement. A relatively new project is The Southwark Travellers' Action Group whose part-time workers support the four local travellers sites. Activities include literacy, environmental improvements, a woman's support group and a Youth Group for Travellers' children twice a week. Sure Start, a new national initiative to improve the health and well being of children under four, is a reminder of both the old care committees and Head Start. The Settlement is on the agenda for the local police's induction day, and in return schoolgirls working at the Settlement visit the police station as part of their community experience. A cultural day of drama, dance and drumming workshops, and other live music took place in 1999, to which over 200 people came. Other dramatic productions are enacted in the Settlement hall. As stated in the Report on the Settlement *"There are four main areas of community work, namely young people, the elderly, unemployed people and advice" [109]* which is a familiar echo of the work and activities of the Settlement from the past hundred years.

Chapter 4

The Religious Influence

From its conception, the work of the UGS was based upon a definitive religious footing and fundamentally the established church, the Church of England. The term 'mission' was one which did not disappear even when the original religious nature had been forgotten. Although the service part of the mission was seen as very important, there was the intention also to increase the number of practising Christians, and to relieve the perceived spiritual deprivation amongst the poor of the area. The Mission was to be at the forefront of achieving better social conditions and the spiritual needs of the poor were considered an integral part of this purpose, *"To provide social activities and practical assistance to the poverty stricken population as meeting spiritual needs" [110]*. A similar statement appeared in all the local mission reports with a very heavy emphasis on moral and spiritual training.

The foundation head teachers were all staunch churchgoers and committed Christians. The girls' schools mostly had a Church of England foundation. Daily acts of formal worship were a feature of all the schools at that time. The ethos of the privileged giving alms and service to the poor and needy was a Christian principle fostered by the heads of these schools. The church and other organisations closely associated with the Christian religion took on most of the responsibility for the welfare of the poor. The Pilgrim Trust, a large and quite wealthy church charitable trust, undertook a survey of unemployment in 1929 and the author, Dr H Singer, concluded in one interim paper that *"the position of the unemployed within the community presents a challenge to the Christian Conscience which is not being fully faced… …remedial measures* (must be) *adopted to mitigate the lot of the unemployed especially by voluntary agencies" [111]*. The influence and power of the Church and the quite formidable women of the time were a potent force.

48 Reverend Harry Veasey

From the early days there was a ready correspondence between the founding heads and the clergy of the day including the Rev Harry Veasey and Bishop Talbot. Miss Dove suggested the following inscription to be put on the first Settlement building. *"Female pupils of many schools will go forth from this* (building) *in the glory of God" [Translation from the Latin] [112]*. It is not clear whether this was adopted. Until the 1970s, there was an inscription over the blue door of the present building carved in wood, and remembered by many generations of schoolgirls and Settlement workers. *"Pax intrantibus, salus habitantibus, spes exeuntibus"* [enter in peace, abide with comfort, leave with hope] *[Film Documentary] [113]*. At the opening of the Staffordshire Street Settlement, the Bishop of Southwark declared that the motto be *"to the glory of God in the Service of life" [114]*, and certainly this became a catch phrase for the next thirty years, as *"an outward expression of the recognition of the girls of 185 schools that their religion, their education and opportunity gave them responsibility towards those whose lot had fallen in places less fortunate than their own" [115].*

By 1908 the second mission district of St Andrew's had been added, not without some heated discussion between the Rev Harry Veasey and Bishop Talbot. The adoption of the second parish was strongly recommended by Veasey but this would mean reduced help for St Mark's. The matter was put to the vote and it fell to the Bishop to give a casting vote. He referred the matter for further discussion, whereupon Harry Veasey said, *"'My lord, I... ...did not vote'. The bishop said... ...with a twinkle in his eye... ...'then I think you are a very foolish man' which we all received with much delight" [Miss Alsop] [116].* The Bishop was so impressed that he wrote a letter later which endorsed the addition of St Andrew's as the second mission. That same year Miss Dove addressed the Ruri-decanal Conference on the subject of the UGSM, where she emphasised the systematic and concentrated giving both of money and service - a dictum she earnestly enforced at Wycombe Abbey. Also in 1908 the Melanesian Mission in the South Seas was started. In 1924 the third mission in the poorest district of St Chrysostom's was added to the Settlement's supervision. A publicity pamphlet issued from the Mission in 1915 emphasised that the object of the mission was *"to bring brightness and hope into the dark, monotonous and often hopeless lives and homes; to help men and women to realise they are the children of God, the Great Father, and not un-cared for straws on life's ocean" [117].*

Prayer was considered a very important part of this service to others and certainly prayers and often a hymn attended every function connected with the Mission until well into the 1970s. Bishop Talbot had drawn up a prayer in 1915 and sent a copy to all schools and OGAs, with the request to pray constantly to God for the mission. *"Bless, O Lord, our Mission, teach us how to serve it with love and self denial and be pleased to use it for the help of Thy people and the service of Thy Kingdom for Jesus' sake, our Saviour and Redeemer. Amen" [118].* The original prayer was revived after the Second World War and the girls were asked to learn it by heart.

Formal Church Services

The annual service of thanksgiving in Southwark Cathedral was first mentioned in 1926, although it is likely it had been held before this date. When Mary Datchelor School joined the UGS in 1909, the school provided a choir at the annual service. *"The service has always been a great inspiration and the singing of the girls' congregation most impressive" [Miss Alsop] [119].* One thousand and five hundred girls attended the Cathedral service in 1929 and wore distinctive colours and white straw hats. In 1939 there was a suggestion that the annual service could alternate between St Martin in the Fields and Southwark Cathedral so that free churchmen could preach. This does not seem to have happened, although the annual service was held at St Martin's in 1935. The regular services at Southwark Cathedral had been reinstated by 1947, after the Second World War.

The Service was a highlight of both the Settlement and the Schools' calendars. After the Second World War there seemed to be a resurgence of the missionary ethos and until the late 1960s the numbers of girls and students visiting the Settlement were large. The annual service at Southwark Cathedral in May was a memorable event for the girls even if they did sit behind one of the many pillars. The sight of coaches and buses disgorging hundreds of schoolgirls to march in line to the cathedral, and the wonder of the blocks of colour produced by the various school uniforms are recurrent memories. The attendance at Southwark Cathedral was one of tradition and pride for the girls, *"an atmosphere of friendship and devotion to the cause of the UGS" [M. Taverner, Schoolgirl] [120]*, and was by all accounts an awe-inspiring affair. It was also an occasion not only to present a purse of a specially collected donation from each school and OGA, but also to return to the Settlement or to one of the parishes for tea to meet everyone and to see the place for which they raised money. Tea cost one shilling and the cost of a coach to Peckham was one and sixpence in 1957. The privilege of attending this day was one which the girls really appreciated, and the school magazines always carried reports of this annual event. *"We went home feeling... ...we were ready to do still more for the UGS" [Mary Bonsall, Schoolgirl] [121]; "The unity of purpose of various schools present was clearly realised" [Schoolgirl report] [122]; "The* (Bishop of Croydon) *was a very good speaker and the amplifying system was really unnecessary for his voice" [UL, Schoolgirl][123]; "(We) were fortunate in having seats in the main body of the packed cathedral near the pulpit" [EB, Schoolgirl.] [124]; "The singing of the assembled schools sounded whole-hearted and impressive" [SCT and PMS, Schoolgirls] [125]*. Members of invited schools formed the choir on these occasions. The Mary Datchelor choir also had the honour of singing for the Diamond Jubilee service in the Festival Hall. In 1955 the service was held on May 18th, where 42 schools and OGA s were present. *"We arrived at 2.40 pm to find the church already crowded, although the service was not due to begin until 3 pm. Because of this we had to sit in the south transept beneath the organ loft and we could not see the choir (ours was one) of three schools. After listening to Rev Reindorp, we went back out into the sunshine again" [Veronica Basford, Schoolgirl] [126]*.

At each service either the Bishop of Southwark or a visiting preacher elucidated the message of service to others. In 1947 the Bishop of Kingston exhorted the girls *"to pray, to learn about the UGS and to come down and see" [127]*. The essence was to gather the supporting schools together and to emphasise the needs of the Settlement. *"We found ourselves in a mass of various uniforms... ...the colours began to co-ordinate and we realised how vast is the number of schools supporting the Mission. When Rev Canon Lloyd of Winchester spoke we began to realise the multiplicity of tasks which the Settlement has to confront" [SRJ, Schoolgirl][128]; "The sermon brought to our attention the need for even greater social service in the coming year" [M. Taverner, Schoolgirl] [129]; "The sermon, although long, was very interesting and told us how UGS helps children of Peckham by means of youth centres and play groups" [Brenda Charles, Schoolgirl] [130]; "It is not often that so many members of the Union in which are included schools as widely apart as Birmingham and Portsmouth, and the West Country can obtain so comprehensive idea of the work they support" [Janet Shaw-Smith, Schoolgirl] [131]*.

Supporting schools banded together also to hold services in their local parish churches from the early days. There is a report in 1950 that the three supporting schools in Bournemouth had a service where Miss Waite spoke, comparing life in Bournemouth to 'the rather drab existence in Peckham'. The East Sussex Schools had separated themselves from the yearly event soon after the Second World War and held their own religious service which followed a fund raising sports' day. 3,251 service sheets were sent to 12 schools to arrange identical services in their own areas in 1967. Nevertheless, 884 girls attended Southwark Cathedral representing 38 schools, and 176 of these had tea at the Settlement later, quite a daunting number for so small a staff.

In 1956 there was a break in tradition when the annual service was held at the Royal Festival Hall instead. Because it was the Diamond Jubilee of the Settlement, the purses were made of 'white moiré silk and embroidered with the school's crest'. This was a most magnificent occasion, where Lady Ogilvie, Principal of St Anne's College, Oxford, emphasised *"the need for schoolgirl help, without whose time, money and skill, the Settlement could not exist" [132].* Princess Margaret, the Patron of the Settlement, was there to receive the purses. *"Miss Benyon made a beautiful purse......It was cold and grey when we arrived and from all sides parties of schoolgirls were hurrying into the building... ...The school was greatly honoured by being asked to choose one of its members to present* (Princess Margaret) *with a bouquet... ...an inspiration to everyone who went" [Schoolgirl] [133].*

49 Wing Commander Baker Reading the Lesson at the Annual Service

50 School Girls Attending the Annual Service, Southwark Cathedral, 1960s

In 1959 it appeared that a new ruling at Southwark Cathedral might have prevented the Settlement taking up a collection on its own behalf. There was much discussion, and a threat was made to move the Annual Service to Westminster Abbey or even to St Mark's. It is not recorded how this was resolved but the service did continue at Southwark for a few more years. By 1966 it was quite obvious that this service was becoming an organisational nightmare. The purses in the last few years had yielded only just over £300 each and although celebrities like Des Wilson were invited to give the sermon it was not enough to raise the donations. However, the service was felt to be a necessary part of the Settlement's annual events for the schools. *"This feat of organisation which involves much planning and travelling, gives us an opportunity to give thanks for the many things achieved and to dedicate ourselves once more to the complex and challenging work we have set ourselves in South East London" [Annual Report] [134]*. Then in 1974 it was felt that the logistics and expense of preparing for a service some miles away from the Settlement were inappropriate. The last annual service at Southwark Cathedral in 1974 *"resounded with guitars amplified through microphones and the unconventional atmosphere was completed by specially written prayers and poems about Peckham, both its problems and its plans for the future" [James Allen's School Magazine] [135]*.

51 The Parish Church of St John's 1966

The new church of St John's in Meeting House Lane had been consecrated in 1969. This had been built to replace St Chrysostom's and St Jude's churches which had crumbled to bomb damage and dry rot. The service was first held at St John's in 1975 in a delightful modern building where there was a Caribbean flavour to the music.

The 80th anniversary thanksgiving service was back at Southwark Cathedral on 17th November with Rev Edward Martin, vicar of St John's, and Rev John Lane, the Director, taking the service where the address was given by the Bishop, Mervyn Stockwood, with Blackheath High School providing the choir. The annual service now coincided with the annual general meeting, instead of in the traditional May. The Bishop of Woolwich gave the address at the next annual service which was printed in full in the Peckham Mirror.

By 1980 several letters had been received from schools saying they were unable to support the service. The reports of the annual service in school magazines declined quite rapidly from that date, the interest and the numbers had dwindled, the yearly event was discontinued, and perhaps some of the unity of supporting schools was lost too.

Barbara Hill suggested in 1975 that all schools should have a special Settlement school assembly at which a collection could be taken, and offered to send photographs and other material to help. Elspeth Howe organised the 80th birthday celebrations with a special service and reception for about 250 people at Goldsmith Hall in 1976.

There were services to celebrate the 90-year and centenary anniversaries, both held at St John's and the Archbishop of Canterbury, Robert Runcie, celebrated Eucharist and addressed the congregations. Afterwards, the Archbishop attended the Settlement for tea where his well-deserved reputation of being able to 'float' socially and make people feel happy and comfortable was so apparent and is remembered with affection. His visit *"made lasting impact and everyone was greatly impressed by the real interest* (he) *took in their affairs" [Letter of thanks to The Archbishop, November 1986] [136].*

52 The Right Reverend Mervyn Stockwood, The Right Reverend Michael Marshall, Lady Howe and the Pearly King and Queen of Peckham at the 80th Birthday Event, 1976

90TH
BIRTHDAY
EUCHARIST
for
The Peckham Settlement
held at
The Church of St. John with St. Andrew, Peckham
Celebrated by
The Archbishop of Canterbury
on
5th November 1986

53 The Cover for the Order of Service for the 90th Birthday Celebrations, 1986

54 Archbishop of Canterbury at the Settlement, 1986

Kitty Leek wrote after the 90-year service *"Of equal importance was the feeling of partnership between the Church and the Settlement and we hope that this experience of sharing can be repeated in the future" [Letter to Rev Malcolm Johnson, November 1986][137]*, but this partnership seems to be a forlorn hope in the present climate. Although no formal church services have taken place since, there was a service at St John's in 1989 following the fatal gas explosion at Edinburgh Settlement. The London Settlements staff and users were invited and many attended. The Director and Committee officers of Edinburgh Settlement also attended the service.

The Mission Work

From its inception the spirit of the Mission was *"to set forth by deed and word a Christianity that is bright and joyous... ...and that aims at making the Kingdom of Heaven begin here on earth" [UGSM Record] [138]*. The certainty that the Settlement was doing God's work was paramount until the 1970s and the describers of activities always included some religious phrase. The religious nature of the foundation was also emphasised at the Social Service conferences. In 1959 there was a talk about church work for women, and in the following year on the nature of parish work by a female parish worker. Typical comments of the time were *"the UGS is united in the common work for the glory of God. Service to others is probably the most valuable lesson we can learn" [Executive Committee Minutes] [139]*, and *"by kindling a sense of responsibility in those who work with us as well as those whom they try to serve we can best achieve that help of thy people and service of thy kingdom for which we all pray" [ibid.][140]*.

There were various attempts to include other branches of the Christian faith and, later in the 60s, other religions. When the name changed to 'Union' it was perhaps to reconcile the deferring sects of Christian religion by not emphasising the word 'Mission'. The word stuck though and schools were reporting on Mission work for at least another forty years. From early days, the missionary aspect of the work was emphasised. Bishop Talbot wrote "*soul life was almost non-existent, crushed or crowded out. No one went to church, hardly any said prayers. Few children attended Sunday school. As to the standard of behaviour it has not kept pace with that. It was a clever thing rather than a wrong thing to tell a lie. Stealing means to get your fair share. God didn't care - you come to care not even for yourself" [141]*. Some fifty years later, Elsie Bowerman reiterated this feeling, *"owing to the deterioration of spiritual welfare the need is not less but greater" [142]*. In 1937 the Bishop of Kingston declared at a Committee meeting *"since the move from Peckham Road to Stafford Street there has been a gradual and unconscious slipping back from a positive and explicit religious base to the work" [143]*. It was strongly suggested that there should be religious training of the children, prayers at the beginning and end of each club activity and at the beginning and end of the day. The older children were obliged to go to a dedication service. Services were held at the beginning and end of term for volunteers and students. Bible study courses were proposed but there was *"one Roman Catholic, one Jew and several members of the free churches and they might cause difficulties" [Executive Committee Minutes] [144]*, but Elsie Bowerman felt it was most important to express as a body the Christian principles underlying the work.

There was another expression about the lack of religion in 1945. The Executive Committee heard that most children had little connection with the church. This was perhaps not surprising considering most of the buildings had been very badly damaged in the war and many children had been evacuated from the area. It was decided the children needed informal discussion and teaching. A tally of religions in the clubs revealed 46 Church of England, 18 Roman Catholics and 28 Free Church members. It appeared that both the children's clubs and the mothers' clubs had no prayers now. The committee resolved to

"1. Reaffirm the Christian basis and nature of the work
2. People of all denominations could come to the Settlement but staff should be people with definite committed Christian convictions.
3. That money should be set aside for religious instruction, and religious books for a club library.
4. Monthly meetings between staff at the Settlement and the parishes should discuss common problems.
5. There was a need to set up a chapel" [145].

A lively debate had occurred in 1934 as to the size of the chapel. Before he died, Rev Bailey had wanted to provide a small chapel for 25 people but the Executive Committee felt a small chapel was quite contrary to the spirit of the UGS work.

The Committee felt it ought to be large enough to be used as a centre for the Life of the Settlement. This took some time to resolve and the Bishop of Kingston did not dedicate the chapel until 1949. The other resolutions were going to prove an uphill battle.

In 1957 the Executive Committee was much concerned about the many social problems which

55 The Chapel, 1965

were perceived to have arisen as a result of the development of the welfare state. *"Material poverty is not now so much our main preoccupation as moral and spiritual indulgence and the apparent decay of a sense of responsibility. The charity which suffereth long and is kind now must find new ways of penetrating the iron curtain of paganism which darkens so many of the homes in our land today. Never have we been more in need of the faith to persevere" [Executive Committee Minutes] [146].* This seems to be a rather puritanical way of expressing concerns which would have been unlikely to achieve a positive response from the people the Settlement was trying to help. The Seniors at Wycombe Abbey were told that the Settlement's main work was now to *"to make friends in the neighbourhood, to break down paganism which prevails and try through various activities to teach the people what are the underlying principles of work" [Elsie Bowerman] [147].* At the opening of the rest room in the same year there were dedications both at the beginning and end of the service, and Bishop Simpson reiterated that there were *"many ardent spirits who long to bring the spirit of our Lord into social work of the Welfare state" [148].*

The staff were required to be committed Christians, although the cosmopolitan nature of the people using the Settlement was a point in reports of 1951 and 1960. The students who came to help were from India, New Zealand, China, Scandinavia, South Africa, Germany, Italy, USA and Nigeria, *"people of different nations, faiths and parties meet and make friends, and probably there never was a time when such opportunities for mutual understanding were of greater value" [Dorothy Shove, Honorary Treasurer][149].* All were expected to join in the morning and evening prayer ritual. These prayers were often taken by the local clergy as the parish churches were still heavily involved in the Settlement's work. It is not recorded whether any allowance was made for different faiths. When there was a need to appoint a warden in 1962, one candidate was eminently suitable but because she was a Jewess she would not take daily house prayers, so presumably did not get the job. However, when Wing Commander Baker was appointed he made it quite clear that he would not lead the prayers, and as there were now a number of staff who did not embrace the Christian faith, the daily act of worship stopped, and the little chapel became an office. Some staff were ex-missionaries, there were still Church of England services in the hall of the Settlement, and the local parish vicars were on the committee with Bishop Simpson as chairman, *"whose shrewd and firm chairmanship of the Executive Committee was characterised by pithy comments such as 'an academic mind in a pastoral job'" [Mary Welsh] [150].*

When the Triple S Scheme was initiated this actively involved the local Roman Catholic, Baptist, Methodist, and Congregational churches. Although John Lane was a practising minister when he was appointed director in 1972, the religious nature of the Settlement's work was not emphasised. It was conceded that by the middle 1980s the Settlement had ceased to have any religious identity and became 'quite political'.

56 The Right Reverend Bertram Simpson, 1970

From 1990 very little mention is made about the religious foundation of the Settlement. The religious strand is tenuously held because various rooms of the Settlement are let to Pentecostal churches with no building of their own. These churches represent the expansion of black gospel churches in the area and lead to an important spiritual revival. Several of the Settlement users and organisations work under Christian principles. The African clubs all have religious foundations and the Plough Redemption Foundation Trust is a charity which adheres to Christian teaching and beliefs.

57 The Reverend Geoffrey Heal, Vicar of St John's Church, 1964

Miss Dove had suggested in 1929 that if the parishes and Settlement were to be closely linked, the vicars of the missions might be on the Settlement's committees, and the Warden of the Settlement on the parish committees. Indeed, the Bishops of Southwark, Woolwich or Kingston were either Chairs of the Management Council or the Executive Committee until the 1980s, and the vicars of the respective parishes were on the Board until 1999.

When there was a debate in the Executive Committee in 1994 about the need for a celebration of the Centenary, the whole essence of the original Settlement's foundation was questioned. *"The Settlement has little to do with either religion or the founding schools now, and we need to be clear about what we are about, whether we are celebrating the past, the present or the future" [Executive Committee Minutes] [151].* The Bishop of Southwark, the Right Rev Tom Butler and the Right Rev Colin Buchanan, the Bishop of Woolwich have visited and pledged support for the Settlement's work. Maybe the church will have a representative on the Executive Committee again.

Chapter 5

The Neighbourhood and The Settlement Buildings

The first impression of this one hundred and four year old institution is forbidding. The description of a schoolgirl's visit in 1967 seems to be typical. *"Before I had actually seen the Settlement I had pictures in my mind of a building rather like a new block of offices. Therefore my reaction on seeing Staffordshire Street and then the Settlement, was one of great surprise… … it was a rather dingy grim looking street with the Settlement building at the end of it. The front of the building was painted red, reminding me of a fire station and altogether it looked far too small to be of much value" [Angela Davies, Schoolgirl] [152].* Other observations have been - *"outside, the Settlement looks like a prison" [Joyce Baxter, Warden] [153]; "a large rambling building" [Ruth Muffet, student worker] [154]; "it's like a tardis" [Kate Lindsey, Nursery Deputy] [155]; "a beleaguered fortress in the middle of a battlefield" [Peckham Settlement News] [156].*

58 Peckham Settlement, 2000

59 Peckham Settlement showing the Old Wesleyan Chapel, 2000

The Mission had already moved premises once before, when Queen Mary opened the Settlement in 1931 in Stafford Street (renamed Staffordshire Street in 1937). The opening was on March 18th.

A reception at the main entrance consisted of the Mayor of Camberwell, the Right Reverend Lord Bishops of Southwark and Kingston, the Architect and Dr Gertrude Willoughby, the Warden. Queen Mary declared the building open and received purses from the schoolgirls who were *"dressed in white with black shoes and stockings and their name of their school on a label"* and who *"filed past making a low bob. The purses just about cleared the debt on the building" [UGS Record] [157].*

60 Queen Mary Passing Heard's Sweet Shop on Her Way to Open the Settlement, 1931

A feeling of doom and crisis had preceded this event. *"The Council has descended on the Settlement like a dignified hurricane and would shortly sweep it away" [Times report] [158]. "In Camberwell, the movement had recently met with great catastrophe as the LCC required their Settlement as a site for small houses and in three months all the centres* (Kempshead, Calmington and Peckham Road sites) *would be scrapped" [Times report] [159].* The Committee cast around for suitable premises and was facing a possible bill of £7,000. A survey was commissioned before the move to Stafford Street, which proposed three plans to suit the activities of the Settlement.

61 Queen Mary Receiving Purses at the Opening of the Settlement, 1931

It pointed out that the residential and public places had to be kept separate with separate entrances. Teak stairs at the southern end of the Settlement are mentioned but it is not clear whether these are the spiral stairs. The stone stairs at the north end are still there. The survey further proposed to build a new second floor to accommodate three to four bedrooms and a bathroom for residences. It does seem that some of this work was completed. The purchase of the building, which had been a Wesleyan Methodist Chapel from 1834 and then later a Wesleyan Sunday and Day School, was made for £4,000. Wycombe Abbey had raised £1,000, and the Settlement paid £2,150. It is to be surmised, although this is not documented, that the balance was donated by one of the founder head teachers. The transfer of the sites was completed in 1931, whereupon the Settlement became an Incorporated Association so that it could hold property and make contracts. Later, in 1933, Mrs Ursula Townsend donated the five adjacent houses in Goldsmith Road which initially became the residences for students and staff. Mrs Townsend was a Wycombe Abbey Senior who did much philanthropic work chiefly in connection with the ICAA. She took a prominent part in the management of the Settlement for most of her life.

62 UGS Settlement, 1935

She had bought these houses from Mr Archibald Robinson in 1931. One of the conditions had been that *"no manufacturing or sale of intoxicating liquors, or theatre, dancing or music" [160]* was to take place on the premises.

An impassioned letter from the President, Lady Abel Smith, the vice – president, Lady Isobel Lawrence, and the Bishop of Kingston in the Times of 1933 beseeched everybody to attend a Christmas market, which was to be opened by Princess

63 The Goldsmith Road Houses, 2000

Alice, Countess of Athlone and the actress Edith Evans, to wipe out the debt caused by the move. The letter quotes the sum of £11,000 of which £3,000 remained outstanding. This amount does not seem to tally with the stated sums in the contract, and may have included some remuneration for the Goldsmith Road houses, or the alterations which had to be done to the buildings. In 1940 the building was insured for £14,250. This conglomeration of buildings was to become the home of the UGSSS [The Union of Girls' Schools for Social Service] or Peckham Settlement for the next 70 years.

Situated off the main roads of the 'village' of Peckham, the Settlement has endured a world war, massive alterations to the built environment, population and cultural changes, and seemingly unchanging social deprivations which have existed in various guises since the Reverend Harry Veasey''s inception of 'the little thing on little wings'. The Bishop of Kingston''s sermon in 1947 at the Annual Service described *"a little area down in Camberwell where the people are as a whole very poor, who live in over crowded houses, where the children have not much comfort and care when they are ill, where it is hard to get amusement and gaiety except on the street and where old men and women are cared for very little" [161].*

The Neighbourhood

The environs of the Settlement, bounded by Old Kent Road to the north, East Dulwich Road to the south, Lausanne Road to the east and Rye Lane and Peckham Hill Street to the west, have been bulldozed, built up, demolished, rebuilt and partly gentrified. Gone are the soda water and the baby food factories, *"the sweet factory, a bottle works, a paper factory which employs girls as rag pickers and a birdcage factory. Sausage skins are prepared not far from our doors, and there are a number of laundries" [Dr Willoughby, Warden] [162].* Gone are *"the hot waves of jelly and parsley sauce and eels which blow over the queue outside the post office"* and *"the cart and horse (coming) for the pig swill" [Jessica Broomhall, UGS Record] [163].* The pickle factory across the road has been demolished. This was where *"workers seemed cheerful. Some had been there as long as 25 years and we were impressed by the lightness of the whole building and modern facilities" [Schoolgirl Report] [164]* but where *"the ever pervading smell of the onions"* [Jill Andrews, *Student Worker] [165]* would be a lasting memory for many people.

64 The Pickle Factory, circa 1950

Gone are the baker's shop on the corner of Marmont Road run by an Austrian family, the little sweet shop on the corner of Lower Park Road [now Friary Road] where *"Mr Heard sold sweets often wrapped in small paper pokes" [Phyllis Hughes, Resident] [166]* and 'The Mansions', a block of courtyard flats in Goldsmith Road. Here *"families lived in two rooms, sharing a tap and a loo with several other families" [Jill Andrews, Student Worker] [167]* and where *"the (rather boisterous) Worsfold twins lived and who had regularly to* (visit) *the cleansing station with impetigo and dirty heads" [Phyllis Hughes, Resident] [168]*. Gone are the original Mission churches of St Mark's, and St Chrysostom's and many of the *"drab, dark rooms in tiny terraced houses with no facilities, in a badly planned and overcrowded area" [UGS Annual Report] [169]* where *" people have few amenities, children's educational opportunities are few and they have far too little good food and fresh air" [Joyce Baxter, Warden] [170]*. A Nigerian congregation now uses St Andrew's Church, the other Mission parish.

65 Demolition of the Pickle Factory.
The Wildlife Garden is seen in the Background, 1996

A report in 1958 painted a gloomy and depressing picture. *"People here have the disadvantage of living in unbeautiful quarters of SE London where there is still dereliction of bomb damage. High rise flats are being built, but many people still live in terraced houses with no bathrooms and a loo in the yard" [Rev Canon Lloyd of Winchester] [171]*. Five hundred and twenty-four flats were nearing completion. These were part of the Acorn Estate finished in 1963. Surely this estate must have been preferable to the previous dwellings shown by the following descriptions. *"The poverty and deprivation certainly made an impression. One lady……did not even have a front door. It had rotted away - just a heavy brown curtain over the doorway to the street" [Susan Waggitt, Student Worker] [172]* and *"an old couple lived in Verney Road where a great deal of redevelopment was in progress. Ten old houses were left in their row. They lived on the ground floor… … and had tenants on the upper floor. Both inside and out the house is extremely shabby. On one side it is overshadowed by a recently built warehouse which keeps light out of their rooms. Their only lavatory is outside. They have no electricity, and light and heat is provided by gas and a coal burning stove" [Anne McFadyen, Schoolgirl] [173]*. The modern flats may have seemed a luxury compared to the houses they were replacing, but seven years later, Peckham appeared still to be *"an area of squalor and decay where the families* (were) *obliged to live in houses next door to empty rat-infested ones" [Patty Paice, Settlement Worker] [174]*.

66 The Environs of the Settlement, circa 1975

The move to the high-rise flats was *"utterly bewildering to so many of the old people whose roots are in the past. Their homes adequate in their eyes are being pulled down to make way for redevelopment" [Annual Report] [175].* The Settlement went through almost a bereavement process when this building was taking place. As families moved out and away to new modern flats the old community was breaking up. *"Those of you who remember hearing about the Mansions will be glad to know that this very bad slum has been condemned and most of the families have already been moved to other parts of London. We are glad for them because we know they now have far better accommodation, but we do miss the children terribly and shall be quite lost without* (them)*......Until (they) finish pulling down the old houses and building the new flats there will be a shortage of children for our clubs and we do feel rather lost at the moment" [UGS Settlement News] [176].*

The high-rise flats may have solved some housing problems but they exacerbated and possibly initiated some of the social problems, many of which were brought to the doors of the Settlement for help, support and advice. *"A club started for mothers of children in the nursery, as they were tied in* (high-rise block) *homes with small children until they felt like screaming for lack of adult conversation" [Mary Welsh, Volunteer] [177]; "They* (the flats) *created problems of loneliness and isolation, especially for the elderly whose homes were pulled down to make way for the development. They become captive in their new flats, because the lift does not work and the caring neighbours have disappeared......and there is a lack of community life" [Peckham Mirror] [178].* John Lane, the director of the Settlement from 1972 to 1978, wrote in an appeal letter of his particular concern *"with the needs of the old people who feel cut off because they have been rehoused and don't know their neighbours probably for the first time in their lives" [179].* A description of visits made in the days before the high-rise flats belies this apparent lack of community spirit. *"I had several conversations through letter-boxes with people who refused to open their doors. It is said communities were closer and more caring in the past, but I found few neighbours who seemed to care about or even know the names of many people I visited" [Susan Waggitt, Student Worker] [180].*

A description tendered by a long time resident in Peckham, depicts the scene from the top of the Settlement. *"One could see high tall dark buildings, and Keddy's and Costa's were there. There was an off licence on the corner. Just up the road was the boot shop. Opposite the boot shop were big gates and behind these a white Rolls Royce, which the bloke used to keep for weddings, and then everything started to diminish, diminish, diminish. The council decided to build a gypsy's encampment...... the area was split in half and the gypsies had one half and Sims the builder had the other. Sims decided to clear out and the council decided to clear the gypsies out of here, take them off the hard standing because there was water but no bathing facilities or portable loos, down into Hilldon Road into purpose built houses. I used to come up here and you used to hear a cockerel crow, and a dog bark. They cleared them away and the site was derelict for a while" [George Smith, Settlement Worker] [181].*

67 The New Housing in Staffordshire Street. The Travellers' Site is in the Background, 2000

In 1967 the area was mainly working class with a large proportion of people in social groups 4 and 5, with low-grade housing and a significant number of immigrant families. In 1982 Peckham was designated a low-income area with 17.4% of the adults out of work. It had an ethnic population of 15%. Southwark was the London borough with most council tenants and a quarter of the people living in sub-standard housing. Peckham was designated an Urban Priority area in 1986 and the Government set up a Task Force there. Twenty years on the area could still be coloured violet, the colour used by Charles Booth in 'Life and Labour in London' (1904) to denote the poorest districts. Things seemed to have changed little when Southwark scored the second highest deprivation level on the Index of Local Conditions in England and Wales in 1996. Of the three wards closely connected to the Settlement,

Friary Ward, the most deprived, scored 18.96, Liddle, the second most deprived ward, scored 17.62, and Consort came seventh out of the twenty-five wards in Southwark with a score of 16.48. These scores are based on the selected thirteen indicators introduced by the Department of the Environment to measure relative levels of deprivation in the 366 local authority districts. The indicators include low earning, overcrowded households, unemployed persons, and the number of 17-year-olds in educational participation.

The dreary portrayal of *"filthy streets, covered in newspaper, cigarette packets and other rubbish, and some of the streets look as if they haven't been swept for years......where the homes look neglected with peeling paint, broken windows, and dark gloomy insides......and where the general impression... ...is one of poverty and neglect" [Angela Davies, Schoolgirl] [182]* did not extend into the Settlement building.

The Settlement Building

There are many reports of the friendly and congenial atmosphere inside the big grey building. *"Everybody is made to feel welcome" [E. Allen, Schoolgirl] [183]; "As soon as you walk through the front door, you can see the Settlement is a going concern. The atmosphere is alive and vital - there is a feeling of optimism and enthusiasm about" [John Lane, Director] [184]; "There is a relaxed atmosphere and we all have a good laugh" [Tania McPherson, Settlement Worker] [185]; "We had happy times here because they are all such nice people" [George Smith, Settlement Worker] [186].* One description reasoned *"there is......a great deal of character......in the old buildings. I think the appearance makes people feel at home and at ease, whereas a very modern building might put them off by seeming too artificial" [Angela Davies, Schoolgirl] [187].*

Not withstanding the agreeable, sympathetic atmosphere and the friendly, welcoming people, the records show a running battle with the deficiencies of the building and the eternal search for money and goods in kind to complete even the basic maintenance. The building was often described by the people who worked there as a nightmare. Alterations, modifications, modernisation, renovation and constant, almost daily, patching-up are the themes of many reports. A note of triumph also emerges through these reports where despite everything the Settlement manages to continue its excellent work.

A visit from Miss Havergal, from St Swithun's School in August 1941, describes, *"a beautifully kept old house, a winding staircase, nicely carpeted (leading) into a comfortable sitting room ... ...with oak tables and chairs" [Diary of Visit][188].* There she awaited the arrival of Miss Ellis, the warden. The Settlement was almost completely empty, because the nursery school had been evacuated and all evening and many daytime activities had been closed down on the order of the local authorities.

The building had a complete structural survey in 1953 where it was found the roof was in danger of collapsing, probably caused by 'the bombing having given the buildings a severe shaking'. The building was given a huge face lift resulting in complete rebuilding of the Goldsmith and Stafford Street Corner, resulting in many apologetic letters and notices for the inconveniences. The exterior was painted (in the famous 'fire station' red?) and the stone facade facing Staffordshire Street renovated. The reconstruction of the entrance was wholly financed by Wycombe Abbey. A section of this site was a disused burial ground. In 1930 The Bishop of Kingston, Mary Douglas, the President, and Mr Thomas Hawkin, an accountant, had signed an agreement to remove any extension and to re-instate the burial ground if called upon by the London County Council. There does exist a plan showing the graves in this area.

In 1961 a town-planning proposal seems to have involved the Settlement. Apparently it was known that after the war the Settlement site could be demolished within the next twenty years.

The Settlement appeared to be living on borrowed time. A letter was sent to all the supporters of the UGS in May informing them of the expected changes and that the Settlement might be reopened in another district. Apparently the new flats commanded higher rents, the poorest families had been moved out, the new inhabitants were very different and the work had drastically altered. However, nothing more was said about this removal.

68 The Entrance to the Settlement in Goldsmith Road, 1997

A detailed surveyor's report in 1963 advised that the Settlement should look for new premises as the building was in too poor a shape to refurbish. This report led to an Executive Committee discussion but no decision was made to move.

Appeals for money to do essential repairs were sent out regularly. The tone was always very apologetic and wardens admitted, *"these repairs lack(ed) glamour but (are) so vital" [Joyce Baxter, Warden] [189]. "Of the £8,000 required, the UGS* (the schools) *has collected or has promised £4,000. An Appeals Committee is discussing ways and means of raising the rest. Meanwhile the builders have to be paid and the hard pressed general fund is bearing the burden until new projects bring in additional income" [ibid.] [190].* One wonders whether this was all too much for Miss Baxter. Despite her sterling work and commitment she resigned shortly after this. The roofing problems alone had taken three years to solve because the funds for the roof repairs were diverted to a new heating system. Appeals went on through 1954 and 1955, where the target had just been reached only to be followed very quickly by the collapse of the 'distressed' wall above the Nursery School, which required £3,000 to be made safe. The constant worry about the building was evident from the impassioned letters to Wycombe Abbey School, a frequent life-saver in times of crises.

Rev Geoffrey Heal, the acting warden in 1964, wrote in The Annual Report that the Settlement had embarked on the *"most urgent and crucial structural defects. There is much to be done but at least now we are in a position where we can choose from a given list of priorities where next to begin. Whilst the builders are in occupation it is not possible to entertain many visitors from schools" [191]* especially as the structural defects were threatening to eat up all spare resources. Two years later it was decided to set aside at least £500 annually, later increased to £1,000, for dilapidation and repairs.

The UGS Review [a successor to the UGS Record] was sent out to all the supporting schools regularly and the state of the buildings was mentioned frequently. In the 1965 issue, Eve Keatley wrote a very stirring piece, rather reminiscent of Kitchener's war message, detailing what had been done and what else was needed. The roofs needed repair, dry rot had to be eliminated and the entrance and kitchen remodelled. During this time there is no mention of other pecuniary aid, and it is to be supposed that the schools gave most of the financial support for these repairs. By 1973 the sum needed for redecoration, modernisation and repairs had risen to £60,000. Four years later the lighting and heating were renovated and other costly repairs done. That apologetic statement was repeated. *"We recognise that donors may not find a building the most attractive of causes, but we urgently need the money because our programme can only be really effective in a properly completed building" [Martin Pickstone, Director] [192].*

The 1980s and early 1990s saw *"widespread rebuilding, closure of many local industries, a large immigrant population and a rapid turnover of people" [Draft Proposal probably written by Martin Pickstone] [193]* with the Settlement constantly reassessing its position in the local community, part of the nursery school rebuilt, the Youth Wing enlarged, and the ubiquitous dry rot appearing again. *"We had to have the money just to keep the building from leaking, and to accommodate the extra staff" [Kitty Leek, Director] [194].* In fact the building appeared to have been rebuilt around the users and the workers as in 1964 and there was heartfelt relief expressed in the newsletters when all this was finished. Nearly five years on there was a photograph in the newsletter of the leaking and dangerous roof which required urgent attention.

The Interior Rooms

The numerous different-sized rooms, the long passages and the flights of stairs can confuse first comers. The myriads of rooms have changed their function through the years, often as much to do with the sad state of repairs as with the requirements of different activities, needs or new ideas. Dr Groves remembers the concrete ceiling of her office crashing down just before she was due to take up her appointment, so another room had to be designated as her office space.

The Rest Room by the side of the stage in the main hall was a lively topic for a number of years. The original concept was to have a *"room … …with a lovely kitchen and armchairs so that elderly people could come in for a cup of tea and a chat" [Florrie Whale, Thursday Club] [195]*, a sanctuary from their homes and maybe also a quieter haven away from the very lively pensioners' clubs which abounded every afternoon then. The Rest Room was opened in 1957, but not before the usual pleas for furniture had been issued. Finishing touches had taken at least five years from concept to actuality, and it had cost over £9,000. Just two years later it needed to be redecorated. One wonders what the pensioners were doing in it. In later years this room served in turn as a café, a bar and a store.

The chapel was an important feature for over 30 years. Elsie Bowerman had donated the apricot, blue and gold altar frontal in 1948. The chapel was moved into the centre of the Settlement when the façade was rebuilt and re-dedicated by the Bishop of Woolwich on July 26th in 1955. Appeals were made for an altar, rails and reading desk, matting for the floor and a large curtain 7' by 4'. Strict specifications were issued for the creation of the kneelers each school was expected to provide for the chapel. *"The cross stitch on canvas should be embroidered with the school crest taking up 11 inches by 8 inches" [UGS Record] [196].* By 1956, the year of the Diamond Jubilee, this 'lovely little chapel' was fully furnished and used for daily prayers. In 1972 it was converted into an office, as it was no longer needed.

The basement is also mentioned many times. The original jumble shop run by Mary Pittard was situated there. Children's clubs, the day nursery and the youth clubs all inhabited the basement at one time. The Youth Club decorated it in 1957 turning it from scarlet to yellow and mushroom. In 1972 it was utilised as a workshop to make furniture then rented out to the PDCCA organisation. Later, the basement *"a dreadful, dirty, filthy* (place) *which needing painting" [Kitty Leek, Director] [197]* and which had been flooded in the late 80s, was decorated. It is now the home for the Latch Key Project.

The main hall, the original chapel of the Wesleyan Church, has been used as a dining room for pensioners, a clubroom for every age group nearly every hour of every day, a theatre, and a gymnasium. It sports a polished floor for dancing. The local Baptist churches used the hall in the 1940s and St Chrysostom's and St Jude's Church held services, Sunday schools and baptisms there whilst the new Church of St John's was being built in the 1960s. There was a grand opening by the Mayor of Camberwell in 1958 of the new stage, which the local fire station crew had built and provided the stage curtains.

69 The Stage in the Hall 1960

A report in 1982 said the hall was unrecognisable to the old people with its new comfy chairs and carpeting, *"a bit different from the chipped tangerine and lilac paint they were used to" [Barbara Hill, Settlement Worker] [198]*. Later in that decade, the Crystal Prospect, a theatre group under the supervision of Graham Gluck, wanted the hall painted black, and various lighting effects and twinkly disco balls installed. Some of the lighting was fixed but a compromise was reached and the hall decorated in grey. When the local school, Peckham Park, suffered a teacher shortage in 1989, it used the hall for several days as a makeshift classroom. It was described seven years afterwards as a 'truly hideous hall' and was decorated again just in time for Princess Margaret's visit to the Settlement in 1999 in a tasteful green and cream. The hall has always been considered as the Settlement's biggest asset.

70 The Hall Showing the Polished Dance Floor, 2000

The main kitchens, which had done such Herculean work since the first days of the Settlement, were closed in 1987. As complete modernisation had taken place nearly thirty years before when the Aga cookers were replaced with gas cookers, and fluorescent lights installed, it was perhaps not surprising the kitchens needed new premises. A small kitchen is in use now just off the main hall.

The spiral staircase was refurbished in 1956 in time for the Jubilee celebrations. The staircase is still there, even though someone tried to sell it in the 1980s. It is now carpeted and it is not quite so easy to slip or be heard as you climb up to the top floors to where the bed-sitters used to be.

71 The Spiral Staircase, 2000

Detailed plans for the decoration and alteration of the whole interior were drawn up in 1979, which included the installation of fire doors, smoke and heat detectors to comply with standard building regulations of the time. A reception office became essential and was re-sited in 1986, next door to the Director's office which had moved from upstairs. A sign of the times, security measures were installed in the same year.

There were many 'funny little' rooms upstairs, which were used for residences and for other activities. The mother and toddler group [forerunner of the All Nations Nursery] occupied the first two resident rooms and then the big airy room with large windows on the second floor. This room was later taken over by the Urban Studies Centre and then by the Friary Open Learning Centre. The day nursery moved downstairs into the old nursery school area in 1994 when the nursery school moved out to refurbished premises in Meeting House Lane. There was also a large reading room, now a conference room, a study area, a dark room and a print room.

Some of the staff lived on site in the residents' rooms from 1930. The purpose of residential settlements was to enable the church and social worker's to live in the midst of the district they were serving and to provide accommodation for students to live and gain first hand experience in the area and to research into local social conditions. All the residents in such settlements were expected to take part in the communal activities of the settlement, and there was always a chapel where the residents met for prayers. In 1951 there was an appeal to the Wycombe Abbey Seniors to use these rooms if they were *"prepared to give at least a few hours a week... ...*(The Settlement) *is on the direct bus route to Victoria and Marble Arch, and can offer convenient accommodation for anyone wanting practical experience" [Elsie Bowerman, Volunteer Settlement Worker] [199].* The rooms were small, had the bare comforts and were often very cold and miserable in the winter. In 1936 there had been efforts to get the schools to adopt a room, decorate it in attractive colours and provide money for maintenance. A naming of rooms ceremony took place in 1937. There was of course a Wycombe Abbey bedroom in pale primrose and deep brownish red; a Mickelfield room with *"a comfortable divan bed ......an upholstered chair......and a most attractive grey and red rug" [Settlement Newsletter] [200];* the Downs School room was green and white; a Malvern College room; Bexhill's room was a sprigged design of yellow and red on a cream background. The Bournemouth School room had *"pale blue walls, and cream paint, light wood furniture... ...which can be painted cream, with cherry red bedspreads, curtains and cushions" [The Milestone] [201].* In 1964 schools were asked to give £200 for decoration and furnishings of a room which would then display an inscription. Sydenham High and Hitchin Grammar School both took part. A party of girls from Walthamstow Hall painted their room white and pale blue and then went on to decorate an old lady's house in two shades of pink! Students were able to live rent free in the early days after the war, in exchange for doing some work with the clubs, visiting or even helping out with the teaching, typing and cooking. They stayed there for a weekend, a week or sometimes for a few months. Certainly having a room in that part of London was a perk for both the girls and the Settlement. Dr Groves lived on site in a room 'off the spiral staircase' as did two full-time students, and there was encouragement for short stays. The residences could accommodate 40 or more if some people brought sleeping bags. The rooms became emergency crash pads for homeless people in 1972. Ten years later it was reported the Secretary was living and working there, but the rooms were otherwise occupied by tenants who were not contributing to the work of the Settlement, and legal proceedings were taken to evict them. At one stage in the 1990s, the rooms were completely empty. Now, still bearing the signs of bed-sitters, the rooms are rented out to organisations wanting office space.

The garden area was a topic of comment several times. It was taken up with a vast shelter (provided by the LCC) in 1941. It had an outdoor cooking stove with an oven and chimney to provide a feeding station in case of blitz. The area appears to have been leased to the Settlement from the LCC for a period of seven years from 1973. The issue of who owned this land arose when the Settlement wished to divide the area into two so that each nursery could have its own play area. In 1983 it was deemed the local council owned this land on the corner of Goldsmith Road and Marmont Road which was only on temporary loan to the Settlement. The Settlement managed to negotiate a peppercorn rent with London Borough of Southwark for its use as a play space for the Nursery School and signed a contract to maintain the land, the perimeter fence and gates. Southwark Council proposed to sell the area for housing in 1998. Negotiation took place for Southwark to gift the site to the Settlement, but this did not happen. Southwark did say that its continued use by the nursery was not under threat and it retains ownership of the land. In October of the same year Anderson Consultants spent two challenge days at the Settlement during which they decorated the bottom floor of the nursery, the computer room's kitchen, an office and passageway, tided and planted the garden and painted a splendid mural on the garden wall.

72 Painting the Mural, 1999

73 The Finished Mural, 1999

The area now sports some very smart equipment for the nursery children who take every opportunity of using the enclosed garden in most weathers. This year, the Settlement were the recipients of the Capital Cares Day when 30 volunteers came for one day and managed to decorate the lobby, the general office and the photocopier room, the dining room and the toilets, as well as clearing and preparing a piece of the garden for a climbing frame.

74 The New Improved Play Area, 2000

The dreams of a new building were raised again in 1994.

75 The Old Wesleyan School Building is Exposed after the Demolition of Surrounding Buildings, 1996

Southwark Borough Council decided to redevelop the Staffordshire Street area as much of it was in a derelict state. Adjacent to the Settlement was a large food warehouse and opposite was the old disused pickle factory both owned by Costa's. Although the whole area was designated an Employment zone, Southwark sought to buy the freeholds of the various properties and turn the whole area over to housing. The Executive Committee welcomed the idea initially but stated that the Settlement would want to be in a position which would enable it to continue to serve the community. It would be preferable to have a smaller more efficient building on the same site, especially as it was considered that 67% of the present building was under utilised, an observation that had been made in 1982 as well. However, the Settlement would consider moving to another site if the terms were favourable.

A report in the Wycombe Abbey Gazette heralded the decision that a new Settlement could be built in a different location, hopefully not too far from its present position. *"The buildings are old and inconvenient. Certainly parts of the building look almost as they did when* (Miss Dove) *helped to found them" [Gill Fletcher-Watson, Wycombe Abbey Senior] [202].* Southwark made no offer at this juncture. In March 1996, the developers expressed their interest in buying the Settlement land but confirmed that this would not be at a premium rate so no further negotiations took place. By this time the roof had to be repaired again at the cost of £42,000, the boiler needed replacing and other major maintenance was urgent. Expenditure seemed fruitless and better directed to a new building. After a visit by the Executive Committee to St Hilda's East Community Centre in Tower Hamlets, where a similar situation had occurred and been resolved, a feasibility study was conducted on Peckham. Six options were considered. The estimated cost of refurbishment was £1,086,000, a new building costs varied between £941,000 and £1,037.000. As an interesting comparison, the reinstatement cost for insurance purposes had been estimated in 1985 at £913,000. The Executive Committee concluded that refurbishment was not a viable option. An appeal was launched and bids made for regeneration funds.

It is interesting to note that the girls' reports of their time and experience at the Settlement rarely mention the buildings except as a first impression and certainly never recall the inconveniences and uncomfortable nature of the building. The activities were obviously more important than the surroundings. Although there may be misgivings, *"pity if this was pulled down and another built in its place. Once the Peckham Settlement is gone you've lost the image, it's part of the area" [George Smith, Settlement Worker] [203],* there is a recognition of a new age for the Settlement in the new millennium.

76 Paddy Cribb, the Chairman of the Executive Council Presents Leaving Certificates to George and Ann Smith, Caretaker and Cleaner of the Settlement Building for Many Years, 1997

"Anyone who is familiar with Peckham Settlement will know that the centre is a collection of different buildings which have been joined up and adapted over the years. Because of their age and the absence of regular maintenance they are both expensive to operate and repair. All major services need renewing and the Executive Committee, having looked at the options of renovation or rebuilding, rightly decided in favour of redevelopment" [David Kitchen, Director] [204].

Chapter 6

The Role Of The Supporting Schools

When the head teachers of the first twelve schools formed the United Girls' Schools Mission, it is to be doubted they envisaged it would still be in existence, albeit with quite radical changes, over 100 years later. There might appear to be, to the modern eye, a paternalistic and patronising approach from better-off classes giving time and money to the poor unfortunate lower classes, or as a typical report cites *"the gracious patronage of the wealthy easing their conscience by carrying out duties to the Peckham poor" [C Rouse, Newspaper Reporter] [205]*, but to the original schools it was much more than this. It was a service and a privilege to think of others less fortunate than themselves. Miss Williamson commented in 1899 on *"the wonderful service… …and if so much has been done in two short years what may not the future have in store" [206]*. Within five years, there were 90 affiliated schools, and by 1914, 160 schools had joined with 64 separate Old Girls' Associations (OGA).

It is clear from many reports that neither the girls nor the Settlement users took a patronising attitude at all. The old people, the young mums and children alike welcomed and looked forward to the visits to and from the schools. The girls were overwhelming in their gratitude and thankfulness that they were able to visit this part of London legitimately. Many firm friendships were cemented. It is recorded that a Wycombe Abbey girl corresponded with a 'Mish' kid for several years after his visit to the school. Another wrote, *"in the summer term of 1925, a party of Mish kids and their Sunday School teachers came by train to Wycombe Abbey for the day. As a new girl I had to find (a Mish Kid)… …a sweet little girl of about seven wandering in the Abbey gardens. I invited her to be my 'Mission Child.' I do not remember if or when the friendship ended. I used… …to write a friendly letter about once a month… … On Mission day in 1926 and 1927 I welcomed her, saw she had a good lunch and tea and saw the gardens, especially mine. Then in the hols we arranged for her to spend the day at my home… …My brother went and fetched her from her Peckham home. He said her mother reminded him of our old Nanny. We tried to give her a happy day" [Marion Gain, Wycombe Abbey Senior] [207]*. The Centenary magazine of Wycombe Abbey contains many reminiscences of these Mission days. Girls from Bournemouth School wrote regularly to some old people in Peckham long after the initial meeting. Two of these friends were invited to celebrate the school's Golden Jubilee in 1968. Another girl corresponded with 'my old lady' for about twenty years until that lady's death. Another lady from Troy Town wrote to the head of Mickelfield School, *"I am so sorry I won't be seeing Sylvia again. I have written to her for a year since our last meeting" [Mrs Gamble, Pensioner] [208]*. There is much evidence that these friendships were not unusual. The girls, the students, the staff and the recipients all speak of the Settlement with great affection. *"I know the girls are wealthier than we are, they come from lovely homes but they don't get snobby… …we have a lovely time" [Peggy Weller, Friday Club pensioner] [209]*. It is only in begging letters to various schools that the hint of paternalism enters. *"Come and be that (leisured) class, not in a patronising spirit, but in the spirit of neighbourliness. You will find there is more for you to learn than to teach" [Canon Barnett] [210]*.

How the Schools and OGAs Supported the Settlement

Throughout most of its 104 years, the supporting schools, OGAs and further education colleges have sent volunteers in large and small numbers to the Settlement, who came to savour the work and the problems faced by the people who live in Peckham. Throughout this time the Warden, later the Director, the Organising Secretary or a Schools' Liaison Officer worked very hard to visit schools and report on the Settlement's function and describe its work in the hope that the schools would be fired with enough enthusiasm to provide support, volunteers and to raise money. *"The schools... ...are the Settlement's lifeblood" [Jessica Broomhall, Warden] [211].*

A UGS record, review or school supplement was sent out at regular intervals to update the schools on the activities of the Settlement and to reinforce the message of need. The girls contributed to this review and to their own school magazine in the section called 'Social Service'. These articles are a rich resource of social service since the Second World War as undertaken by girls in public schools of that time. They reflect the changing social pressures of each decade. The reports not only relate the fun, enjoyment, and hard work these girls obviously experienced but also convey a profound and empathetic respect for people who lived a very different life to themselves.

The schools have supported the Settlement in three main ways. They raised money for the Settlement either by donations, or by conducting sales of work and other fund-raising ventures at school. They invited people from various clubs at Peckham to their school for a day, and entertained them with tea, games or plays. They visited the Settlement and worked with the clubs, visited people in their homes, or put on plays and other entertainment at the Settlement. The schools were situated all over Britain but mainly in the south, and a substantial number were in London. For a while in the 50s, there was an ardent supporting school in New Zealand, Woodford School, possibly influenced by the one-time head of Wycombe Abbey, Miss Whitelaw, who went to live in New Zealand for some time. Until 1962 these schools were exclusively female, but then boys' schools (Dulwich College, Peckham Manor School, Wilson's, and Eton) and mixed schools (Peckham Park and Warwick Park) became involved.

<u>Gifts to the Settlement</u>

The weekly donation of a penny, or sixpence in some cases, was a tradition in many schools both pre-war and post-war. This was probably the most painless way of collecting for charity which instilled the habit of giving to good causes. *"Every form was expected to make some money* (for the Settlement) *and we set the target as equivalent to 1d per child per week" [Joan Kirby, Executive Committee member] [212].* The habits imbued at school are sometimes hard to break. There is a lovely letter from Miss Bray, one time pupil, later school secretary and very staunch supporter of the OGA of Bournemouth School for Girls, in which she writes she has put a sum of money aside regularly since she was twelve. For well over 70 years until her death last year, she sent donations each Christmas to the Settlement.

The sales of work are well remembered by many girls, and probably their mothers. *"We worked in threes on a pleated blue serge gym tunic, a white shirt and navy blue knickers. The gym tunic fell to me. I think I managed it but it was an alarming effort" [Marian Gain, Wycombe Abbey Senior] [213];*

"I struggled to knit lop sided cardigans" [Morwenna Hocking, Wycombe Abbey Senior] [214]; "We had to make something for the (summer) sale (of work) but I was not a very creative child so my mother provided cotton yarn for knitting dishcloths. I progressed to embroidering wobbly tray cloths. I think there was always a crisis of finishing them on time and seem to remember my mother having to do it on the last night. She would then have to turn up at the big event the next day and buy the item, so honour was upheld all round. I remember this event as something of a millstone" [Hilary Pincott, Executive Committee member][215]; "There was much knitting of squares, which were sewn together to form blankets by long suffering members of staff and of the sixth form" [James Allen's School Magazine] [216]. Miss Baxter thanked Wycombe Abbey for the bright bed jackets and the 'fifteen gay' blankets which cheered up the dismal rooms of old people and wrote of her joy at seeing her 'ragged little neighbours rushing about in their new things'. *"From the beginning of its history, the Settlement has been supplied with clothing from the schools......(in the early days) girls were expected to make at least one Mission garment a year......the piles of red flannel petticoats, voluminous nighties and serge frocks have given place to more attractive...... woollies and pretty frocks" [UGS Settlement News] [217].* In 1974 Wycombe Abbey decided not to send their girls' creations of *"knitted garments... ...pyjamas, children's blouses, dresses and boys' pullovers and cardigans" [Wycombe Abbey Gazette] [218]* to the Settlement but to sell these articles at school instead. They raised £200 for this effort, a donation which of course was gratefully received by the Settlement.

Gifts to the Settlement took all shapes and sizes. There was an armchair for the clubroom, lamp standards and shades for the common room which cost £9.12s.6d. in 1962, vases, toolkits for the nursery, percussion instruments for the children's band, pictures for the display boards, a Hobart Mixer for the kitchen staff in 1959, a cine camera, 'Christmas boxes of toys, books and tinned goods in 6 packing cases' and Christmas decorations.

Many beautiful flowers, especially bluebells, were sent from the country schools to 'dreary Peckham'. This practice had started in 1903 when schools were asked to send flowers to an area with 'not a blade of grass or a tree'. Later botanical specimens for the nursery school were sent from Newbury School, and many schools participated in a flower sale in 1953 which raised £60. In the UGS Review there was some advice for the packers of flowers.

Flowers with care

1. If all the boxes of delight
And fragrance that you fondly pack
Arrived in good condition, we
Should have the flowers we often lack

2. But some strew flowers into a box
Tie it with string and send away
But they get shaken on the road
And do not live to see the day.

3. Or flowers are picked too fully blown
Or put into a flimsy box
Or made to spend a long weekend
In transit vile, with postman's knocks.

4. So when the flowers that bloom in Spring
Bring spring to Peckham's dreary heart
Remember, those who love to give,
That PACKING is a major art. [UGS Record] [219]

The flowers usually graced the pensioners' tables when they were having their midday meal and bunches were sent out with Meals on Wheels, but the practice had generally stopped by the 1960s because the cost of transporting the flowers many miles was too much for the schools.

Easter Eggs were collected and sent to the Settlement. It seemed that often volunteer drivers would undertake to deliver these to Peckham. There is a slight discrepancy about these eggs. In 1962 Easter Eggs were sent to the nursery school apparently for the first time ever by Sydenham High, but Bournemouth had been sending them for at least six years before that. Coal was also sent and in 1964 six hundredweight of coal was distributed to twelve households. A regular gift for many years were the overalls made for the nursery school by Christ's Hospital, and there was quite a heartfelt statement in the UGS Review of 1970 when Joan Serle, the head, commented, *"we are delighted that we no longer have to make aprons for the children" [220]* and the pupils of the schools were probably also very pleased they no longer had this onerous task.

Harvest parcels were a regular feature from each school. *"A school at Newbury sent a whole lorry load... ...including fifteen sacks of vegetable marrows. The dinner club pensioners nearly went on strike over the number of times marrow was served. All the harvest had to be sorted, packed up and delivered so I quickly got to know the area as I went round delivering produce" [Jill Andrews, Student Worker] [221].* In 1967, 453 carrier bags of harvest goods were distributed to the Peckham old people. One hopes they did not have too many marrows to eat. The tradition of sending harvest produce is still observed by St Bartholomew's School in Newbury, Sydenham High School and Camelot School in Peckham.

Produce and goods were sent to the Settlement each Christmas and the club members at the Settlement had a good time sifting and sorting and in true jumble sale fashion getting the best bits first. *"Clothes, toys, cakes, books, jewellery, cosmetics were taken to one of the rooms upstairs and we would sort it out and price it all... ...The stalls would be laid out with the smaller stuff and second hand clothes (in the hall)... ...Then the firemen from Talfourd Road fire station would take over the stage... ...with all the things that used to be auctioned off and didn't they do well... ...and then the stampede was on when the stalls opened... ...we were quite proud of the money we made... ...(we) went home tired out but with our little bargains that we would put away for the children at Christmas... ...a second hand dress or coat for me perhaps and a tie for Dad if he was lucky" [Florrie Whale, Thursday Club] [222].*

The Settlement had their own sales of work too and on one famous occasion Anita Harris opened one of these sales and bought some dresses for her nieces. They had been made by one of the staff and cost 'all of 2/6d'. A student resident recalled another occasion. *"Someone suggested that we should have a bottle stall, so Felicity and I spent several afternoons going round the local pubs and off licences (of which there were plenty) asking for bottles - everyone we asked gave us something - which was good because I don't suppose profits were that easy" [Jill Andrews, Student Worker] [223].*

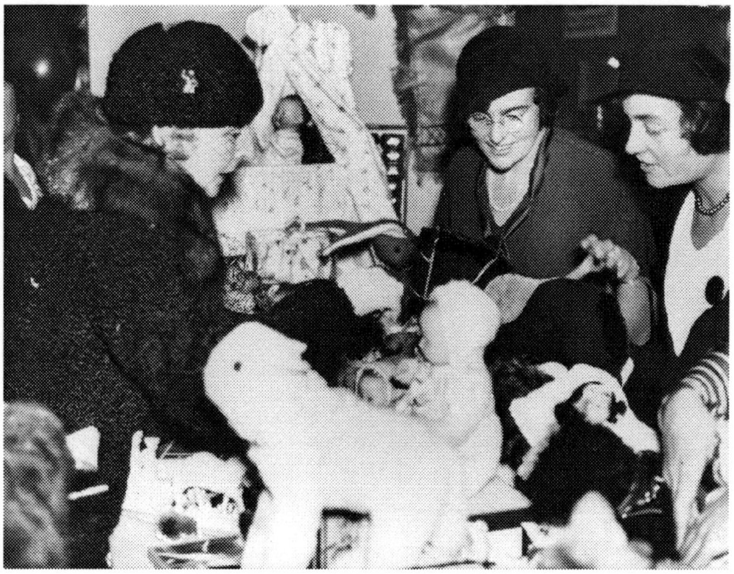

77 Jumble Sales in the 1940s and 1970s

Parties and Outings

The real enjoyment and the most descriptive records are the parties held at the schools for the clubs from the Settlement or from the parishes of Peckham. The members of the clubs were entertained by a preview of the latest school play, or Morris dancing, or even a ventriloquist and conjuror. The pensioners were invited for a January and a summer tea. Whatever the occasion, the graphic descriptions effuse with affection, enjoyment and clarity. *"Unfortunately the weather was very cold, and the old people, although considerably cheered by the sight of the blazing fire in the hall, felt the need of their coats indoors......*(they) *were entertained to country and Morris dancing, a tea......and were delighted with their scarves and bed socks. They went home saying they had had a lovely time" [J Oakes, Schoolgirl] [224].*

In 1947 each of the clubs at the Settlement went to one of the schools. The Mums' Club went to Brighton and then on to Downs School, Seaford. This outing is remembered fondly. *"What a day that was......we were dropped off......on the beach for a couple of hours...... we used to have a quick dip in the sea......then we were picked up to go on to the school to sit down to a lunch we couldn't take our eyes off... ...then would come up those lovely strawberries and cream. Then the entertainment from the schoolgirls......we would have tea and cakes and when we left, the girls used to line up with little posies of flowers each and some goodies......it was a real break for all of us because* (the) *dads knew it was the one day a year they would have to take off from work to look after the children ......It was like a holiday for us with a whole two shillings to spend" [Florrie Whale, Thursday Club] [225].* One party in 1950 cost the school £7.9s.1d when the club went to James Allen's for a tea. *"A real treat for us who didn't have money for cakes" [ibid.] [226].* In the early school magazines, the annual visit from the old people was always known as the Peckham party and *"the guests were chosen from those who lived alone" [UGS Record] [227].* At another party, the old ladies were given *"a woollen shawl and the men a pair of woolly gloves" [J Oakes, Schoolgirl] [228].*

Wycombe Abbey was the first school to hold these parties. Large numbers of men, women and children came from the Mission by omnibus and train and were treated to milk and buns.

78 Mission Day at Wycombe Abbey, 1904

The school entertained forty ladies in 1972. They had a conducted tour of the school, played bingo and charades and had some community singing. *"Each was given a little nosegay... ...they boarded the coach - some surprisingly nimbly, some with great difficulty and several have written since" [Wycombe Abbey Gazette] [229].* The Ivy (Thursday) club still visits each Spring and sees the dress rehearsal of the school play. The Friday club visit Bellerby's College (an amalgamation of two previous supporting schools, Mickelfield and Wadhurst) and Walthamstow Hall annually to this day.

79 The Pensioners Visit to Sydenham High School, 1999

80 The Friday Club Visit to Bellerby's College, 1999

The children of Peckham probably did quite well because it seems likely that they managed to have at least two or maybe more parties each year. Most of the Home County and London schools held a Christmas and a summer party for the children. Falling in the lake at Wycombe Abbey was a time-honoured tradition and obviously an annual event for at least one of the 'Mish' kids, who took to the lake 'like lemmings'. There are regular reports from 1926 of this occurrence. *"Wycombe Abbey invited the children's club and Billy Jacks fell into the lake" [Jennie Fisher, Social Worker] [230].*

81 The Thursday Club Prepare to Visit Wycombe Abbey, 1999

There was a visit by the Black Eagles, boys of 6 years to 10 years old, to Winceby House, Bexhill on Sea. Twenty-six arrived by coach, and they went to the beach. *"Some had never seen the sea before... ... they paddled... ... hunted crabs, played cricket, they had tea and ices. They had a bag of goodies and two and six for each boy" [Fifth Form Report] [231].* James Allen's entertained 222 children to a Christmas party in 1959. This seemed an inordinate number but for ten years there were never less than a hundred children at these parties. All the children had *"a continuous flow of fun and games. Tea was bread, butter and jam, buns and cakes, lemonade, ice cream and jelly... ...there was a treasure hunt and (they) went home happily after a very eventful party" [Enid Binstead, Schoolgirl] [232].* A student resident who was helping at the Settlement recalls taking a whole group of Brownies to a campsite. As a coach was beyond their means, they went by furniture van. In 1958 children were invited to Haberdashers' Aske's School for a picnic. *"We started having the picnics in the school as we kept having wet days... ...we sent them home with a bag of goodies after a large tea of buns and jelly... ... Around the late 60s, we gave up the picnics and sent Harvest gifts instead" [Joan Kirby, Executive Committee Member] [233].* By the 1980s, the outings were to Margate, Bognor Regis and Thorpe Park, instead of to schools.

82 A 'Mish' Kid at Wycombe Abbey, 1920s

Visits to the Settlement

In the early years the main function of the supporting schools was to raise money and for many years afterwards that was still the principal task. But very quickly, the need for volunteers to help at the Settlement with all the many activities was apparent and who better than girls willing to give up their time and who cost the Settlement only the price of a meal and maybe a small room if they stayed overnight. Rev Harry Veasey's ideal was to *"bring about a real, personal interest between the schools and the people of Peckham and in many different ways the schools have been able to come in real touch with the life of the place" [234]*. And come they did, often many times. Some of the London schools are reported to have sent girls to help every week in 1903 with the children's clubs. In 1931 Mary Datchelor girls were helping regularly with the Band of Hope children every Monday evening. The Second World War disrupted the volunteer help but by 1947 there was a concerted effort to re-establish the volunteers. A volunteer from the London School of Economics wrote, *"I helped with the Squirrels club who were girls of 8 to 10 years...... every Friday. I stayed to supper and then assisted at the evening youth club" [Susan Wright, Student Worker][235]*. These visits made a deep impression on many of the schoolgirls. There is a detailed description of a week's visit to the Settlement in 1956 from a City of London schoolgirl. Descriptions in the UGS Review of the late 1960s were equally graphic and vivid. In the 1957 UGS Record it is recorded that student volunteers were living and working in London, and working at the Settlement in their spare time with the old people's clubs (Monday and Wednesday), the Mothers' club and the children's clubs. There were also seven students helping with the secretarial and general work. Most of these had been drafted in by the OGAs. One such student worked as a full-time volunteer for three months in 1957, and then continued helping in the evening whilst holding down a full-time job as a secretary in the City. With her, she had two university students, one gap year student, a nursery nurse and another student who combined a job with bookkeeping at the Settlement. Her duties included visiting, sorting and delivering harvest food, helping in the nursery, Meals on Wheels, cleaning the gent's loo, assisting at the Christmas fair, and helping with the parish Brownie pack. It could not have been a boring life, because there was a camaraderie amongst the young people. They supported each other, had much fun and a good social life too.

Visiting the people in their own homes was a very important part of the Settlement's work, and the schoolgirls were often part of the visiting teams. They went to have a chat and a cup of tea with the old and housebound. *"Often they (the visitors) are the only people the poor dears have seen to talk to for days on end" [Theo Waite, Organising Secretary] [236]; "As I was leaving, an old man (who had seemed to live in abject poverty) unlocked a door to show me his parlour which he kept for best. It was a lovely room with beautiful chairs and china ornaments" [Susan Waggitt, Student Worker] [237]*. In 1966 Haberdashers' Aske's, James Allen's, Honor Oak and Silverthorne Schools made up the visiting teams. Not only were the housing conditions appraised but *"old people are easier to talk to than our parents" [Schoolgirl] [238]; "We were pressed to have a cup of tea......and we needed no effort to stimulate conversation as they were only too anxious to praise the Settlement and its work" [Lindsay Darling, Schoolgirl] [239]*. There was a great deal of commitment on both sides. *"If she doesn't call every week, she rings me up" [Resident] [240]; "I won't allow them to come on these dark evenings- I am frightened about them going home, but we write to each other each week" [Resident] [241]; "It is a great joy to look forward to the visits of MY schoolgirls on Saturdays, and to chat of cabbages,*

Kings, and many things" [Resident] [242]. Jennie Fisher remembers *"ticking some visiting schoolgirls off for wearing trousers to deliver Christmas parcels" [243].* At that time the girls were all still expected to wear school uniform. These young volunteers also put on pantomimes and other entertainment and these were all a great source of fun. *"The audience seemed to enjoy it as well. We wrote it ourselves and had a wonderful time. Doing the pantomime meant we learnt many old time songs for the community singing. This has proved amazingly useful through the years" [Susan Waggitt, Student Worker] [244].*

The 50s and 60s saw a steady stream of student and schoolgirl volunteers but by the 1970s the emphasis on volunteer help was slightly reduced because the Settlement was able to get grants from Government sources and because the staff were now being paid. In the publicity brochure of 1973 it said *"UGS is still the main source of voluntary support for the Settlement and we're proud of this... ...students and Old Girls share in many Settlement activities...... training and experience are provided for residents and visitors including members of the supporting schools" [Geoffrey Heal, Executive Committee Member] [245].* The girls were still helping in the holidays mainly with the play schemes. If they did not live in London, they paid their own way. In the 1980s reports of schoolgirls and student volunteers are very few, partly because they had been discouraged from visiting Peckham during the riots and unrest happening in the area. Downe House girls helped with the drop-in centre and the second-hand clothes shop in the holidays. Malvern College sent girls every summer and they stayed with the Director. A group of students came from Bellerby's College to visit the Settlement in 1998. The following halting English description is from one schoolgirl, whose native land is Russia, *"Today we went to London. We have been visiting old ladies and little children. And after we played in Bingo with the old ladies. I enjoyed it very much. The ladies were kind and friendly. We done a lot of photos with them. When we were playing Bingo I won a prize. And I was have to choose something from the food. I took the corn and gave it to one old lady...... After we went to the little children. They were so quiet......they always smiled at everything. I liked them very much. It was the nice day. And I'm happy that I spent this day with this old ladies" [Julia Beredznay] [246].*

The Settlement had a tradition of holding Open Days not just for the schoolgirls but also for all interested people in Peckham. It is in the UGS Reviews and school magazines that the open days are mostly described. These were begun in the 1950s and nearly always included a sermon from the local vicar, or a religious service. There were keep fit exhibitions from the Mothers' club as well as singing from the nursery school. The Open Days continue, and there are records of the supporting schools sending pupils to them.

Training and Education

"The primary aim of the founders was ......that it (the Mission) *should be part of the character education of the girls themselves" [Rev Harry Veasey] [247].* From the beginning the Settlement was seen as a training ground for social work, and by 1906 it was an established centre. The London School of Economics, Bedford College, The Royal College of Nursing, Leicester and Nottingham Universities and the Church Work for Women sent students regularly for training. From 1951, influenced by Elsie Bowerman, the Norland Nurses came to the Settlement as part of their course. Teacher training colleges and voluntary associations from other countries, notably America, also sent students to observe and learn as well as help with the activities of the Settlement. Many of these students would have been

pupils in the supporting schools. Usually they lived at the Settlement or nearby, often rent free in exchange for work in the clubs, or with visiting. At the Annual Service, the sermon reminded the schools that *"the union was formed to bring the need, the interest and the joy of social service before all girls' schools. (The Settlement) has been established where girls leaving school can obtain experience of conditions in an artisan neighbourhood as well as of the social and educational activities which best serve it and can, if they wish, qualify for social work by a definite course of training" [Times Report][248]*. It was recorded in 1930 that 100 students had gained practical experience for their respective courses. The training element was rekindled after the Second World War. Seventeen students from various university social science departments spent anything from two weeks to two months at the Settlement in 1955.

Many of the volunteers went to work at the Settlement after they had been to one of the Social Service weeks or weekends. Jennie Fisher attended a social service week as a schoolgirl from St Mary's and St Anne's, a supporting school. She came back as a volunteer for several months and then in 1964 returned as a fully qualified social worker to work at the Settlement for some years.

83 Jennie Fisher Lighting Candles at the Old People's Christmas Party, 1966

Not only did these weeks fire the enthusiasm of the girls and bring the problems of Peckham to reality, but they also inspired so many girls, and later boys too, to take up professions in the social work field. Some of these girls were and are pioneers in certain fields of social work, and it is not too strong or fanciful to say that the Peckham Settlement was responsible for these famous ladies. The Emeritus Professor of the University of Warwick, Meg Stacey, took a Social Science Certificate at the London School of Economics mainly because she had stayed and worked at the Peckham Settlement, during the early years of the Second World War. The trainees did have a good example in the original group of head teachers, but the work at the Settlement was a stimulus and a good foundation to their own thoughts and actions. Eve Keatley visited the Settlement in 1949 as a schoolgirl from Wycombe Abbey.

84 Eve Keatley (on the left of the picture) Helping at the Old People's Christmas Party, 1966

She stayed with the local vicar who delighted in showing her the poor post-war state of the area. It was a revelation to her. She returned in the 1960s to work voluntarily as Organising Secretary, a member of the Executive Committee and Editor of the UGS Review. Even if the girls did not pursue social work as a career, these original visits often inspired them to take up voluntary work either in the Settlement or elsewhere.

Social Service Conferences

The first social service week appears to have been held in 1924 in Oxford. Later these were held in Cambridge too and then at the Settlement. It was an action packed week for sixth formers and some fifth formers, who stayed at the Settlement, took part in the Settlement activities, listened to talks by practitioners, and visited other institutions connected with the week's specific theme. The descriptions of these weeks from the girls are explicit and vivid. The week obviously made a huge impression even years afterwards. From 1947 these conferences were regular events every spring. The range of activities and lectures was truly amazing and comprehensive. The quality of visiting speakers was very high and the arranged visits to relevant places were many and diverse. The girls were invited to discuss, debate, have hands-on experience of real life problems, and there was the lighter side of making friends and visiting the theatre. The girls were treated like university students and the conferences were run like seminars, a possible reason for their popularity. The Settlement acted as a meeting place, an active learning environment and a source of a good and lasting education.

A conference entitled 'The Physically Handicapped' took place in 1950. During this week the girls heard talks on teaching a deaf child to speak at the unit for the hearing impaired which had opened in 1948 at Peckham Park School, after care of cripples, the work of an occupational therapist, and Lady Althea Eliot gave a talk on the Extension Guides. They visited schools for the deaf and educationally sub-normal children, the workshops of both Lord Roberts and the London Association for the Blind, and a hostel for crippled girls. In 1955, 44 girls from 17 schools, 33 of whom were resident, attended the conference. 'Social work as a career' was the title for 1959. At this conference the girls heard from a woman police officer, a housing welfare officer, an old people's welfare officer, one describing women in Church work, and a person from the Migrant Service Division about the problems of integration for the West Indian population. They visited St Bartholomew's Hospital and a local school, as well as the theatre to see 'Salad Days'. The title was repeated in 1960 but the programme was different. There were talks from a Public Health Officer, a probation officer, a home teacher for the blind and a parish worker, visits to the local school to see how deaf children were integrated into mainstream school, to King's College Hospital and to the theatre to see 'My Fair Lady'. The girls also helped each day with the old people's lunch clubs.

Apparently the middle 60s was a turbulent time for the Settlement when staff changes and the building programme had produced some problems but *"one cheerful factor is the enquiring interest and enthusiasm of succeeding generations of schoolgirls" [Annual Report] [249]*. The resurgence of interest in the conferences was fuelled by Eve Keatley and David Collett, the Warden of Blackfriars Settlement. Mindful of the original quest to find a place which was 'predominately children', the themes of the Social Service conferences in 1964 and 1966 were on child care and 'The Social Needs of Pre-school Children'. There were talks from a juvenile court officer, a children's Church of England home warden, a child-fund officer, a head teacher of a nursery school and from Dr Bernstein of the Institute of Education on the early environment for pre-school children. There were visits to Great Ormond Street Hospital, and a school for mentally challenged children where *"we were surprised to learn how often these children can be trained to do simple repetitive jobs and therefore help to pay their way" [G Tuffnell and H Weinberg, Schoolgirls] [250]*. Other conferences were on Leisure (1951), careers in the field of Human Misdemeanour (1963) which included talks by prison officers (to which 26 residential students and 33 others came from 28 different schools). In 1967 Elspeth Howe, as a Juvenile Court magistrate and care committee worker, gave a talk on the scope of volunteer work with children in playgroup organisations and school care committee work. Later, she became Lady Howe and President of the Settlement. This conference was attended by 36 residents and 25 non-residents from 28 schools. 'Living in a Redevelopment Area' was discussed over three days in 1970.

<u>The Urban Studies Centre</u>

In 1972 a change to these conferences took place. The newly inaugurated Urban Studies Centre was designed to serve the schools and the local community with practical courses, seminars and education to promote the understanding between local residents, planners, councillors and the schools with a focus on the voluntary sector. ILEA gave funding for two full-time teachers. The centre was run by Barbara Hill, whose brief was to involve the local schools to promote an awareness of the needs of the inner city, and aimed to provide practical situations for theoretical viewpoints. There was a social work sub-committee headed by Ann Vickery, a trainer at the South West London Institute of Social Work Training. The weekends continued with studies on housing, structured first hand observation on ward trails and collecting of data. The centre developed courses *"to help young people become responsible citizens, able to cope with civic issues, competing needs like industrial changes, housing redevelopment, traffic congestion, how local government works and how they can participate" [John Lane, Director] [251]*. There were audio-visual facilities, a large reading/study room, a darkroom and a print-room. Fieldwork was emphasised. In 1973 a survey was conducted by fifth formers from Sydenham High School on the local housing estates. Debates and discussions took place on redevelopment, education, ageing and social community work. Barbara Hill was particularly adept at designing role-play and simulation games. At a weekend in 1974, the subject was 'Defining the Problem' and the young people walked around Peckham, visited an adventure playground, talked to community workers and African youth workers. In 1975 a report from two Wycombe Abbey girls describes such a weekend. *"The object of our weekend……was to discover in which ways the community had altered with redevelopment and in particular to see how old people had coped with a drastic change in the environment… …Throughout the weekend, Mrs Hill stimulated us through talks, films, encounters with the occupants of high-rise flats and old age homes… …and to analyse… …the redevelopment scheme" [E Duncan and C Lancaster, Schoolgirls] [252]; "We walked around……Peckham; some of the things we noticed were vandalism, lack of care and involvement in the community. We were … …involved in role play… … we were all given characters who had different decisions to make and afterwards a member of a local council talked to us about our decisions" [L Pickup and V Hinks, Schoolgirls] [253]*. Roedean, Malvern and St Alban's were some of the supporting schools who took part in these activities.

85 The Urban Studies Centre at the Settlement, 1977

From 1979 these weekends were reduced to days because funding was cut. An outcry in the press heralded the appointment of George Nicholson as head of the Centre. He was a Southwark councillor and could be viewed as well versed in the workings of the council with the community it served. Not only was George a left-winger but also he had not been educated in the traditional way. Nevertheless, he was strongly supported by the British Youth Council, the Schools' Council and ILEA. He was funded for three days a week, and given a grant to provide a comprehensive programme to give schoolchildren a political awareness of the area, housing problems and lack of community facilities. Several urban trails were set up from which schools could glean information and debate some of the developmental issues about local government. George designed a Social Skills course and in 1982 helped with four secondary schools to design three ward trails and present these in a very professional booklet. The Urban Studies Centre had the services of part-time teachers from the Southwark Infotech Centre as well. In 1984 a slide show was produced to take round the supporting schools. The courses included designing play schemes, looking at the implications of the new shopping development, and access for disabled people. The Centre also became the home of Peckham Properties, an old people's memory resource bank. In 1985 the centre was moved to Willowbrook and was affiliated to BASSAC. It retained an office at the Settlement for a few years.

86 Students on an Urban Trail, 1982

Training and Education in the Latter Years of the Last Century

In the late 70s education days were organised by Mary Rose Bateman, the Schools Liaison Officer (one time head teacher of Berkhamstead School and later of Perse School, Cambridge, both institutions being long time supporting schools). There was an attempt to bring back the three-day conferences under the BASSAC label. This was to follow a talk to be given by Leon Brittan, then Home Secretary, on 'The Role of the Settlements'. The decision to hold this meeting at the Settlement was reversed at the last minute. There had been intimations of left wing dissension and threats of disturbances and protests. Even though the Settlement was a non-political charity, the venue was moved to the Royal Commonwealth Society Hall in the West End. It was an excellent lecture and well attended by a cross section of society. After this any visits to the Settlement were really left in the hands of the schools to organise what they wanted to do.

When Kitty Leek became director in 1985 she encouraged the schools to send girls to the Settlement, trying to foster a two-way exchange, in which the girls set the agenda. *"They wanted to visit the estates and talk to a social worker. We organised that... ...another day we arranged a visit from a police officer and the girls were shown round the estates" [Kitty Leek, Director] [254].* On one memorable day girls from Roedean, Benenden and Newbury Schools were *"ready to go on their walk around and all of a sudden one of my staff came to me with a huge paper bag and said, 'We must lock this into the safe'. I asked, 'What is it?' and she said, 'It's all the girls' jewellery. I warned them to take it all off because they were going round the Peckham estates" [ibid] [255].* The member of staff lived in the area, walked to and fro from work and wore jewellery. Another instance of the perception looming larger than the reality is illustrated by several pensioners some years before. They commented on the large number of muggings and burglaries even though none of them had had direct experience of these crimes.

In an appeal letter of 1992 the two-way exchange was emphasised again. *"Schools support our work with cash donations, harvest festivals, Christmas gifts and hospitality to our pensioners. In return we invite pupils to visit us and experience first hand the life of an inner city community. Some schools send pupils on work experience while others arrange day visits to look at a topic of specific interest, for instance housing, work with the under-fives" [Kitty Leek, Director] [256].* Today the Settlement is still providing training and work experience. This is mainly directed towards the local schools, although some students do come from the supporting schools and work with the staff in the Settlement for a week. They stay with the Director or with one of the Executive Committee members. One of the by-products for the participating schoolgirls is an addition on their CV forms for university entrance.

The Old Girls' Associations

The Old Girls' Associations formed the foundation of the enthusiasm and support for the Settlement. Wycombe Abbey Seniors had pledged collective support for the Mission in 1898 and each member undertook to do such work as lay in her power to promote that cause. Most girls at other schools were expected to become members of their OGAs. There was an implicit understanding that the girls had been exceptionally lucky to have had a good education and that for this they must give something back to the community. There was a loyalty to the old school but also a genuine sense of loving duty which kept these ties going. In many schools the OGAs worked hard and long for the Settlement. They sent money, provided personnel to step in at a moment's notice to help with activities, were a breeding ground for trainees and students, held positions on the staff, and on the various committees. This set of attributes has never really died, although the numbers of Old Girls are fewer. In fact they did and still do provide the link from the past to the future. *"Groups of old girls particularly people from the 1948-1955 era had their own groups, and sent money and (other things) and still do" [Joan Kirby, Executive Committee Member] [257]*. In 1913 there was a reminder to the Seniors of Wycombe Abbey from Miss Whitelaw that the Mission was *"a claim directly on the present school for money, on all past and present for the interest and for prayer" [258]*.

In 1924 *"The UGSS is full of OGs*
Rushing around as busy as bees,
Still more are wanted so each OGA
Should urge its members to come and stay"
[UGSM School Sheet] [259].

In 1933 James Allen's, along with other schools, formulated a service roll of OGs to help the Settlement. In 1946 the City of London School was saying *"that the Settlement will always have the strong support of the girls' schools to enable it to continue its valuable work" [260]*. With the fifty-year celebrations, representatives of OGAs were entertained to a special meeting, no doubt to encourage the Associations to continue to help the Settlement. In 1951 Wycombe Abbey Seniors were told by the Organising Secretary, Elsie Bowerman, *"the continued support and financial aid from the schools during these hard times was really miraculous" [261]*. The next year another reminder was given. *"Last July a Senior had a glorious anniversary. She had been doing voluntary work in St Mark's Parish for fifty years...... That kind of service has been the glory and life-blood of the UGS. It was the impact of educated and devoted women and girls, who with no hint of patronage, came and took the lead in the work, that enabled St Mark's to do such wonders among the people of the parish......Now for a variety of reasons the stream of personal workers has nearly dried up and the results are very serious. Partly because of the long tradition of outside help, there has not been any strong leadership among the local people. Those who are most able are the first to move out into more salubrious neighbourhoods, and the type of education in LCC schools is not yet producing leaders" [A MacGregor Lewis, Wycombe Abbey Senior] [262]*. In 1957 most volunteers at the Settlement were Old Girls. They came from Godolphin, Wycombe Abbey, St Swithun's, Benenden, Malvern, the Bexhill schools, Mary Datchelor and James Allen's.

When the nature of the Settlement changed in the early 1970s this did not seem to deter the Friends of the UGS from contacting all 46 OGAs to raise interest and also funds. Mary Datchelor was still exhorting its Old Girls to support the Settlement. *"Past members of the school would find something familiar in the continuing support of the UGSS in Peckham" [263]*. But by 1980 the OGA support of the Settlement was not very strong, and although there was a move to involve the Associations in the committee work again in 1990, the links never really recovered the strength of the previous 50 years.

The Changing Nature of Social Service Support by the Schools

The debate concerning the schools' support for the Settlement started in the very early days, and has fluctuated throughout the years with the changing social service scene and the required educational curriculum.

Who Owned the Settlement?

The dedication of the founder ladies may have given rise to the proprietorial possessiveness which permeates the early records. As early as 1905, some head teachers were disagreeing with the Settlement's policies and some difficulties in liaison and communication became evident. The dissension often took the form of a naughty child being disciplined because it had stepped out of line. Miss Wilson, the head of Boston House Eastbourne wrote to the warden.

"Dear Madam, I am much astonished at the contents of your letter of November 7th and fail to understand your demand for £1.1s. when annually you receive £10.10s and several articles of clothing from our Old Girls' Branch. (It was at my suggestion that we joined ......your Mission and I made it quite clear at the time that the school had no part in this) I hear also that our Hon. Sec. to the Old Girls' Association has been likewise annoyed and now the climax is reached with your informing me that I owe £1.1s to the General Fund. We hold our meeting on 6th December and I shall move - and I am sure the Hon. Sec. will second it - that we select another outlet for our surplus funds. Indeed this year we devoted a third elsewhere because we were much annoyed that the garments sent by the Hon. Sec. in 1904 were sold for the benefit of some foreign mission instead of being given or sold cheaply to the poor we intended them for" [264].

In the next year there were a series of letters from Miss Dove's secretary to Harry Veasey or directly to Bishop Talbot about the running of the Settlement. *"If Miss Nutt forms too many OGAs then WA* (Wycombe Abbey) *circles would find other work NOT in connexion with the UGSM at all" [AR Burne Secretary to Jane Dove] [265]; "Plenty of Seniors are ready and able and specially fitted to do the work both as officials and on the committee" [Jane Dove] [266]; "I feel very anxious about the new Settlement. The enthusiasm of all our Seniors has been stirred and it will be a fatal mistake if by any mischance it is not utilised. But from what I hear Miss Gooch is better at arousing enthusiasm than at making use of it... ...It will not on any account do to mix up Society ladies and the more luxurious kind of life they will expect with the girls who ought to have a perfectly simple life......There should be one general referee who should hold in his or her hands all the threads and co-ordinate everything" [ibid] [267].* There was also concern about Harry Veasey's work in the parish. Miss Dove did not think he was able to devote enough time to the Settlement. She suggested that the Bishop of Woolwich be made warden or that Harry Veasey should retire from St Mark's and give himself wholly to the Settlement. *"If this were done I, personally, and I believe many others also, would have absolute confidence in the conduct of affairs......He knows the bishop's wishes, he has an unique knowledge of the schools and commands their confidence and his devotions and powers of organisation are remarkable... ...I am sending a copy of this letter to every member of the Committee excepting Miss Gooch who is of course now an official" [ibid] [268].* The proprietorial interest was catching. Miss Williamson wrote to Harry Veasey about the constitution arrangements in 1907. She disagreed with the proposals and withdrew her support from the Committee.

There was obviously some concern about keeping the girls' interest in the Settlement once they had left school. In 1908 Miss Dove wrote it was *"too early to bring notice of the Settlement to the girls in Upper Sixth forms. We don't at all want the claims of the Settlement brought before them too soon. We still have the feeling strongly towards the Settlement's influence that it tends to alienate our Seniors from us in some unconscious and mysterious way. We felt it very much again at the Seniors' meeting in June and later on too" [269].* Miss Dove expressed concern about the large *"numbers of schools and the large and varied body of supporters" [270].* In 1919 she wrote a two-page paper putting forward issues for the development of the Settlement. She suggested that as all the schools seem to be working for St Mark's Parish that the schools be divided into groups and assigned to other parishes in London. She believed this would keep the interest of a schoolgirl after she had left school. She also advised that the word 'mission' should be dropped and that all schools' donations be sent to a UGSM bureau for social services to finance the Settlement. She mooted that schools take on one activity and concentrate on developing and supporting that activity. She used Badminton as an example of one school which was then wholly financing a convalescent home. *"If any school wished to withdraw its support and start an entirely new activity elsewhere an enquiry should first be held. All schools and OGAs which belong should regard themselves morally bound to give the UGSM their utmost support. Each one should be asked at once what support it can undertake to give" [271].* Her other proposals were *"there should be a travelling Secretary to keep the schools and the OGAs in touch... ...that the 160 schools and the OGAs be divided into three groups and each group to work autonomously through committees of its own. They should appoint representatives who would have the duty of keeping the schools in touch with the work" [272].* Certainly by the end of the Second World War, many of these suggestions were implemented.

John Lane wrote that when the Executive Committee decided to drop the name UGS and become the Peckham Settlement, it caused some dissension in the ranks. *"When I went there, there were a substantial number of ex-heads on the management committee......a big bust-up was inevitable because we were saying to the girls, 'Come down here to learn not to patronise'. Secondly, they were not to come in their uniforms so that was dynamite stuff really... ...The change came over culture or maybe class and what role the settlement was to have... ...I went to one school in a hall with 700 girls in serried rows......I remember nearly losing my temper when one girl asked about the poor people" [273].* Nine years earlier Dr Groves had commented on the age of the venerable committee, none of whom were local people, the proprietorial attitude of the retired headmistress treasurer and the Organising Secretary, Isabel Granger, who saw herself as 'ruling the roost'. Isabel was also described as charismatic and full of ideas. John Lane managed to overturn this attitude which did herald the beginning of a new role for the schools but it was not popular amongst the mistresses of the supporting schools.

Personal Commitment

Much of the support from schools came from the energy and enthusiasm of a designated mistress at the individual school, an Old Girl Representative, the Organising Secretary or a Schools Liaison Officer. Indeed without this personal commitment from these ladies, some schools would probably have relinquished their support many years before they did. Some of the mistresses took their role very seriously. When Mary Datchelor School joined the Union in 1909 *"Canon Veasey very badly wanted a clock for the parish of St. Mark's... ... so that his parishioners could be punctual at their work. Miss Smith* (the assigned Mission teacher) *set her heart on getting one for him. Her efforts were so successful that enough money was collected not only to buy a clock but to pay for the tower in which it was placed. The money had to be invested till after the war* (1st World War) *and Miss Smith (1877-1914) did not live to see the Datchelor Clock" [Story of Mary Datchelor School] [274].* The headmistresses formed a close band of devotees. Bournemouth School for Girls joined the Union in 1918 because the new head had been head at Manchester High School for Girls, a member of the UGS and *"under her enthusiastic guidance a regular plan of giving was established" [The Milestone, BSG magazine] [275].* There are records too of Old Girls becoming head teachers and immediately joining their school to the UGS.

Miss Alsop had been newly appointed to Tiffin's Girls' School in Kingston when the *"staff were told by Miss Flavell* (the head mistress of Tiffin's) *that the chairman of governors had recommended to her notice a new organisation in South London for the betterment of social conditions" [M. Alsop] [276].* Miss Flavell appointed Miss Alsop on to the Settlement committee. *"It was an undenominational school but no dissension ever arose. In those days we were by no means a rich school - many of our girls had begun in elementary schools and there were no county council scholarships" [ibid] [277].* Miss Alsop was obviously delighted at having been chosen for the role and she describes in detail 'the thrilling event of a sale of work' for the Settlement funds. She continued for some years as mistress in charge and kept in contact with the Settlement even in her retirement, a trend that was repeated many times with serving mistresses of the girls' schools. This era of the mostly single lady, usually comfortably off, giving unremitting service, would last until well into the 1960s. They would devote hours of leisure time to voluntary work and continue this loyal service for many years. The Settlement could not have managed without them. They would take on various roles, although many of them had a career as well, and were thoroughly committed to the work.

Elsie Bowerman is a name that constantly appears in the records for about thirty years. She was described by those who knew her as highly intelligent, flexible, rather formidable, but understanding, very kindly and a fine woman. She was a barrister with sympathy for the Suffragette Movement and as a small child she had survived the sinking of the Titanic. She worked for the Settlement for years, acting as a voluntary worker visiting housebound people and as Honorary Secretary and Treasurer. She served on the Executive Committee for many years. She took on the arduous role of Organising Secretary and campaigned for the Settlement not just in her old school, Wycombe Abbey, as the school representative, but visited and talked to many other schools. She stepped in as temporary Warden in the 1960s and wrote many articles acclaiming the need for the Settlement. She became President towards the end of her life. Elsie left all her money to Wycombe Abbey knowing that the school would look after the Settlement. Her foresight and professional knowledge were evident when, with the help of Sir Geoffrey Howe, Lady Howe's husband, she established the Dove-Bowerman Trust Fund in 1971. At that time public schools were at a real risk of closure. The fund was to be *"free from State control and could further at will whatever objects might be considered worthy" [Lorna Flint] [278].* The Settlement has been and still is a recipient of money invested in this trust of about £3,000 a year for specified purposes. Just before her death, she asked both Eve Keatley and Lady Howe to ensure the Settlement was in always in good hands.

87 Elsie Bowerman, 1947

Mary Douglas was one of the original foundation members, the head of Godolphin School in Salisbury. She worked for years as a voluntary worker and as a member of the Executive Board, the forerunner of the present Executive Committee. Bettie Skinner was a teacher at James Allen's Girls' School and was a classic example of a dedicated and loyal volunteer worker who served on the Executive Committee, the Nursery School Committee and was Secretary to the Friends. Grace Griffiths was a Wycombe Abbey Senior who visited the Settlement and stayed for at least fifteen years. She was a centre of fun and energetic, giving huge amounts of time. *"She carries out an intensive programme of visiting people in their homes... ...she is always to be found looking calm and cheerful whenever there is extra work to be done or a crisis to be smoothed over" [Wycombe Abbey Gazette] [279].*

88 Grace Griffiths (standing) at the Christmas Party, 1966

May Lee and Constance Irons were two more ladies who had found a niche which they loved and which enabled them to contribute in untold ways to society, but there were many others like them both in the Settlement and in the schools.

A form mistress at Honor Oak School would send Phyllis Hughes, a pupil at the school and who lived near the Settlement, to the nursery with a batch of homemade gingerbread or malt bread, regularly every week. In 1943 the City of London Girls' School gave a presentation to Miss Page for her untiring work for the UGSM, and in 1977 it is recorded that Mary Datchelor School celebrated Miss Baker, who had been responsible for the organisation of the school's work for the UGS for twenty-eight years. Joan Kirby, a pupil at Blackheath School, later a teacher at James Allen's, and head teacher at Haberdashers' Aske's (all Supporting Schools) has worked as Schools Liaison Officer, head of various committees and a long time member of the Executive Committee.

89 Joan Kirby OBE Talking to Princess Margaret, 1999

When the enthusiastic mistress in the school retired or died, or the dedicated representative opted out, they were not replaced by other enthusiasts and the remoteness of some schools to the Settlement gave them few opportunities to serve the UGS in person.

Communicating with the Schools

An Old Girl in each school was invariably appointed to act as the Settlement's Representative, giving annual reports on the work at the Settlement, and keeping the Old Girls' Associations in touch with their inheritance. Communication was further assured by the succession of Organising Secretaries, usually Old Girls, who worked very hard, publicising all activities, writing awareness passages for the UGS Record and later the Review, visiting schools to demonstrate the extent of the Settlement's work, and continually writing to schools not only to thank them for donations but also to appeal for funds. The visiting of schools by the Secretaries and members of the Settlement staff to inform schools of its work was always taken seriously, but it did often look as if the Settlement and its volunteers over-extended themselves in doing this.

Numbers were disappointing for the Social Service Week in 1947 and the Organising Secretary, Theo Waite, held a conference for the representative mistresses from the supporting schools and began a settlement bulletin in which news of the Settlement's activities was distributed to schools. In 1953 there was the aim to speak to each generation of schoolgirls twice in their school lives at the then 125 supporting schools. Three years later Miss Waite visited 24 schools in the summer term. In 1963 Isobel Granger visited and spoke to 27 Schools. When Wing-Commander Baker was appointed warden in 1964 he set a target of visiting 23 schools a year. Later this task seemed to have been left to very busy volunteers who all had other full-time jobs. One such person was Mary Welsh, described as a clear-minded and competent administrator, who was on the Nursery School and the Executive Committees. She had been a teacher at Sydenham High School and became the school representative at the behest of the head teacher, Miss Yardley. She remembers being asked to visit schools as far away as Somerset and Northamptonshire. *"I didn't take any material with me and I don't think there was any collection of money made at the time. I made these visits as a member of the Executive Committee. I was at the time a vice-principal of a small college in Clapham, training women for church work. I went to Bruton by train as I was without a car......I was made welcome but have very little recollection of the details of that visit. At Northampton High School I was asked to speak at morning assembly. By then I had a Mini in which I set out at something like 6 o'clock in order to get there in time...... My brief was to describe the work going on at the Settlement and certainly to encourage the schools to continue to make contributions to it" [280].*

The lack of regular communication with schools was apparent from the late 1970s, and played a large part in the demise of support. This was the result of a combination of things. Firstly a paid education officer whose role was to develop the Urban Studies Centre post had replaced the Organising Secretary. A more vigilant role was being taken by authorities into lone schoolchildren visiting places of apparent danger, and Peckham was becoming a place of unrest and occasional trouble. There was also *"a lot of suspicion because a lot of the work......was with young black youths and we opened up the premises to black organizations" [John Lane, Director] [281].* With the accompanying cessation of both the Social Service weeks and the Annual Service, reasons for visiting the Settlement were few and unclear. Many of the schools were now closing in the new Thatcherite economic climate, and others were merging, amalgamating or changing their status. With these changes came a new set of traditions and ethos which often did not include the Settlement. A questionnaire was sent by the Settlement to all supporting schools around the late 80s but the response was very low. There was also evidence of lack of response from the Settlement end too. Blackheath High and Bruton both asked for a visiting speaker but no one went. Godolphin and Latimer in London asked for details about the Urban Studies Centre, and Princess Helena College and James Allen's wanted girls on placement. Nothing was done. There was a letter to Mickelfield to ask why the school was not on the donation list and yet the school had been sending regular contributions for a room that hadn't existed for about thirty years.

Mary Rose Bateman became the Representative for the UGSS and helped reform the Schools Liaison Group which first met in September 1981. The group was particularly concerned with the role the schools could play. For some years she assiduously organised educational and open days, but found there was *"a general reluctance in the attitude of some of the Settlement staff towards the school" [Peckham Schools Liaison Minutes][282]*. Four years later it was recorded that as only four members of staff were available for the schools open day, only four small groups of girls could tour the Settlement. Nevertheless, the group sent out newsletters regularly telling schools what their roots were and what the Settlement was all about, trying to personalise some activities which needed help and detailing where each pound went. It arranged for speakers to go schools as well. Mary Rose introduced a wall-chart of Then and Now as well as conducting a poll with the schools to discover how their role could be increased, and wrote to all the OGAs separately. The liaison group consisted of representatives from Sydenham High, Godstowe, Bournemouth School, Walthamstow Hall, Sexeys School, St Swithun's, Benenden and Wycombe Abbey. All the members were busy teachers who met at the weekends to discuss further plans. By the beginning of 1984, the group was becoming very dispirited and unwanted. It felt it had little support. Only nine head teachers came for a specially arranged day. When the constitution was rewritten in 1985, the group expressed its utter dismay at the strongly worded paragraph stating that only local people should serve on the council, and therefore the schools would cease to be a controlling body. The group had previously campaigned that the schools be given invitations to the AGMs and that the girls should be encouraged to attend. Before an Open Day in 1986 twenty schools had responded saying they wanted to be more closely involved but on the actual day only four schools came with fifty girls and five teachers. Mary Rose organised the sponsored walk in Windsor Great Park for the 90th birthday celebrations in 1986.

90 Mary Rose Bateman (centre) with Girls Who Took Part in the Windsor Great Park Sponsored Walk, 1986

The lack of response and the little return for all the effort took its toll. Such voluntary dedication could not continue and Mary Rose wrote to all schools disbanding the schools liaison group.

Another effort was made when eight schools came to an open day in 1987 where they saw displays, visited the pensioner's group and where the police showed them around the area. One teacher even wrote in the thank you letter, *"I must say I had thought the parting of the ways had come. I now feel differently. After today I do feel we are wanted – well done" [Director's Report] [283].* However this welcome report did not influence the general feeling. In 1988 the birthday celebration service was very poorly attended. Bournemouth School responded to a personal letter in 1990 saying, *"the school had changed its arrangement for charitable giving and the pupils had voted to support more local charities" [284].*

Alternative Causes for Support

The difficulties in communication and liaison combined, certainly in later years, with the attraction of different and more exciting causes. An appraisal of the social service support to the Settlement was inevitable. Many entreaties for support tended to concentrate on the financial aspect rather than hands-on experience. The habit of the weekly penny was hard to break, but the round of annual fairs, picnics and other money raising activities were obviously becoming monotonous and dull as well as yielding very little return. The radical change in schools began in the1970s where they had a more mixed and certainly multi-ethnic roll. This coincided with the changing nature of the Settlement. In many schools the girls were taking consensual decisions about the social service they would support. Inevitably the more aggressive charities won the girls' hearts. Emotional presentations of tragic events such as famines, refugee problems or environmental issues were more attractive. Many causes were also one-off events into which much energy could be poured because it did not have to be sustained. The Settlement could not compete, especially as most communication with the schools still concentrated on a financial need for many unspecified purposes.

The dilemma had shown itself before. A debate was raised in 1914 when it was realised that three-fifths of the Settlement's income was coming from schools outside London. It was argued that there might be a separate mission set up in particular areas of the country but in the end there was a unanimous decision that there should be only one UGSM for the whole United Kingdom. With the more distant schools, the head teachers decided if a *"sufficient number of schools will group themselves together to furnish enough help to justify undertaking a local Mission district, the executive committee might arrange for development in that direction......to face practically the eventual limiting of UGSM to Home Counties and Southern third of England i.e. schools within easy reach of London" [Jane Dove] [285].* Harry Veasey was not happy with this decision partly because Malvern had sent £130 in 1910, and he issued the invitation *"Shall I...... visit the school. I could bring the lantern slide if you have a lantern" [286].* Of the eighteen elected members to the Executive Committee, ten represented schools outside the confines of London, and, of the nine Old Girls' associations, five were from outside London. The fact that many of the schools were not close to the Settlement did play an important part in the decline of support. One example was St Mary's and St. Anne's School in Abbots Bromley. The school decided to resign in 1918 because it was felt that it's contribution was not important to the Settlement. Distance from the Settlement was a factor in the resignation. At some stage the school must have returned to the fold, as its name was certainly on the Settlement's register of Supporting Schools in 1971.

Schools were looking further afield at other charities in 1947. One report from The Green School, Isleworth, mentioned Doctor Barnardo homes, Save the Children Fund, the Red Cross, St Dunstan's, adopting a Polish school, and sending clothes and goods to Holland and France. James Allen's was collecting for TB, Cancer Research and Guide Dogs for the Blind. The City of London School was favouring the Florence Nightingale Hospital, Mission to Seamen, NSPCC, RSPCA, and the National Spastics Society as well as the Settlement. Although *"the pattern of support was much the same - collections of Christmas gifts, knitting of squares, flowers sent regularly, attending the Southwark Cathedral service and social service conferences, money for special appeals and equipment for the clubs" [The Milestone, BSG Magazine][287],* this sameness was beginning to pall with some schools. *"When I became head we were still doing the same thing......many of my colleagues assumed it would go on for ever" [Joan Kirby] [288].* James Allen's School discussed this in 1969. *"This year has seen a change in our social service programme and the school's attitude towards it. Although we carried on with the UGS visiting scheme, washing up at the Dulwich Cheshire Home on Sundays and the weekly collections, it was becoming increasingly obvious that only a few girls in each year were taking any active interest. The weekly collection had become so much a matter of routine that they achieved only perfunctory notice and even the termly meetings of representatives were becoming stereotyped and inhibiting" [JAGS magazine] [289].* It was decided instead to introduce new activities to give practical help and the girls took part energetically in the Triple S Scheme at the Settlement.

The Schools' Inheritance

There was seen, however, a much stronger reason for the continuation of support, that of duty and responsibility to others, the fact that the Settlement is held in trust for the girls' schools, that this was their inheritance which they shouldn't discard lightly. It was also evident that links with the Settlement were very hard to break. Wycombe Abbey Seniors were constantly reminded of their inheritance and the need to continue support. In 1964 the City of London Girls' School debated whether to help with £5,000 to repair the building as it was considered there was *"a duty towards the Settlement, as this was a commitment inherited by us from girls who were in the school in the past generation" [290].* However by 1970 there was no mention of the UGS in the school magazines although the Peckham Party still featured as late as 1982. At Haberdashers' Aske's School, *"I sensed* (as head teacher) *we should send about half the money we made overseas and the other half to charities in this country, but we always insisted we keep Peckham. Sometimes people asked why have we got to raise money, why does our Christmas box go to Peckham, and I would explain this was something we inherited. We were one of the first schools" [Joan Kirby] [291].* In 1979 Bournemouth School decided *"after...... a visit to Peckham Settlement by the head mistress, serious consideration was given as to how best the school could retain its links with the Settlement and this resulted in some changes being made in the nature of the school support" [The Milestone, BSG Magazine] [292].* There was even heart searching at Wycombe Abbey. *"Since June 1897, when Mr Veasey brought 89 children from the UGS Mission to Wycombe Abbey, there has been a long and close link between the school and what has simply become known as 'Peckham'. This link remains as does the one started in 1898 with the Melanesian Mission, but its nature has changed and its need has become an increasingly financial one. In addition, the proliferation of charitable organisations, the frequent disaster appeal funds, the present emphasis on medical research and world-wide coverage by the media of conditions elsewhere that must concern us all have produced increasing pressure from within the school to try to meet other demands on our resources. A wish to fulfil these demands brings with it a need to choose carefully how they can best be met without forgetting our existing obligations" [JY, Wycombe Abbey Gazette] [293].* Each of the school houses had taken up special charities of which 20% of money raised went automatically to the Settlement. However, *"although all charitable organisations are worthwhile, are some more worthwhile than others? We must not evade our responsibilities in tackling this question and making positive decisions about it in the coming year" [ibid][294].*

Mary Rose Bateman conceded there was *"no longer any role for the schools in it even as fundraisers as so much money came from other sources. By the middle 80s support had really dried up because there was unrest in many areas of London and the safety factor came into play. But my school at Berkhamstead continued to send money every single term and to include it* (the Settlement) *in prayers every single Thursday" [295].* Susan Wright (nee Ruegg) wrote about the 1980s when she was representative for Wycombe Abbey Seniors. *"It was hard work getting people to understand what was going on in a modern age" [296].* The distance from the Settlement was one factor which affected support. King Edward Grammar School in Louth resigned in 1964 because local problems were more relevant for support. Mickelfield in Sussex was the only out of London school to take part in a market in 1973, and felt that it couldn't attend the annual service or the tea party any more. Harrogate College conceded in 1986 that *"we are too far away to be useful but could help financially from time to time" [297].* Fund-raising was now related to huge events and although the girls' schools took part with ushering duties and performing concert pieces, they were much more an adjunct to this rather than helping with its organisation.

However, many people believed that the schools did still have a role to play in the Settlement, and this was written into the Aims of the Settlement in 1990. In 1991, when the very successful holiday play schemes were launched, schools were invited to come and help. *"An aspect of the work is also to provide opportunities for staff and pupils of schools (which founded the Settlement) and others in comparable circumstances to serve the local communities and gain better understanding of its value and the circumstances of life in Peckham" [Executive Committee Minutes] [298].* An audit in 1992 revealed that it was still believed that the schools and the OGAs gave backing for all its work, and a proposed new constitution was sent to all the supporting schools for comment. There was this rider. *"1996 will be our centenary year and we intend to give full recognition to the role of the schools and OGAs and their importance to the vital work that Peckham Settlement has done and continues to do in this hard pressed inner city area" [ibid] [299].* The Settlement looked to the schools to provide the choir, to write and compose a special anthem and to enter a competition for a special centenary prayer. There is no record of these plans materialising, and the centenary celebrations were quite low key. The role of the schools is still seen as a most positive thing *"because girls ……are likely to be in leadership positions and it is a……good thing they should understand the issues of the inner city and the resilience of the people of Peckham" [Malcolm Johnson] [300].*

Other Influences Concerning the Schools' Support

In the early 70s there was a concentrated effort to discourage the perceived elitism and sexism, which was felt by many connected with the Settlement, to be inherent in its reliance and encouragement of the girls' public schools, despite the traditional reason for the establishment of the Settlement. There seemed to be two reasons for this change of thought.

One was the need to widen the scope of the Settlement and include boys' schools, co-educational schools (especially as some of the supporting schools had become mixed) and the local schools. The UGSS name was changed to the Union of Schools or 'US' to endorse the feeling. This was quite fortuitous for the Settlement as Dulwich College, a local boys' public school, raised some very large amounts of money for the Settlement. The Union idea was shelved when the name 'Peckham Settlement' was adopted to identify the Settlement more closely with the community around it. [It is interesting to note that the Settlement was not formally registered as Peckham Settlement until December 1992 and in 1995, it was discovered that the Seal was still inscribed UGSS.] However, this thinking rebounded on the Settlement in one way. Students in the local public and state schools were reluctant to view it as a charity for which to raise money. Many of the girls either lived in the area or their grandparents or other members of the family lived in Peckham and used the Settlement. A more distant charitable cause was preferable.

The other reason was to prevent the Settlement from losing funds. The local authorities of the day were very left wing, and any suspicion of elitism or monied privilege was anathema to them. It was felt that the authorities might discriminate and deprive the Settlement of its rightful funds, because of a perception that the Settlement had wealthy patronage. In the event, the funds were forthcoming and quite abundant.

Despite the decline of support, it must still be recorded that like many other things the Settlement started, its influence on the girls is lasting and enduring. *"That's why I chose to go in for social science at the London School of Economics" [Ruth Plant] [301]; "My early exposure to Settlement work undoubtedly played a part in my choice of a career in social work which I have now pursued for 42 years……the more things change, the more they stay the same" [Elizabeth Grace] [302];* "(The Settlement) *gave me the confidence to approach the unknown at a relatively young age……I don't think it ever occurred to me how fortunate we were to have a UGS Settlement so close by that we could have regular hands on experience and see where the money went and why it was so worthwhile……All the school friends whom I still know manage to do some sort of voluntary work, however busy their careers, because it simply wouldn't occur to us not to" [Susan Waggitt] [303]; "I went on to be a social worker and still retain an interest in working with issues of poverty at home and overseas" [Jill Andrews] [304]; "(After my experience at the Settlement) for four years I ran a church youth club. I changed from teaching to social work and much later trained as a Jungian analyst/psychotherapist" [Ruth Muffett] [305]; "The Peckham Settlement changed my life" [Gill Fletcher -Watson] [306]; "It was a happy time for me although looking back I could have contributed much more with more experience and training. From the Settlement I went on to do a Social Science course at Leeds University" [Maureen Marshall] [307].*

Two schoolgirls who were on work placement from Malvern College said, *"This is classed as an inner city project. Its been great fun even the filing. We thought it would be really boring, but it's so worthwhile. We've learned a lot about the different foundations. I didn't know what went on…… This is a complete eye-opener, how there is much more to it, the hard work, the fund-raising. And what's behind it. We have to produce a report and produce an assembly to tell the rest of the school about it. It's so well run and well organised" [308]*. Thousands of schoolgirls came, saw, worked and went on to make worthwhile and long lasting careers, or to give many long hours to voluntary work because they spent time at the Settlement. As Mrs Philip Snowden, wife of the Chancellor of the Exchequer, said at the AGM in 1929, *"If members were to follow the gleam (an illusion to Merlin in Tennyson's poem) they would reap an immense joy in selfless service" [Times Report] [309]*. Schoolgirls are still coming for community experience which is influencing their further education and choice of work. That fact cannot be dismissed.

91 Members from Supporting Schools at Princess Margaret's Visit to the Settlement, 1999 Lady Howe, Gill Fletcher-Watson, Reverend Richard Warden (all from Wycombe Abbey) and Jennifer Stephens (James Allen's Girls' School)

Chapter 7

Income And Expenditure

In any organisation, financial affairs loom large as one of the major factors and not least with the Peckham Settlement. For most of its hundred years, income came from donations, fund-raising events, grants, trust funds, bequests, rents and subscriptions. Expenditure was mainly on the building, salaries, publicity and projects. The records make constant references to the problems of achieving a financial equilibrium and at only two periods in the whole hundred years did this seem to be achieved. *"The great weakness of voluntary organisations is that they are always short of money, they have to find funds where they can" [Newsletter [310].* This phrase certainly sums up much of the Settlement's financial history. There are four quite distinct eras of financial management in the history of the Settlement.

From Inception to World War Two

The Mission in Peckham started on the understanding that it be wholly financed by the girls' schools and the Old Girls' Associations. This would be achieved by regular collections of the weekly penny, fetes and sales, intermingled by appeals for contributions for earmarked projects. Sometimes schools would adopt an activity for which to raise money. Wycombe Abbey gave regular amounts to ICAA which was then attached to the Settlement, and James Allen's School gave every term to the Children's Country Holiday Fund. When the warden or member of the managing board made special appeals for an item or an amount of money for a particular purpose, these were usually donated very promptly. By 1902 the schools were contributing £1,200 a year and by 1906 the schools and OGAs had donated an astonishing £12,000.

It was also obvious in the early days that the founding head teachers were giving much of their own money to the cause. Miss Dove, the headmistress of Wycombe Abbey and one of the founders, appeared to have lent the Settlement or one of the three mission parishes copious amounts for various projects. She was in frequent correspondence with both Harry Veasey and Bishop Talbot about money matters. In January 1898 she wrote a postcard to Harry Veasey, *"I have my £35,000 so I can manage the rent of that house* (19, Peckham Road) *quite well......Now if I can borrow £3,000 or £4,000 for the Mission what security is there to offer? We might get the schools to guarantee the interest" [311].* In 1902 Miss Dove gave £300 for the rental of the hall in Calmington Road, and a further £7,000 was lent for the club building. A year later Miss Williamson, the head of Princess Helena College, another founding school, is also recorded as having donated personal amounts of money. Often this money was lent with conditions. Miss Dove would *"send cheques as required and not expect any interest for the lads' club as long as they took frequent if not daily baths" [312].* The money could also be withheld. *"I do <u>not</u> see my way to helping the Building Fund," [313]* wrote Miss Connolly of Haberdashers' Aske's School.

There was trouble over an apparently incompetent treasurer. Miss Nutt reigned in this post from 1900 to 1906, whereupon Miss Dove did remove this *"very unbusiness like lady - no one can get on with her" [314]* only to complain when a Colonel Farrant was appointed to do this work, as he was a man and an outsider. Miss Dove believed there were plenty of Wycombe Abbey Seniors who could take on the accounts even though Mrs Talbot seemed to think that women couldn't do complicated accounts. Another gentleman became treasurer later, a Mr. Satterthwaite, but when he was called for active service in 1914, the post reverted to a lady, Miss Low.

The cost of maintaining the building fabric of the Settlement was already large as was the mission work in St Mark's Parish. Schools were asked to finance three clergy at £450 a year, three ladies at £150 a year and a nurse at £90 a year. This bill was added to that for some warming apparatus, cleaning and restoring St. Mark's church hall, bricks, mortar, bibles and prayer books. There were questions from the donors about the way money was spent and some heated correspondence from one or two heads. Miss Dove wrote in 1909, *"the Mission owes such a quantity of (my) money" [315]* although some was repaid soon after this. She also protested that there had been no bargaining for the price of the house next to Kempshead Road Hall *"and £150 was too much for such a house" [316]*. By 1914 Miss Dove wanted all her money repaid but it is not clear whether this was achieved. She was a trustee of the Settlement but in 1927 resigned saying she *"couldn't support the Settlement anymore" [317]*. Most of the time *"expenses are becoming quite regularly to be in excess of the receipts" [AR Burne, Secretary to Jane Dove] [318]*. This was a trend that was to dog the Settlement for most of its hundred years. Indeed this phrase was repeated almost verbatim ninety years later. *"At the year-end there will be an excess of expenses over income" [Executive Committee Minutes] [319].*

The haphazard nature of the school collections and other money raising activities is made very clear. The Settlement seemed to lurch from one good idea to another but with no definite plan. The need was initiated and the funds expected to follow when entreaties and appeals were issued. The Settlement could not rely on a set amount of income from the schools. The regular appeals were probably necessary because of the turnover of the schoolgirl population. The perpetual and seemingly everlasting appeals were being sent most terms to the schools, mostly for money but also for items of usefulness. The constant plea for money was a source of worry to the Bishop at the commemoration of the 21st anniversary. *"The Schools come to think that all special anniversaries are simply a device for getting money......I know that a certain number of Headmistresses are getting restive and inclined to break off their connection" [320].*

Special appeals such as for the building fund and the infant welfare work were never well endowed. In 1927 the schools raised £270 for the infant welfare work of which £50 went to Amott Road Welfare Centre. Wycombe Abbey usually excelled in its fund-raising. It amassed £1,712 at a Christmas sale for the general fund in 1933. There were mission funds for St Andrew's and St Mark's parishes, an expansion fund appeared to finance the Melanesian Mission and the Settlement in Quesnal, British Columbia, and £50 was paid regularly for Ranyard Nurses to minister to sick and poor people in the Settlement neighbourhood. This first nursing agency had been organised by the London Bible and Domestic Female Mission in 1857. There was a Fresh Air and Outing fund and a general fund. This latter fund appeared to be for emergencies which were usually quite numerous in the early days. It became especially useful when all £300 was drawn out to distribute to wives left without a penny after their husbands were dispatched to the front in 1914.

After the First World War schools were urged to become annual subscribers for one guinea a year, although St. Mary's in Abbots Bromley records that it paid a subscription of three guineas in 1904. This may have been in an effort to stabilise the income, but as many schools would have lost contact during the war this could have been to rekindle interest. By 1926 the subscription was two guineas. This method seemed to work for a time, but by 1934 it is recorded that subscriptions were falling off.

Income was generated from other sources. In 1914, £1,000 was gleaned from residents who used the Settlement bedrooms as cheap accommodation. The Settlement often housed 60 students a year. Girl students had to pay ten guineas per annum whereas students studying at the London School of Economics and other further education places had to pay twelve guineas a year. Casual visitors paid twenty-eight shillings a week. This arrangement continued until well into the 1960s.

Trust and memorial funds were a feature of income. The Georgina Gooch Memorial Trust Fund was instituted in 1908 to give a student money for board and residence at the Settlement for a year. Georgina Gooch was a warden at the Settlement for a short time and a force to be reckoned with as *"she raised confidence and stirred enthusiasm. Her spirit pervaded the Settlement and the work lives on as hers" [EMS, probably Mrs Salmond][321].* Before she died in 1907, Georgina wrote as warden of the Settlement to Harry Veasey to express disapproval at money spent on builders rather than on volunteers. The Gooch Trust Fund has an air of mystery to it. The Trustees were the Bishop of Southwark, Mary Douglas, the Head of Godolphin School in Salisbury and the Treasurer Miss Low. A sum of £384.19.4 was lodged with the Canada Insurance Stock to be administered by the Rochester and Southwark Diocese Church Trust, with the dividend to be paid to the Settlement. The Trustees were *"to invest the money in their names and their discretion towards a payment of the whole or part of the fees of a student at the UGSS. If this cannot be done the money…… can be retained in hand for not more than three years" [Trust Fund deeds][322].* It was to be twenty-five years before any mention is recorded of the scholarship. In October 1932 the first scholarship went to Marjorie Johnson an old girl of Roan School in Greenwich. It is recorded a few times after this that a student did indeed benefit from this fund, although dividends were paid in at regular intervals to the Settlement accounts until 1972. After that there is no mention of the trust although the dividend may have been included under Donations in the accounts. In 1992 a surprise letter from the Diocese Trust stated that the fund should close, as it had gained no interest for some years. The treasurer was obviously in ignorance that such a fund existed and asked for the records. A balance of £777.56 was transferred to the Settlement on 14th October 1992, and the fund closed.

Henrietta McArthur left a legacy in trust which was tapped through the years, but was also a fund that seems to have been lost in the mists of time. The Pilgrim's Trust Fund, which was founded in 1930 by Edward Harkness to finance social welfare to encourage people to become active members of society, gave £500 towards the reduction of the building debt.

Stocks and shares did not seem to be a significant method of obtaining money and values seemed to dwindle quite alarmingly. When the house in Calmington Road was sold in 1939, the Settlement was reputed to be in sore straits, but converted the sale of the house, £2,250, into war loans and conversion loans stock, an area which did not produce much capital. There was a little mileage in property. The site of Peckham Road was sold to the LCC for flats in 1928, but it is not recorded how much was realised although the site had been valued at £4,500.

The nursery school prompted the first application for grants from the statutory authorities. This was partly to achieve recognition but also to get the project well financed. The LCC and the Board of Education allocated these grants. However, there were anguished comments in the executive reports, which might seem very familiar today, that the promised grants had not been forthcoming. Indeed it was not until 1937, two years after the school opened, that the first annual grant was paid. Meanwhile, the Settlement was financing the venture.

In 1939 the Settlement was seeing one of its low periods. A question was raised that the UGS money should not be used for the parish missions but solely for the Staffordshire Street Settlement. The British Association of Residential Settlements (BARS), the forerunner of The British Association of Settlements and Social Action Centres (BASSAC), gave £75 for the repair of the roof in 1940, £5,000 in 1941, and £100 for war work in 1942. The 1941 award seems to be very large but the schools' contributions were almost nil. Many schools had been closed especially in the big towns, some had been evacuated and it seemed too difficult to maintain donations during the Second World War.

Management

In the very early days, the Settlement was managed by the founding head teachers with Harry Veasey appointed as the missioner. His job was to oversee the mission districts attached to the Settlement and liaise between them and the Settlement. The Lord Bishop of Southwark was the Warden and Chairman of the Council. The Executive Committee was chaired by Harry Veasey, with the Lord Bishop, the President, the head of the Settlement, the Honorary Treasurer and Organising Secretary as ex-officio members. The rest of the committee consisted of both elected and nominated members who were representatives of the Old Girls' Associations, teachers of the Supporting Schools and the three parishes. (In 1916, there were forty named people on the committee.) The Committee was divided up into various sub-committees managed by about eight of the committee members.

A constitution seems to have been written in 1924, when the UGSM became the UGSSS (Incorporated), and it declared that schools could involve themselves in both the Settlement and Mission parishes.

When the Settlement moved to Staffordshire Street, Articles of Association were written in which all members of the association who had paid subscriptions were members of the Council and could attend the AGM. The object of the Association was *"to promote religious, social, charitable, educational, artistic and scientific work" [Articles of Association] [323].*

The Executive Committee managed the daily affairs of the Settlement and appointed the sub committees, of which there now five. The Chairman of the Executive Committee was the Bishop of Kingston, Harry Veasey was on the committee and the head of the Settlement was now called the warden (Dr Willoughby). The committee was not to exceed 60 members. In 1931, the committee consisted of 32 ladies from the Supporting Schools with another nine people holding offices. The Chair of the Council remained the Lord Bishop of Southwark. There were no less than six vice-presidents.

The Heyday of the UGSS. 1946-1972

From 1946 to the middle 60s the records seemed to show that the schools really did control the running of the Settlement to a large extent through financial contributions. Until 1961 the donations from the schools and Old Girls were usually double any other money going into the Settlement. The upsurge in interest was probably due both to the renewed vigour after a long war and the desire to help a community which had seen terrible bombing and was obviously in need. Perhaps the real inspiration came from the fact that Princess Margaret consented to become Patron. This was one of her first public duties.

92 Miss Joyce Baxter, Warden of the Settlement, 1955-1957

She was only slightly older than most students who used the Settlement and of course she was Royal. There had been a traditional interest from royal princesses in this area of Peckham and Princess Margaret is a good figurehead. It was plain from the start that she was going to take an active part as Patron, visiting and communicating regularly, and this gave even more credence to the worthwhile nature of the Mission.

Entreaties for money were made at least three times a year. *"Funds are always a problem and though the response from the schools is excellent it is a struggle at all times. Money and Helpers are the Settlement's direst need" [Elsie Bowerman] [324]*. In 1954 there was a debate in the Wycombe Abbey Gazette about this financial need as the Settlement now received Government grants. The Seniors decided that the Settlement should continue to be the chief object of their charitable work and that every effort should be made to support it. It was also pointed out that the UGS and ICAA always received less than the school when a question arose as to the amounts raised. It did seem then (and indeed still does) that Wycombe Abbey was the first call in times of need. The school contributed over £300 every year and there was a regular correspondence between the wardens and the school to ask for equipment, furniture and money for special projects. It may be that Wycombe Abbey was kept more informed or that the Seniors just recorded all such transactions. Many of the workers at the Settlement were Wycombe Abbey Seniors, so would have been more aware of the difficulties. Nevertheless, the school and the Seniors certainly seem to have been asked much more than the other schools for emergency donations. The Seniors frequently helped out with salaries, building work, and club expenditures. In 1951 the Seniors gave £50 to ICAA because the LCC had cut its grant. They sent a child with poor posture for a recuperative holiday to Great Yarmouth for four weeks at the cost of £16.16s. Also in that year there was a letter from the warden explaining that the Settlement would be reducing money to the three Mission parishes, partly because the Settlement needed funds to do extensive building work, but concluded with the veiled plea *"Rev Lewis of St Mark's feels it would be great to have a uniform set of prayer books... ...We do not of course expect you to contribute to all of these... ...you may be sure that however you allocate the money you decide to give us, those who benefit will be extremely grateful" [Theo Waite, Organising Secretary] [325].* The schools and OGAs had been instrumental in providing the roof fund with £670 and £100 respectively of the £800 collected in 1955. In 1958 Wycombe Abbey sent £270, of which £200 was directed to the general fund, £60 was donated for the club leader's salary and £10 to St Chrysostom's rebuilding.

The social service articles in the school magazines mention many fund-raising activities. £10 from selling wool in 1949 came from the City of London Girls' School. In 1954 the school spent more on the old people's party, £10.16s.3d. than it sent as subscription, £5.5s. There was £16 for the Children's Country Holidays Fund in 1953 from James Allen's and £40 for the roof fund was donated by Bournemouth School for Girls in 1954. Donations from the schools were pretty steady at around £3,000 a year, although the schools were asked to raise their subscriptions by another 25% in 1958. This may have been because many schools were still donating the same amount that had been set in 1947. For instance, James Allen's School gave two guineas, the amount did not vary for twelve years. Most schools were still supporting the Settlement with a termly collection. The amounts from the annual service were assiduously recorded where about 50 to 72 schools attended each year and where each purse contained around £2 to six guineas, although Bournemouth School did give £75 in 1964. The Diamond Jubilee celebrations in 1956 gave an impetus to the funds and £1,283 was collected at the annual service in the Royal Festival Hall. The Bishop's (Bishop Simpson) Appeal was launched and directed to the schools and OGAs in 1963 for £5,000 for alterations to the building fabric. Seventy-eight schools contributed £3,828.17.6d, ranging from five guineas to £300 from St Swithun's. Twenty-six OGAs sent £1,079.10s almost immediately. By 1964 over the £5,000 had been raised. Although there was a massive purse of £6,500 at the annual service in 1965, by 1966 the service yielded only £371.7s.7d. The schools now preferred to give in kind or earmark money for special projects rather than just raise money for no particular purpose. Berkhamstead School took on responsibility to finance the Settlement's minibus during this time.

93 The Cover of the UGS Record, Spring, 1949

The UGS Record which started life in 1926 was hardly a money-spinner. It had first been published at the princely cost of one shilling and sixpence and it was declared that it still cost only three shillings in spite of 'war and inflation'. There seem to be no records as to the number sold, presumably to the schools and the Friends of the Settlement, but much work was put into the regular issues and it is doubtful whether there was adequate financial return. In 1957 there was a deficit of £16. Newbury School came to the rescue and paid off the debt, but the rising cost of publication and distribution was too much and the UGS Record closed in 1964.

Donations came from grateful pensioners through bequests such as the £39 from Mr Dunning. He was reputed to have taught music to the Duke of Norfolk at one time and featured in the film of 1956, playing the piano for old time singing. In 1967 a legacy of £263.4s. was given to the Settlement by a Mr Pointer. Mrs Charrington, a long time member of the UGS Executive and Managing Committees, the editor of the UGS Record and a voluntary helper, who was wife of the famous London coal merchant, left £100 to the Settlement.

Income was generated through residents' fees and rents. These were quite substantial through the 50s and 60s. In 1957 a schoolgirl would pay £2.7s.6d. a week, a student, £3.10s. a week or 10/- a day and a visitor £4.4s. a week or 12/- a day. A room with three meals a day cost £3.10s. a week for schoolgirls, £4.10s. for students and £5.10s. for others. The total fees collected in 1967 were £1,298.17s. The nursery school paid rent in 1962 of £3,000, although it was frequently needing financial help. In 1951 Elsie Bowerman wrote *"The nursery school has experienced a crisis......A special appeal to the schools has met with a generous response......But an Honorary Secretary and Treasurer are needed. This would be a very rewarding piece of work for anyone living in or near London" [326].* Self-generating income came from sales, fairs and club subscriptions. A fair held in 1948 raised £700. The clubs gave concerts, one of which raised £10 in 1951. In 1949 the Mothers' club paid about 2/6 a year to attend lessons in the afternoon. Subscriptions were apparently hard to get from some people as there are several references concerning the clubs being subsidised. In 1956 club members were supposed to pay sixpence a week but a condition was made for these non-payers. *"There is a social arranged for next week and only those that have paid* (their subs) *can go to it" [Commentary in Film] [327].* In 1965 the subscriptions from the clubs yielded only £36.4s.7d.

The second hand shop was regularly bringing in anything from £700 a year to £997 a year in 1968 and an astounding £1,000 in 1971.

Local organisations helped in fund-raising. The nearby fire station had adopted the Settlement as its local charity, and maintained a very long connection. The firemen raised £1,500 for an ambulance to bring disabled and housebound people to the Settlement and constructed a stage and all the trimmings for the hall. The Fire Officer of the time recorded *"the small band of friends whose determination......will prove to everyone this is a worthwhile cause" [328]* Other local firms helped in material ways too. For example, Stone's in Deptford, a supplier of railway products, donated a van to carry meals around the neighbourhood in 1956.

An effort to tap the Friends of the Settlement at 2/6 a year began in 1959 with a promise of an up-dated report and, no doubt, appeals for money. The subscription was still the same in 1971.

Two BBC national appeals were made in 1955 and in 1964. Margaret Lockwood, the famous actress, and Jeanne Heal, a prominent BBC broadcaster, made the appeals but the proceeds were quite small, £520 and £318.14s.10d. respectively.

There were small amounts from various trust funds and societies, such as the Queen Alexandra Day Fund especially for old aged pensioners, the Peckham Dramatic and Opera Society, and the strangely named Sunday Cinema Grant. The King George VI Fund gave £1,500 in 1957 for the building fund. The Gooch Memorial Fund gave £224.14s.6d. for student training in 1955. The McArthur Memorial Fund was earmarked for a worker's holiday and in 1967 was worth £246.10s. and the Library Fund gave £100. This latter fund appeared to be the dividend from investment in Consols and War loan stock, but there were other small dividends from the stock and shares. The Smith's Charity gave money towards holidays. As with so many charity donations, it came with restrictions. A Mr. Smith had owned fields in Kennington and had created his income and thereafter the charity from this ownership. The money had to provide holidays for 'ailing and necessitous children', but the money had to be administered by holiday homes and not by an individual. To access this money, Peckham Settlement became registered as a holiday home and was thus able to utilise the money to give a holiday for 21 children in Bexhill in 1959.

There was now a change in the distribution of monies to the Settlement which would impinge on its financial status for the rest of the century. The Local Authority and other statutory bodies, such as the Camberwell Old Age Pensioners Welfare Association, and the Camberwell Borough Council for Holiday and Welfare, gave financial support. In fact, Dr Groves recalls *"although it was believed that the......projects ran on money raised from the supporting schools, the greater part of the finance was, actually, coming from the local authority and the London County Council" [329]*. John Lane confirmed this later after his analysis of the financial state of the Settlement in 1972. The Local Authority provided a salary for the club leader, Daisy Bouckley, of £300 a year with full residency in 1957. The Local Authority also heavily subsidised the Foot Clinic, Meals on Wheels service and the Dinner Clubs for the pensioners. These grants were much reduced when the borough took over complete responsibility for the Meals on Wheels and the Foot Clinic in 1961.

In most of this period expenditure outweighed the income. A bank loan had been taken out and appeared to have been paid off in 1958 but an overdraft at the bank loomed large again in 1972, even though the interest charges appeared to be only 2%. The high cost of staff salaries caused much concern. The staff were paid below the national scale partly because they lived 'above the shop, had full board and lodging with three meals a day', and partly because they were still being regarded as volunteers and doing their jobs for love. In 1951 it was reported *"the Settlement......finds it impossible to run on the grant from the general fund largely because of the increased cost of living and in salaries and wages ......(but) the Settlement Holiday Fund shows an excess of income over expenditure, as does the Foot Clinic" [Theo Waite, Organising Secretary] [330]*. Wycombe Abbey had been asked to donate some money again *"because the members' subscriptions cannot possibly meet the high cost of salaries" [ibid] [331]*. The warden recorded in her diary in 1961. *"Knock at door. Cook to say one of her ladies has not arrived. Exit Domestic Bursar in haste to rearrange duties. Domestic Bursar returns. Mrs R. has agreed to oblige, but that will mean three hours extra on the wages bill" [Margaret Cousins, Warden] [332]*. In 1962 it seemed difficult to raise thirty shillings for three nights to run a much-needed coffee bar for young people. The Warden received £1,000 a year in 1964 with bed and board, and Jennie Fisher recalls that in 1965 as the first paid social worker at the Settlement she received £550 a year when she lived in and £800 a year when she lived out, lower than the average for that era especially in London. The wage bill for 1966 was £4,930.14s.10d. which seems very small in today's terms.

The minutiae of financial management were frequently mentioned, e.g. in 1961 a memo was written referring to buying a small amount of thread for the Junior sewing class, and having to pay an extra eight shillings and nine pence on a hamper which had been delivered to the Settlement. The Settlement was still making grants to the three missions of £100 a year.

During this time most money seemed to be spent on repairs and renovations of the building. A report stated that the building was 'eating up the money' and certainly much written space was taken up with maintenance and renovation. Less money was being spent on salaries and wages and the overheads were crippling.

Wing Commander (Ben) Baker was appointed warden in 1965. Eve Keatley remembers him as being a very efficient manager and administrator who had a good rapport with everybody. Three things occurred during his tenure that were to herald the financial management of the future.

94 Wing Commander C.H. Baker, Warden of the Settlement, 1964 - 1972

One was the assessment of future funding and where this might come from. David Collett was the Warden at Blackfriars Settlement, the former woman's university settlement [WUS], and a frequent adviser and supporter of Peckham in times of stress and trouble. In 1964 he set up a Federation of Settlements which included Peckham, Blackfriars, the Albany Institute, and the Lady Florence Institute in Deptford. Talbot House joined in 1966. At that time a fifth of all the Settlements were in the London Borough of Southwark and all were experiencing the same problems with funding. David Collett relinquished the wardenship of Blackfriars in 1965 and became full-time director of the Federation. He realised that unity of purpose and cooperation would facilitate future work and funding, and give the individual settlements support, advice and solidarity. This far-seeing idea of co-operation was to surface twice more in the Settlement's history. Meetings were held frequently to discuss mutual problems and Eve Keatley was secretary of the Federation for some time. She said that David literally saved

Peckham from closing. In particular, representatives of the Federation sat on the Camberwell Settlements Enquiry, played a part in BARS, and drew up contracts for employers of the individual settlements. David helped Ben Baker with the Plowden Report plans for new nursery schools. But it was his recommendation of the services of Elizabeth Montgomery Campbell, a professional fundraiser, that was to prove a turning point in the Settlement's fortunes. Unfortunately, the Federation disbanded in 1968.

The second thing of note was the application to various and very large trust funds for substantial amounts of money. During Baker's reign, the Gulbenkian Fund gave £4,500 in 1966 and the Sembal Trust promised £2,000 for each of three years. The Sembal Trust's money seemed to emanate from the 1965 Gladys Singerman survey and review for the Camberwell Settlements Enquiry. Commander Baker had to give details of how and where the money would be spent. The grant was given to promote voluntary activities by young people and to develop a knowledge of the opportunities for public work. He aimed to target the schools by improving and expanding the facilities offered by the UGS to young people interested in social work, to introduce a good quality newsletter, to send regular visitors to the schools to talk about the UGS, and to build up the visual materials with slides, photographs and films, by organising social service conferences, introducing school visiting teams to people in the Peckham area with team projects under the supervision of a professional social worker, and publish materials to attract fresh volunteers. A direct result of this assessment was a more strenuous and energetic effort to involve the schools in the Triple S Scheme. Not one penny was allocated for the fabric of the building!

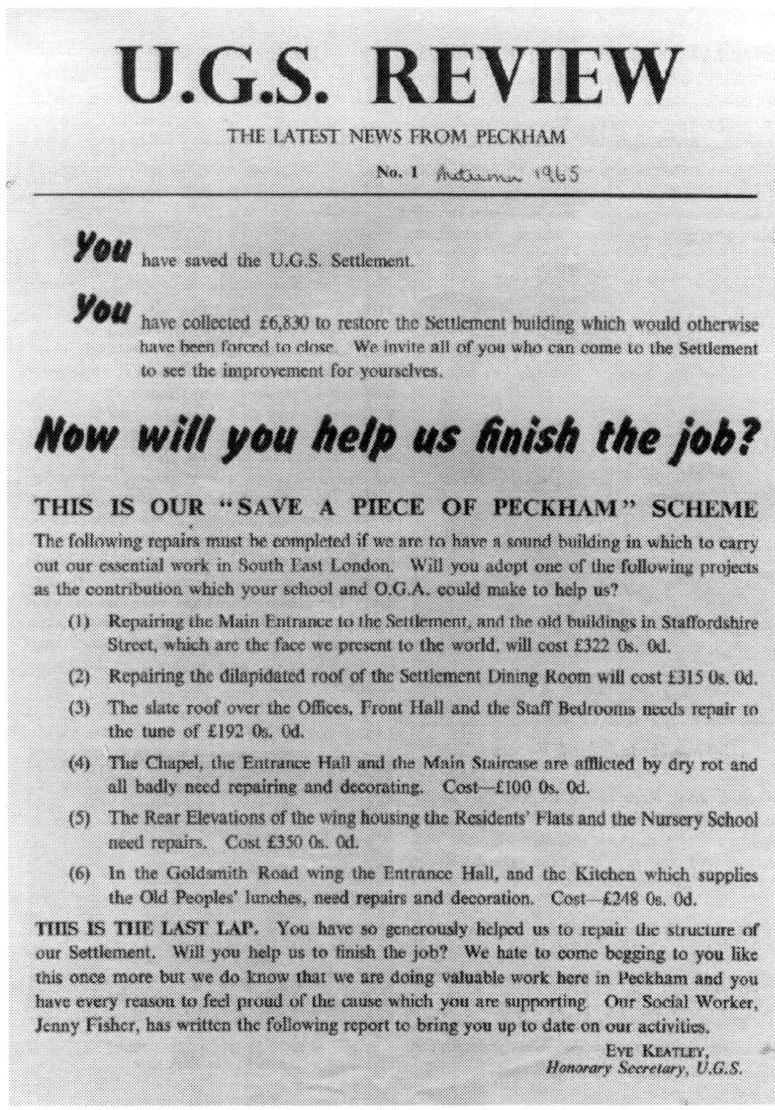

U.G.S. REVIEW

THE LATEST NEWS FROM PECKHAM

No. 1 Autumn 1965

You have saved the U.G.S. Settlement.

You have collected £6,830 to restore the Settlement building which would otherwise have been forced to close. We invite all of you who can come to the Settlement to see the improvement for yourselves.

Now will you help us finish the job?

THIS IS OUR "SAVE A PIECE OF PECKHAM" SCHEME

The following repairs must be completed if we are to have a sound building in which to carry out our essential work in South East London. Will you adopt one of the following projects as the contribution which your school and O.G.A. could make to help us?

(1) Repairing the Main Entrance to the Settlement, and the old buildings in Staffordshire Street, which are the face we present to the world, will cost £322 0s. 0d.

(2) Repairing the dilapidated roof of the Settlement Dining Room will cost £315 0s. 0d.

(3) The slate roof over the Offices, Front Hall and the Staff Bedrooms needs repair to the tune of £192 0s. 0d.

(4) The Chapel, the Entrance Hall and the Main Staircase are afflicted by dry rot and all badly need repairing and decorating. Cost—£100 0s. 0d.

(5) The Rear Elevations of the wing housing the Residents' Flats and the Nursery School need repairs. Cost £350 0s. 0d.

(6) In the Goldsmith Road wing the Entrance Hall, and the Kitchen which supplies the Old Peoples' lunches, need repairs and decoration. Cost—£248 0s. 0d.

THIS IS THE LAST LAP. You have so generously helped us to repair the structure of our Settlement. Will you help us to finish the job? We hate to come begging to you like this once more but we do know that we are doing valuable work here in Peckham and you have every reason to feel proud of the cause which you are supporting. Our Social Worker, Jenny Fisher, has written the following report to bring you up to date on our activities.

EVE KEATLEY,
Honorary Secretary, U.G.S.

95 The UGS Review No. 1 Autumn, 1965

The third issue concerned the UGS Review. It was felt that this publication needed to make a more dynamic and impressive impact. Eve Keatley, who was a Public Relations expert by profession, became the Organising Secretary. In 1965 she created a very professional and eye-catching booklet with the express purpose of regenerating interest in the schools. She inveigled contributions from the Settlement staff and encouraged the schoolgirls to write vivid accounts of the activities. These prove to be a rich resource of history. The booklet was printed locally three times yearly and each issue cost about £200 to produce. As 2,000 copies of each edition were sent out, this activity probably did not break even. For seven years it was distributed widely and there are many girls and workers who have retained their copies. The impact had been made.

The conferences were estimated to cost at least £250 to organise, with the participants paying a fee of 2/6 without residency. It is suspected, though not recorded, that many of the speakers would have given their services free.

The Settlement became a member of the Cambridge Settlement with Cambridge House and Talbot House when the Federation of Settlements disbanded, but it is not recorded whether this brought any pecuniary advantage. Eve Keatley describes this time. *"The Settlement was a prosperous child... ...No longer a sickly infant" [333].* But like all growing children, its expenses kept increasing too.

Management

The overall structure remained the same throughout these years except that the warden took a much more active role in the management of the daily activities. The Executive Committee's role became more that of a governing body. In 1971 it consisted of 14 school representatives, the local ministers, the staff of the Settlement and one or two local authority representatives. The Council was still the very large collection of association members. The Council and the Executive Committee were both chaired by either the Lord Bishops of Southwark or Kingston. There were still a number of sub-committees.

96 A Group of Settlement Residents Meet with John Lane, Director of the Settlement 1972 - 1977 (far right), and Geoffrey Heal

The Expansive Era of 1972 to 1985

1972 to 1977

The Rev John Lane was installed as Warden, later to be termed the Director, in 1972. He was described as being dynamic and having a vision for the Settlement. He was energetic and experienced in the social field with good contacts in the locality. Through him came the first serious business plan.

The age of accountability had dawned, where projects had to be planned in advance, both for feasibility and for financial support. If the Settlement wished to keep its image as a local community centre not only would it have to update on practices and be run like a business rather than a well-meaning neighbourhood centre, but also it would have to compete with the plethora of other South London charitable institutions. The business plan embraced the past, present and future requirements and expenditure of the Settlement. It began as an assessment of resources and income and a survey of needs, and developed into a management programme. John tracked the expenditure and income from the early days, assessing the schools' contribution, household expenses, building costs and overheads. Projects were planned, policies shaped and a budget forecast was given for the next five years. He shook the Settlement out of complacency and contingency management and made far-reaching decisions which changed the whole nature of the Settlement, probably not before time. As he said *"it was easy to predict expenditure, much more difficult to predict income" [334].*

97 The Winner Takes Possession of the Mini-Car, 1976

The income from the schools was steady at around £6,000 a year. It was pointed out that the income from schools had been 29% of the total income in 1929, 49% in 1946 which included the residents' fees, but in 1975 was only 4.6%. John Lane estimated that the schools' contribution just met the household and building overheads. The schools' financial interest in the Settlement during this period was not very lucrative. There had been one very good addition to the funds with the 75th Birthday bazaar at James Allen's School when Diana Rigg, the actress, opened it and there was a competition to win a Mini car. £3,893 was made.

Even pleas to Wycombe Abbey lessened. The emphasis was to obtain financial support in much bigger amounts than was previously envisaged. The new president, Lady Howe, a Wycombe Abbey Senior, made a special appeal in 1975 for schoolgirls to take 80 pence and make as much money as possible with it, but the outcome of this was not recorded. The appointment of a Schools Education and Liaison Officer in the person of Barbara Hill did not help the 'financial contributions'. Rather she encouraged interests in the Social Service conferences, visits to the Settlement and education through the Urban Studies Centre. Instead schools and more notably the 'wealthy old girls' were invited to participate in One-Off Specials, such as the one day market at Chenil Gardens in King's Road and a sale of work in Chelsea Town Hall. A sale in a disused shop in Peckham High Street raised £700, and a Peckham market in 1975 totalled £622.19. The onus was being put on to the Friends and the OGAs to donate money and to send in subscriptions. The need for the inclusion of the schools was driven by knowledge that the Settlement was the trustee of the schools, but no longer could the Settlement continue with a hand to mouth existence. There was a need to obtain a capital sum to produce the funds for projects, *"a need to have enough money, not to be worried about money" [Lady Howe, President][335].*

Fund-raising entered the big league. A number of well-known and influential people were approached and consented to give patronage to the Settlement. Princess Margaret was of course still the Patron of the Settlement and she came to many functions which increased their appeal as well as swelling the coffers. Lady Howe is still a major asset as President. She has a long association with the Settlement both as a schoolgirl and as a visiting speaker to the Social Service conferences. She is a scion in social work ethos and lends great support to public appeals. The role of the Executive Committee became more important, where the members were required to network and bring in useful people who could heighten the profile of the Settlement. During the next twelve years some very distinguished men and women from the diverse fields of politics and business to acting and writing gave their names in support of the work of the Settlement. The public appeals of this time were orchestrated to a large extent by Elizabeth Montgomery Campbell, the professional fundraiser introduced by David Collett. This job was later taken on by Lady Pamela Blackmore. These up-market fund-raising events included a 'very windy evening' at Westminster Abbey which raised £2,000 and where Princess Margaret had to borrow the Bishop's (The Very Reverend David Sheppard) coat to keep warm, even though it was June; a 'very cold' reception at the Tower of London in 1974 which raised £5,000; a visit to Greenwich which raised £4,500; and a reception at Goldsmiths Hall in 1976 during which the AGM was conducted. This latter event coincided with the 80th birthday celebrations. Attendees were asked to bring an object which would have been in use in 1896. The most interesting item was to be given to Princess Margaret and the rest sold by auction.

Publicity was more aggressive too, with publications of the Peckham Mirror supplements, and publicity leaflets distributed around the area, not just to schools. This brought the Settlement to the attention of the local people and the authorities.

The big bone of contention and a budgetary nightmare was that the local authority grants, though quite generous, always came in large amounts and at the end of the financial year, making cash flow difficult at other times of the year. However, John Lane also recorded that the amount spent on the building was 20% of the expenditure in 1929, and only 11% in 1960 which seems to belie those constant appeals for the condemned building. The wage bill also makes interesting reading especially when the early days made much use of volunteer activity. In 1929 it was 48% of the expenditure, in 1946 it was 32%, and in 1970 it was 69%, accounted for by the employment of extra staff for the Triple S Scheme. In 1975 the wage bill was 59 %, although the NALGO rates were less than the government equivalent. The salary structure was beginning to cause a strain. There was more paid staff on salaries and pensions. *"They insisted I had a pension, with the consequential worker protection rights just beginning to show their heads. The other point was that social work was being viewed as a professional piece of work and that volunteers were only there for pin money and love" [John Lane, Director] [336].* He reviewed the expenses of the projects, the office services, the public relations and printing expenses. One of the decisions was to create a defined policy which was more attractive to potential financial supporters and thus increased income. By inference this did not seem to include the schools. Statutory and local authority grants seemed to abound and there was no shortage of money for projects. *"It was in the balmy days of GLC and ILEA and Southwark Council and there was plenty of money around" [John Lane] [337].* By the end of John Lane's tenure, the receipts were actually in excess of the expenditure, and there was a surplus in the bank of £10,000.

Self-generated fund-raising continued with collections in public houses and entertainment centres. These amassed between £3,600 and £6,000 in 1975 and 1976 respectively. The summer play scheme brought in £2,500 in 1976. The shop continued to bring in an average of £1,000 a year. Rental of the little rooms as bedsitters were mainly to people wanting short- term accommodation and who did not work in the Settlement. In the 1980s this was causing problems and so residency was discontinued. Rental income from other rooms to outside organisations accounted for an average of 10% of the total income. Rooms were let to the local authority for short periods and to other agencies, most notably the Karib Association. This latter decision was to have far reaching effects through the next 20 years.

98 Dr Martin Pickstone, Director of the Settlement, 1977 - 1985

<u>1977 to 1985</u>

When Martin Pickstone became director in 1977, the upward financial trend continued for a while. Again a detailed business plan was produced with a projection for the next five years. John Lane had estimated that the running cost of the Settlement for the next three years from 1976 would be £92,580. In 1978 Martin Pickstone estimated that during the period from 1980 to1984, the Settlement would need £389,000. This was a very substantial increase. He estimated that self generated income, trust and private funds and the Local Authority grants would provide £235,000 which left £154,000 to achieve by other means. Maximum Local Authority grants both for projects and building refurbishment were available. Trust and private donations were at a reasonable level and there were several ventures which put money into small short-term projects.

A concerted effort was made by the Executive Committee to generate some income. Lady Howe wrote a personal letter to 200 firms which raised over £20,000, personal requests were made to firms and contacts by Lady Pamela Blackmore, Robin Binks and Paddy Cribb. This resulted in some one-off financial help including a donation from Christ's College, Cambridge of £25,000. The Annual Report of 1981 stated that donations from individuals, schools, trusts and companies were £31,041.66, but by 1982 the Settlement had a debt of £36,000, problems with VAT, and staff was funded only for short-term or part-time.

Schools had been donating around £11,982 a year. Barbara Hill estimated she needed £130,000 to keep the Urban Studies Centre running but it was quite impossible to see how the schools were going to realise this amount. Some schools were even omitted from the donation list, newsletters were delayed and distribution narrowed. There was a reminder in 1983 that schools should be invited to the AGM. Not surprisingly by 1984 it was recorded that the schools and OGA donations had dropped to around £4,000.

The high profile fund-raising continued. Expensive brochures were produced in which advertisements cost £200 a page and tickets for the events were sold at £20 or £25. Events included a private viewing at the National Gallery, the Victoria and Albert Museum, and the Museum of London. There were receptions at London Zoo, in Jeffrey Archer's pent-house flat, and at Guy's Hospital. A Guildhall fashion show, given free by Marks and Spencer's, raised around £10,000, and there was a concert and supper at Lambeth Palace.

Martin Pickstone had a particular talent for wording applications to appeal for money from the Local Authorities and other funds. He was thus able to obtain some substantial grants as well as some private finance. Barclays Bank, Heinz, Barings, the Wolfson Foundation, Bovis Court, and the Rank Organisation all contributed substantial amounts. The maximum grants awarded from the DES and ILEA were in the region of £100,000. In 1983 Martin made a proposal that seven of the Southwark Settlements combine into a federation to apply for local authority funding from a stronger position. Pitt Street, Bede House, Cambridge House, Charterhouse, Blackfriars, the Advice Centre in the Blue and Peckham cooperated to obtain £85,600 from the Borough and a further £30,362 from the Community Affairs Committee. The charitable trusts, such as the City Parochial Foundation, who funded two part-time workers for three years at £30,000, Freeman's Trust and the Smith's Charity regularly donated large sums. Appeal brochures were still produced at regular intervals although it is not clear just where these were distributed.

ILEA was actually paying some grants in advance but a warning note was sounded at the Executive Committee meeting in 1982 when it was reported that the GLC and LBS were constantly bailing out Peckham especially for building repairs. The GLC decided to give only 50% of £13,000 requested. London Borough of Southwark granted £1,150 for fireproofing the cellars. One-off grants were awarded for some projects such as the Crystal and the ARTS Projects. The Urban Aid grant of £8,000 was renewed for five years.

Only one bequest appears to have been made in this era. Miss Isobel Turner, the one time Honorary Secretary and Chairman of the Nursery School committee, left the Settlement £500 in 1982.

By the end of 1985 the beginnings of financial trouble were showing. The Settlement was vastly in deficit and interest in sustaining huge fund-raising events was waning. The Local Authorities were cutting back on grants and aid. The London Borough of Southwark became subject to rate capping. The schools were asked to do more fund-raising but many of them had withdrawn altogether from Settlement connections. The trust funds were looking at donations with a more critical eye. The Settlement building was showing signs of severe deterioration and the local unrest added to the problems. As the 90th birthday celebrations in 1986 were put in motion, a new director was appointed who had to pick up all this trouble.

99 Mr E. F. T. (Paddy) Cribb, Chairman of the Executive Committee since 1981

Management

The Council existed as a membership body chaired by the Bishop of Southwark. The Executive Committee made all the decisions based largely on the Director's recommendations. The Committee was smaller with well-connected and active people concerned with governing, fund-raising, networking, and financial control of the Settlement. On the Committee were leaders of local organisations, councillors and local authority representatives, voluntary workers in the Settlement and heads of the supporting schools. In 1985, the Committee had 26 members. Three strategic planning groups were set up to monitor and advise each type of programme in the Settlement and these groups included the staff who were most closely involved and one or two members of the Executive Committee. Peckham did not have the authority over all the organisations using the Settlement building now, but acted as a liaison and their activities were reported to the Committee meetings.

100 Mrs Kitty Leek, Director of the Settlement, 1986 - 1997

The Years of Difficulty

There was a delay before Kitty Leek took over as Director in 1986. The Settlement were fortunate to appoint a part-time director, Louise Pankhurst, who had been head of the Women's Committee Support Unit in the GLC and before that had been deputy director of the Albany Institute in Deptford. ILEA had stipulated that the director was to be qualified for youth workers and community centre workers because of the educational aspects which it was funding. Such a qualification had not hitherto been regarded as a requirement. Kitty Leek began her directorship in the latter part of 1986. She had been a youth worker for ILEA since 1975 for both the statutory and voluntary sectors. She brought considerable management skills to the post and quickly established a disciplined approach to the Settlement's activities and staff. She exercised a strict control over the expenditure as she was immediately confronted by vast financial problems.

The trend now was not to rely on fund-raising but to get local authority and government funding, but the GLC, ILEA and LBS were giving grants only to the nursery school. The rate capping continued and increasingly affected the voluntary sector. It was now becoming much more difficult to promote new ideas and projects and get funding for them with public money. The Settlement was given permission to borrow money from the bank by the Charity Commissioners, the sum was not to exceed £25,000. The local authority funding became worse. In 1988 all funds for the pensioners' clubs and the Arts projects were withdrawn. Indeed this latter project had spent £7,000 of money which 'wasn't there'. Kitty Leek estimated that in 1989 the Settlement was losing statutory income of £10,000 a year. The Government and Local Authorities were expecting organisations to rely on self-help and private funding.

Derek Lowman wrote a consultative paper about raising revenue. One suggestion was to sell off part of the site but keep the use of this on a favourable lease basis. In 1990 a real blow fell when the ILEA grant of £2,000 was withheld never to be reinstated with the demise of ILEA the next year. For many of the following years no one could predict what the local authorities would do. This led to great uncertainty, planning was very restricted and initiatives were limited. The GLC was only part funding Kitty's and the other professional community workers' posts. So began the move away from grant aid to contracts, and a development of public and private voluntary sector partnerships. When staff left, they were not replaced and the Settlement managed for some time on apprentices and unqualified staff. A local council review of settlements was conducted in 1991 and concluded that the council would have to decide if settlements were valid organisations in the voluntary sector and could receive core funding. But there is no record afterwards whether a decision to give core funding was made. There was certainly no appearance of core funding in the accounts. An asset and debits profile revealed that there was no waste, but there was lack of adequate resourcing, poor building and work conditions for staff, difficulty in getting statutory funding, constant penny-pinching, and below standard equipment. The news that the Nell Gwyn Nursery could be moved out of the Settlement was seen as a financial bonus rather than a severance of a sixty-year-old link.

Surprise grants were made. The Community Development Project gave £20,840 in 1991 and the London Borough of Southwark gave £15,000 the next year to enable the expansion of the day nursery. The Southwark Race Equality Unit gave £32,631 to promote West Indian services in 1989. This money was given principally to fund the work of the Peckham and Dulwich Caribbean Association or the PDCCA, who had rented the basement in the Settlement since 1981. However, it became obvious that PDCCA had not paid rent for many years despite all this extra funding. There was a huge debt of £17,690.26 in back rent. It took six long years of legal action before this amount was paid.

The main emphasis was on transitional and short term funding, but the few grants that were forthcoming never seemed to cover the costs of the project. A fund-raising day in aid of voluntary organisations took place in Southwark on 18th May 1988, but there is no record that the Settlement received any money from this. BASSAC had taken on a rigorous programme for tackling poverty and injustice in the Inner Cities in 1992 and was expected to invest money for this through the settlements. In 1995 it was holding £500,000 for distribution to its members, and the Settlement was on the reserve list for £18,000 but again it is not clear whether the Settlement did receive this money.

The other legacy, which caused anxiety, was the house in Linden Grove, originally rented from Southwark Borough Council for a peppercorn rent, and who now wanted to reclaim the property. They issued a writ to Peckham Settlement for £8,000 for the lease and again this took a few years to sort out. Eventually the house reverted to the London Borough of Southwark without the Settlement losing out financially.

There was an enormous overdraft at the bank. The schools' contribution had diminished to almost nothing. In 1990 there were only thirteen registered schools and eleven OGAs, although Mickelfield, Wycombe Abbey and St Swithun's were still sending in regular amounts. A bright spark was the 20% generated from Dulwich College's summer fetes which in 1991 came to £6,000. Lady Pamela Blackmore had retired as a voluntary fundraiser and there was just no money to employ a new person. A sponsored walk in Windsor Park raised £2,000 but other amounts were very low.

Appeals for private funding were also disappointing. An appeal to local firms was launched but only eighteen replied and with reasonably small amounts. The charitable funding continued with the Hilden Trust, City Parochial Foundation, the Mercers' Company and Freeman's still donating regular sums of around £1,000 to £2,000 a year. The Dove-Bowerman Trust gave £1,000 in 1990 and another £1,000 to the nursery school in 1992. £500 came from the Police Property Fund. The McArthur and the Library Funds were still functioning at £150 and £252 respectively. Personal bequests were few although Jane Johnson, the stalwart of the Wednesday Housebound Club, left £1,000 to the Settlement.

<u>Pitt Street</u>

The proceeds from the closure of the Pitt Street Settlement in 1994 were transferred to Peckham. Charles Lisle Watson was a retired army captain and had started a boy scout troop which extended into an old cowshed in Pitt Street in 1910. The aim of this mission was *"to further the objectives for providing spiritual, moral, mental and physical education and training for young men and boys* (later amended in 1932 to people under 25) *who were in needy circumstances" [Deeds of Charity][338].* Watson was a deeply religious man who bequeathed most of his worldly goods to the upkeep of the chapel in the settlement. After he died in 1970, Pitt Street expanded many of its services and was complementing many of Peckham's activities. When the funding of its 22 voluntary groups was cut drastically, Pitt Street never recovered and had to close. The building was to be sold and the assets transferred to Peckham. There were three trustees, one of whom had worked at Peckham for a time, and they were invited onto the Executive Committee.

Pitt Street was also trustee for the Camberwell Relief in Need Charity. This relief was for Camberwell residents only, originally the Camberwell Costers' Benevolent Association and South London Home for Donkeys and Ponies. It's purpose was *"to relieve people who resided in the Camberwell area who were in need, hardship or distress ……to pay for items, services and facilities calculated to reduce this need" [Trust Deeds][339]* and preference was to be given to street traders. The relief had to be a one-off payment and could not be used for taxes and rates. Such conditions made things very difficult for Peckham. The boundaries of Camberwell had to be researched so that any relief was submitted in accordance with the requirements. Then application was made to the Charity Commissioners for advice on investment and whether the money could be used for rebuilding Peckham Settlement. Eventually the Commissioners replied in the affirmative as long as the capital was used for young people under 25.

Everything was formally handed over in 1998 and Peckham assumed complete control as trustees of both charities in March 1999.

Bids for grant aid and private funding took much time and work which was just too much for the remaining Settlement staff. Fund-raising was reduced to tombolas, busking, carol singing (in 1987 this raised £139.40), small in-house fairs and sales. A street party in 1986, the 90th anniversary, was opened by the Mayor of Southwark and raised over £2,000.

The second hand shop income came to an end in 1987 when Mary Pittard died.

The building was showing severe signs of degeneration with extensive dry rot. The nursery repairs alone were estimated at £35,775 in 1988. Southwark Community Affairs did give £8,300 to cover roof, boiler repairs and burglar alarms, London Borough of Southwark and the Dove-Bowerman Trust gave £3,000 in 1997 for the refurbishment of the kitchens, but patching-up was all that was possible.

Rental from the rooms was minimal. The schoolgirls funded themselves when they came to work in the Settlement. Single interest groups rented the rooms instead. *"It was becoming a rental agency with no vision of its own" [Christine Richards] [340].* By 1997 there was a deficit of funds of £27,000.

But it was not all doom and gloom. In 1994, VAT of £35,331 was paid back, after the Settlement de-registered. One of the highlights was the Summer Play Scheme which became very popular. It was extremely hard work, organising programmes and volunteer schoolgirls for the whole of the summer and Easter holidays. The Settlement did get special grants from the Hilden Trust, Children in Need and The Smith's Fund. In 1991 there was funding from The Leisure and Recreation Fund in Southwark, as long as the Settlement used volunteers from local schools. Another grant from Southwark in 1992 amounted to £1,475, but there was never enough money. One of the local Peckham Police was detailed to tour the local shops to obtain some funds by asking, *"What is it worth to you to get the children off the street?" [Gill Fletcher-Watson][341].* Very little press coverage was given to this scheme, and praise for the tremendous efforts of the Settlement and the police in tackling a severe community problem was in very short supply. A Wycombe Abbey Senior *"came away deeply impressed by all that Kitty... ...had managed to achieve under such very difficult circumstances." [Sheila Robertson, Wycombe Abbey Senior] [342]* and Kitty was celebrated as *"an incredible woman, a real trooper" [Lady Howe, President] [343].* The centenary celebrations never really got underway. Possibly a fund-raising opportunity was lost, but day-to-day pressures were just too difficult to allow a concerted effort to be made for this exercise. It was *"extremely difficult some weeks to just keep up with normal daily work and therefore impossible to pursue ...... future initiatives." [Kitty Leek] [344]*

Management

By 1991, the Council had ceased to exist. All authority was invested in the Executive Committee as a governing body. The director and staff were invited and expected to attend the monthly meetings. The project groups, the nursery school and the community development groups reported their activities to these meetings. A new constitution was written in 1992 and the Memorandum and Articles of Association were up-dated. A new concept of membership was introduced where individuals, groups and schools were invited to become members of the Settlement and pay a subscription. The AGM elected the Executive Committee and all members who had contributed and participated in the Settlement's activities could vote. Certain decisions would require a percentage vote from the supporting schools. The assets of the Settlement could not be sold without the schools' consent, and they were to have a slight veto if the Settlement wished to sell its property. They were also able to appoint three members to the Executive Committee. More local people and Settlement users were invited onto the Committee. There were now 17 people on the committee consisting of honorary members, leaders of local organisations, a local minister, councillors, Settlement users and a representative for the schools.

101 Mr David Kitchen, MBE, the Present Director of the Settlement with a Child in the Nursery

The Present, 1997 to 2000

David Kitchen faced a daunting exercise when he was appointed Director in 1997. Not only was there little investment, but also the building was under utilized and in bad repair and the few staff were demoralised. The familiar phrase 'the Settlement has spent more than it has raised' was repeated. However, things were gradually coming in full cycle again. David Kitchen had worked with David Collett at Blackfriars Settlement in the Triple S Scheme days, and had great experience as Director of St. Hilda's in the East End. He wrote a paper on possible funding options and a priority list of actions. The suggestions included the refurbishment of the nursery, the biggest asset of the Settlement, raising the fees for the nursery as these were the lowest in the borough, asking the members of the association to make covenants, targeting charitable trusts and employing a fund-raiser. In the next few months a part-time fund-raiser, Hazel Clayton, was appointed who promptly secured £4,000 from various trusts. Another substantial sum of £10,000 came from the Christopher H Reeves Trust. There was a consideration to discontinue some of the smaller funds such as the Library and the Henrietta McArthur Fund which were yielding very little amounts. When the Barry Richards Charitable Settlement was wound up, assets to the tune of £13,119.13 were transferred to Peckham.

The name of the game is now bidding for funds, many of which concern areas predetermined by central government. The quality of the bid rests on experience, expertise, efficiency and speed, as there are often strict formulae and deadlines for accessing the money. In 1996, some of the Executive Committee attended a professional fund raising training day. Here guidelines were given for accessing funding from the National Lottery Board. The bidding system represents a substantial amount of work. As Director, David has to keep aware of the current position of available grants by attending seminars, liaising with other voluntary organisations and keeping in close touch with the local authority and other colleagues. This is now an absolute requisite for voluntary organisations as competition for these funds is so great.

For the third time in its history Peckham became affiliated to like-minded organisations. David Kitchen secured a partnership with the East Peckham Consortium to provide a consolidated front and effective support when entering the annual regeneration fund rounds. The East Peckham Consortium consists of community, faith and tenant groups in the Friary and Consort Wards who are seeking to improve facilities and conditions for local residents. It is hoped that part of the Settlement rebuilding costs can be raised through this alliance.

Also the Settlement bought into a Golden Bond for the London Marathon, another feature of charities and voluntary organisations. The Bond was for five places in each of the next five years. This means the Settlement has to find five willing runners for each of the years who will raise sponsorship. In the first year four runners, two were local police and one was David's son, amassed over £4,000 for the Settlement. The year 2000 sees a healthy black bank balance for the second time in the Settlement's history.

Management

102 David Kitchen, Florrie Whale, Michael Franks and Derek Lowman serving out Christmas Dinner at the Settlement, 1998

From 1995 the numbers of local people on the Executive Committee were very few. On several occasions it was also difficult to obtain a quorum for the meetings and so management decisions were often delayed. After much discussion and debate, the new Director set up a management sub-committee, which consisted of staff, local people and users and two members of the Executive Committee. The sub-committee meets regularly and manages day-to-day affairs and proposes new projects. It has four representative groups concerning finance, fundraising, project development and the redevelopment of Peckham Settlement. The Executive Committee meets less frequently and has taken on the role of trustee. It will maintain overall and financial control. Staff and submit up-to-date reports on their work. Other individual organisations who rent space are allowed to attend and contribute to the meetings, receive the minutes and the Annual Report.

Chapter 8

The Visits Of The Patron, HRH The Princess Margaret

1947 October 17th.

"Her Majesty, the Queen, has graciously consented to HRH The Princess Margaret becoming Patron of the Union of Girls' Schools for Social Service. Our gratitude to Her Majesty and Her Royal Highness for showing their appreciation in this very gracious way, of the work the Union of Girls' Schools is doing. Her Royal Highness had expressed her wish to visit the Settlement, quite informally, in the near future." [UGS Record]

103 Princess Margaret 1947

1948

"A very important event took place in the life of the Union when Princess Margaret Rose became Patron and visited the Settlement. She was introduced to the various activities carried on there and sixteen representatives from South London schools were presented to her, among them Mary Currie from JAGS. The girls then had tea and chatted informally with her." [James Allen's Girls' School Magazine]

104 Princess Margaret at the Settlement 1948

1956 May 9th

Princess Margaret attended the Diamond Jubilee Service of the Settlement at the Royal Festival Hall. " The schoolgirl audience behaved beautifully throughout – those in the Hall itself, the two-hundred strong choir who had met each other for the first time at 2.00 pm on the day, and the 75 purse-bearers who without any rehearsal presented their schools' gifts with such dignity and pleasantness." [The Settlement Newsletter, Issues No.9. July 1956] Wycombe Abbey was greatly honoured by being asked to choose one of its members to present her with a bouquet. Princess Margaret received white moiré purses from representatives of seventy-five schools and Old Girls' Associations, contributions for the Rest Room.

The Settlement received a letter written by Iris Peake, Lady-in Waiting for The Princess Margaret.

"Dear Mrs Charrington (Editor of the UGS Record), Princess Margaret has asked me to write and tell you how very greatly she enjoyed coming to the Royal Festival Hall yesterday… … The Princess hopes you will convey a message of her warmest thanks to everyone who helped to make it such a happy afternoon." [UGS Record, Summer, 1956]

105 Princess Margaret 1956

106 Princess Margaret at the Royal Festival Hall, May 9th 1956

1960 November 8th

"Our Patron, HRH The Princess Margaret honoured us by coming to see the work of the Settlement and her great kindness and general interest, particularly in the welfare of the housebound, made her visit an unforgettable experience for those who were privileged to share in it. A concrete example of her kindness and concern for the welfare of the old and housebound was the wonderful gift of two huge boxes of chocolates for the party on Christmas Day."[Annual Report, 1960/1961]

"We were told that she would stop at every fourth person. When it came to the point… … she spoke to every single (old person in the row)… …We have a Nigerian student… …she appeared in national costume with a very elaborate headdress. The Princess spoke to her for several minutes and we guess her next letter home would be full of it." [Settlement News, November 1960]

"(The Princess Margaret) was seen to join in softly with 'Oh, What a beautiful morning' and 'You wore a tulip' " [South London Press, November 11, 1960]

"There were ten girls altogether, two from a private boarding school, two from a public one and six from grammar schools in different parts of South England. At last the moment arrived and almost before we realised it the Princess was in the room with us. We were struck by her petiteness and her charming and friendly personality. During the tea the Princess chatted about our different schools ... ... she was intrigued by the ways in which we raise the money to support it. The tea party was quickly over and when the Princess had gone downstairs to see the chapel before leaving, we all made a rush to bedroom windows which overlooked the doors." [R Taylor - Hitchin Girls' Grammar School]

"With my back to the door, I was first aware of a wonderful perfume, and was in a sort of daze as we were all in turn presented to the Princess and I was eventually shaking hands with her myself and making my curtsey as well as possible. When we had each sat down on the nearest chair the Princess asked us to draw our chairs closer to her instead of sitting around the walls. We were all sorry when she went and I know we shall remember this day for the rest of our lives."[M Mouland and C Parsons - Bournemouth School for Girls]

"An invitation to have tea with Princess Margaret when she visited the Settlement in her capacity as Patron ... ..." As the result of a ballot, five schools were invited to send two representatives- The Downs, Seaford; Ancaster House, Bexhill; St Saviour's and St Olave's London; Hitchin Grammar School for Girls and Bournemouth School for Girls. The news leaked out and when the Princess arrived at 3.00 pm a large crowd had gathered to welcome her. The Princess, dressed in a grey velvet suit with black accessories and a charming feather hat, was greeted by the Mayor and Mayoress of Camberwell, Bishop Simpson and Miss Cousins, the Warden of the Settlement. A guard of honour formed by the Fire Brigade stood to attention as the Princess entered the hall. A concert was in progress to entertain members of the Old Peoples' Clubs and invalid people who received Meals on Wheels.

The concert party, dressed in Pierrot costumes, sang a series of old time music hall favourites in which Princess Margaret joined in from time to time. At the end … … the Princess went on to the platform to be presented with a bouquet of freesias by John and David Timlin, five-year-old members of the Sparrows club. She then went down into the hall and chatted to... ... the old people... ... As the car slowly faded into the November gloom the memory of a radiant personality remained with us for all time." [C Parsons and M Mouland – Bournemouth School for Girls]

107 Princess Margaret Visits the Settlement, 1960

"We were delighted and honoured to have a visit from our Patron, Princess Margaret, when she visited the Settlement. She was very interested in the children and in their work which was on show. Children were entirely uninhibited and they sang with gusto at her request for a song, regardless of tune and not always of one mind, but she enjoyed it all and we hope she will come again."[UGS Record 1961]

1972 November 13th

Princess Margaret was accompanied by the Right Reverend Mervyn Stockwood, the Bishop of Southwark. With the Reverend Geoffrey Heal (Parish Priest of St John's Church) and the Reverend John Lane (The Director of the Settlement), they lunched at St John's Vicarage using Win Jordan's (a Friend of the Settlement) tablecloth, before going on to the Settlement.

"Fifth Formers from Sydenham High School squatted on the floor in an informal chat with the Princess Margaret. The schoolgirls are researching the problems of loneliness of old people in tower black flats … … Pensioners entertained the Princess in traditional style on Monday with an old time singsong … …The Princess met Mrs Ivy Sowerton, leader of the Mum's Club, which started in 1913 for wives of service men. Over the years it developed into an old people's club… … Ivy remembered serving tea to Queen Mary in 1931… …Mrs Joan Serle had to cope with pre-visit coyness on the part of seven of the children who had been asked to present the Princess with a posy of flowers." [South London Press, November 17, 1972]

1982 June 17th

108 Princess Margaret Visits the Settlement, 1972

"South London was treated to another visit by the Royal family. She met toddlers of the Mother and Toddler club, the unemployed teenagers and the nursery school... ...After Paul (McLean) aged 16, demonstrated his superior skill on the (snooker) table, the Princess politely turned down his offer (of a match)... ... Paul said, ' She's got a great suntan'... ...Doris Wheddon (a pensioner) quoted "She's still as lovely as she was (in 1972)" [South London Press, June 18, 1982]

109 Princess Margaret Meets Members of the Youth Club, 1982

"Princess Margaret, the Settlement's patron, is due to arrive at 1.30 pm. Various members of the Settlement Staff, looking more dishevelled than usual, rush about trying to effect order out of chaos. The net result is that, while most of the rooms were full of piles of rubbish before the onslaught, they are now full of tidy pieces of rubbish. Martin, the Settlement Director, is busy trying to unblock the drains (hope he remembers to have a bath before he has to shake hands) and to add to the excitement, Security Staff with dogs have arrived to check the premises for explosives. (Expletives, yes- Explosives- no) By 12 noon the Settlement is clean and the staff are very dirty. Princess Margaret arrives on time, of course, is very charming to everyone and everything seems to go remarkably well. She tours the building, accompanied by the Mayor and Mayoress of Southwark, is sung to by the Old People's Clubs, and has tea with members of the Executive Committee. During all this the Staff are still looking like nervous wrecks, but the people who use the Settlement are taking it all in their stride

... ... The old people chat to her as if they did this kind of thing every day and tell her she hasn't changed a bit since the last time she came visiting. They certainly enjoyed her visit; we hope she did too. We have lots of lovely photographs." [Peckham Settlement Newsletter-Autumn 1982]

1999 February 11th

"Thursday 11th February 1999 will go down in the history of the Peckham Settlement as a very special day. It was also a special day for Her Royal Highness, the Princess Margaret, Countess of Snowdon, who visited the Settlement to mark her 50 years of patronage... ... the highlight of this year's visit was a presentation to Her Royal Highness by Lady Howe of Aberavon CBE, President of Peckham Settlement of a pewter dish to mark the long and much valued association... ...The Princess arrived on a damp and chilly February afternoon and was greeted by the Chairman of the Settlement, Paddy Cribb... ... the Mayor of Southwark, Councillor Janet Heatley, the Lady Howe and the Director of the Settlement, David Kitchen... ...Her first stop was at the All Nations Nursery which had recently passed its OFSTED with flying colours... ...LatchKey... ...was her second call... ... Finally, the Princess visited the Friary Open Learning Centre and was introduced by Manager Babs Sohna to the young unemployed who are gaining qualifications in computer skills... ...The Princess met and talked informally to patrons, sponsors and pensioners around the hall.

110 Princess Margaret at the Settlement, 1999, with Paddy Cribb, Chairman of the Executive Board, Baroness Howe, President and David Kitchen, Director

In his speech, Paddy Cribb said, 'We have maintained our tradition of service and today the need for this Settlement is as great as it was ever. There is now a growing recognition that services of all kinds must be subjected to value analysis. We are happy to be judged by any objective value assessment, as a mixture of public and private funds, allied to much voluntary work, mean we can deliver value second to none'

The Princess gave Florrie Whale (a very special person in the life of the Settlement) an engraved crystal rose bowl to celebrate her half century at the Settlement which has included being on the staff of the nursery and involvement with various clubs. These days she leads the Thursday Club.

David Kitchen … … paid tribute to the volunteers and individual schools who have played such an important role in keeping the Settlement vibrant. Although the Royal visit had lasted longer than scheduled, all too soon it was time for the princess to leave." [The Peckham Settlement Newsletter, Issue 2, Spring. 1999]

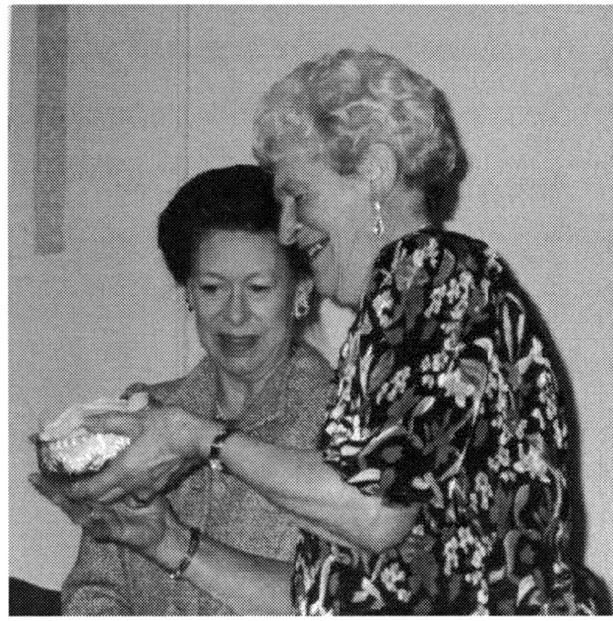

111 Princess Margaret Presents Florrie Whale with a Crystal Bowl, 1999

Viscount Ullswater, Princess Margaret's private secretary wrote from Kensington Palace. "Her Royal Highness was delighted to receive the gift to commemorate her fifty years of patronage and sends you her best wishes and her gratitude for hard work that you undertake to make sure that the Peckham Settlement goes from strength to strength." [February 12 1999]

Dramatis Personae 1896 to 2000

Date	President	Head/Warden/Director	Chair of Executive Committee	Chair of Management Council
1896	Mrs Bailey	Rev Harry Veasey	Rt Rev Edward Stuart Talbot, Bishop of Rochester. Bishop of Southwark (1905-1911)	Rev C R Bailey
1902	Mrs Talbot			
1906		Miss Georgina Gooch	Rev Harry Veasey	
1907		Miss de Burgho-Hodge	Rt Rev Dr Burge, Bishop of Southwark	
1911	Mrs Burge			
1919			Rt Rev Dr Cyril Forster Garbutt, Bishop of Southwark	
1922		Miss Green	Rt Rev Dr Percy Mark Herbert, Bishop of Kingston	
1927		Two Temporary Wardens		
1930	Miss Mary Douglas	Dr Gertrude Willoughby	Rt Rev Dr Frederick O T Hawkes, Bishop of Kingston	Rt Rev Bertram Simpson, Bishop of Southwark
1931	Lady May Abel Smith			
1940		Miss Ellis		
1947		Miss B Gordon-Jones	Rt Rev Robert Stannard, Bishop of Woolwich	
1954		Miss Jessica Broomhall		
1956		Miss Joyce Baxter		
1957		Miss Elsie Bowerman		
1958		Miss Margaret Cousins	Rt Rev Bertram Simpson, Bishop of Southwark	
1959				
1962		Miss C Corteen Miss D Street		
1964		Miss (later Dr) Dulcie Groves Rev Geoffrey Heal		Rev Geoffrey Heal
1965	Miss Elsie Bowerman	Wing Commander C H (Ben) Baker		
1969				Rev John Lane
1971				
1972	Lady Elspeth Howe, CBE. Created Baroness Howe of Idlicote (2001)	Rev John Lane	Rt Rev David Sheppard, Bishop of Woolwich	
1975				
1978		Dr Martin Pickstone	Rev Michael Whinney, Archdeacon of Southwark	Rt Rev Mervyn Stockwood, Bishop of Southwark
1980			Rt Rev Michael Marshall, Bishop of Woolwich	
1981				
1982			Mr E F T (Paddy) Cribb	
1984				
1986		Mrs Louise Pankhurst Mrs Kitty Leek		
1992				
1994				
1997		Mr David Kitchen, MBE		
2000				

Dates are according to Annual Reports and Executive Committee Minutes

References

Chapter 1

1 Samuel Barnett. Quoted from 'Toynbee Hall and Social Reform. 1880-1914'
2 ibid.
3 John Matthews and J Kimmis. 'The History of the English Settlement Movement' 1997

Chapter 2

4 Oration from Henrietta McArthur's Funeral. Manchester Guardian Newspaper. 21 October 1906
5 M Daunt. 'By Peaceful Means-The Story of Time and Talents. 1887-1987' 1989
6 Randall Davidson. Bishop of Rochester. In a letter to Miss McArthur. May 1895. [Wycombe Abbey archives]
7 Letter from Mrs Bailey, reprinted in UGS Record, Spring 1964
8 Miss M C Alsop. 'The UGSM Early Days' 1939
9 Harry Veasey. 'The History of the UGS. 1897-1945'
10 EMS (Probably Mrs Salmond) 'The Settlement 1906-1922' from 'The History of the UGS 1897-1945'

Chapter 3

11 Lord Bishop of Kingston. Introduction to 'The History of the UGS 1897-1945'
12 Harry Veasey. 'The History of the UGS 1897-1945'
13 Bishop Talbot. Taken from UGS Review. 1976
14 From 'The History of the UGS 1897-1945'
15 Report in 'The Times' 10 May 1956
16 John Lane. Personal Reminiscence of 1972 to 1978
17 From Pioneering to Permanence. Article in UGS Record. Spring 1961
18 Mrs Veasey''s 51 years of ministry. St Mark's Magazine. July 1948
19 The Executive Committee and the Schools in 'The History of the UGS1897-1945'
20 John Lane. 'What's Happened at the UGS' 1975
21 ibid.
22 From 'Cambridge House-the First 100 years'
23 John Lane. Personal Reminiscence of 1972 to 1978
24 Paddy Cribb. Personal Reminiscence of 1981-2000
25 Dr Willoughby. UGSM Record 1933
26 Annual Report. 1985-1986
27 Doris Munday. Resident. Personal Conversation. 1999
28 Annual Report. 1985-1986
29 Annual Report. 1961-1962
30 Theo Waite. Organising Secretary. In a letter to Wycombe Abbey Seniors. 7 October 1958
31 Elspeth Howe. Report to Wycombe Abbey Seniors. Wycombe Abbey Gazette. Spring 1971
32 UGS Review. Autumn 1969
33 Mary Pittard. Peckham Mirror. Autumn 1977
34 George Smith. Personal Reminiscence of 1980s
35 Tania McPherson. Personal Reminiscence from 1980s
36 Peckham Settlement Newsletter. Spring 1981
37 Annual Report. 1988-1989
38 Kitty Leek. South London Press. 21 August 1992
39 Report in 'The Times' 11 December 1935
40 A Cobb. Report on the Social Service Week. CLGS Magazine. July 1939
41 ibid.
42 A Cobb. Report on the Social Service Week. CLGS Magazine. July 1940
43 The Story of Mary Datchelor School. 1877-1977
44 Joan Serle. Head Teacher of Nursery School in UGS. Peckham Summer News. 1970
45 Social Service Days. CLGS Magazine. July 1947
46 Theo Waite. Organising Secretary. Letter to Wycombe Abbey Seniors. 14 October 1950
47 Elsie Bowerman. Report to Wycombe Abbey Seniors. December 1951
48 ibid.
49 Commentary in Diamond Jubilee Film, 'In the Service of Life' 1956
50 Report on Nursery School. UGS Record. Autumn 1957
51 ibid.
52 Theo Waite. Organising Secretary. Letter to Wycombe Abbey Seniors 7 October 1958
53 Annual Report. 1961-62
54 UGS Record. Spring 1960
55 Florrie Whale. Personal Reminiscence of 1950s-1960s
56 'The Milestone.' BSG Magazine. June 1961
57 May Lee. UGS Record. Summer 1961
58 UGS Review 1969
59 Executive Committee Minutes. 5 July 1962
60 Peckham Settlement Newsletter. Spring 1981
61 ibid.
62 Appeals Brochure. The Peckham Settlement. 1981
63 Kate Lindsay. Personal Reminiscence of 1998
64 Kitty Leek. Personal Reminiscence of 1986-1997
65 Tania McPherson. Personal Reminiscence from 1980s
66 Peckham Settlement Newsletter. Autumn 1982
67 Kitty Leek. Personal Reminiscence of 1986-1997
68 Trevor Swaby. Report on Community Work. February 1991
69 Kate Lindsay. Personal Reminiscence of 1998
70 Ofsted Report, 521009. No. 1012775, 16 October 1997
71 Mrs Veasey''s 51 years of ministry. St Mark's Magazine. July 1948
72 Annual Report. 1961-62
73 E. Allen. Schoolgirl report. CLGS magazine. December 1956
74 ibid.
75 Jill Andrews (nee Fairclough). Personal Reminiscence of 1955
76 Mary Welsh. Personal Reminiscence of late 1950s
77 Susan Waggitt. Personal Reminiscence of 1963
78 Settlement News, March 1961

79 Maureen Marshall. Personal Reminiscence of 1958
80 UGS Record. Autumn 1961
81 ibid.
82 Jennie Weldon (nee Fisher). Personal Reminiscence of late 1960s
83 Theo Waite. Organising Secretary. In letter to Miss Waddy, Mickelfield School. 28 February 1962
84 UGS Settlement News. April 1962
85 Geoffrey Heal. Annual Report. 1964
86 Eve Keatley. Personal Conversation. 2000
87 'What on earth does visiting mean?' UGS Review. Summer 1967
88 ibid.
89 UGS Review. Autumn 1969
90 James Allen's School Magazine. October 1972
91 Quote from Robin Guthrie, Head of Cambridge House. May 1968. Papers from Blackfriars Settlement
92 Annual Report 1953
93 Wycombe Abbey Gazette. 1971
94 Elsie Bowerman. 'An Inside View of the Settlement' UGS Record. Autumn 1957
95 Martin Pickstone. An Overview of Peckham Settlement. 1980
96 Annual Report. 1955
97 Florrie Whale. Personal Reminiscence of 1950s-1960s
98 E. Allen. Schoolgirl report. CLGS magazine. December 1956
99 Maureen Marshall. Personal Reminiscence of 1958
100 Susan Waggitt. Personal Reminiscence of 1963
101 Florrie Whale. Personal Reminiscence of 1950s-1960s
102 ibid.
103 Susan Wright (nee Ruegg). Personal Reminiscence of mid 1950s
104 E. Allen. Schoolgirl report. CLGS magazine. December 1956
105 Pamela Roach. Personal Conversation. 2000
106 Letter to the Mission treasurer of St Swithun's School, Winchester from Theo Waite, Organising Secretary. 4 February 1959
107 UGS Record. Spring 1963
108 Gill Fletcher-Watson. Report to Wycombe Seniors. 1996
109 David Kitchen. Report on Peckham Settlement. 1998

Chapter 4

110 Harry Veasey in 'The History of the UGS 1897-1945'
111 Dr Singer. Interim paper from 'Regional Distribution of Unemployment' Pilgrim Trust. 1937
112 Miss Dove. Suggestions. Probably written to Harry Veasey. 13 October 1901 [Wycombe Abbey archives]
113 Commentary in Diamond Jubilee Film of 1956. 'In the Service of Life.'
114 Bishop of Southwark. At the opening of the Staffordshire Street site on 18 March 1931
115 ibid.
116 Miss M C Alsop. 'The UGSM Early Days.' 1939
117 UGSM Report. 1915
118 ibid. Later repeated in UGS Record Autumn 1947
119 Miss M C Alsop. 'The UGSM Early Days' 1939
120 M Taverner. Schoolgirl report on 'The Annual Service of the UGS.' CLGS magazine. 1961
121 Mary Bonsall. Schoolgirl report on The Mission service. 'The Milestone'. BSG Magazine. 1950
122 SRJ. Schoolgirl report in 'The Gazette' Wycombe Abbey. July 1958
123 UL. Schoolgirl report in CLGS magazine. December 1949
124 EJB. 'A Visit to UGS Settlement.' Report in 'The Gazette' Wycombe Abbey. July 1953
125 SCT and PMS in 'The Gazette' Wycombe Abbey. July 1950
126 Veronica Basford. Schoolgirl report. CLGS Magazine. September 1955
127 Bishop of Kingston. Sermon at Southwark Cathedral. 3 June 1947.
128 SRJ Schoolgirl report in 'The Gazette' Wycombe Abbey. July 1958
129 M Taverner. Schoolgirl report on 'The Annual Service of the UGS.' CLGS magazine. 1961
130 Brenda Charles. 'My Visit to Southwark Cathedral' UGS Review. Summer 1967
131 Janet Shaw-Smith. Schoolgirl report on UGS Diamond Jubilee Service. CLGS Magazine. December 1956
132 Lady Ogilvie's address at UGS Diamond Jubilee Service. Report in Wycombe Abbey 'The Gazette.' July 1956
133 'The Milestone.' BSG Magazine 1956
134 Annual Report 1966
135 'Social Service.' James Allen's School Magazine. 1974
136 Letter to the Rev and Right Honourable Lord Archbishop of Canterbury from E F T Cribb, Chairman of Executive Committee, 20 November 1986
137 Letter to Rev Malcolm Johnson from Kitty Leek, 18 November 1986
138 UGSM Annual Report. 1915
139 Quoted from Executive Committee Minutes in 'What's Happened at the UGS?' John Lane. 1975
140 ibid.
141 Mrs Veasey's 51 years of ministry. St Mark's Magazine. July 1948
142 Elsie Bowerman. Report to Wycombe Abbey Seniors. December 1953
143 Executive Committee Minutes. 17 February 1937
144 Executive Committee Minutes. 26 May 1937
145 Executive Committee Minutes. 1945
146 Executive Committee Minutes. 1957
147 Elsie Bowerman. Quoted from 'Wycombe Abbey School 1896 to 1996.' Lorna Flint 1996.
148 Annual Report. 1957
149 Dorothy Shove. R-Residential Settlements. UGS Record. Summer. 1951
150 Mary Welsh. Personal Reminiscence of 1960s
151 Executive Committee Minutes. 14 September 1994

Chapter 5

152 Angela Davies. UGS Review. No. 6. Summer 1967
153 Joyce Baxter. Report in 'The Gazette' Wycombe Abbey. March 1956
154 Ruth Muffett. Personal Reminiscence of 1959
155 Kate Lindsay. Personal Reminiscence of 1998
156 Peckham Settlement News. Spring 1981
157 Report in UGS Record. Spring 1994
158 Report in 'The Times' 24 October 1929
159 Report in 'The Times' 15 November 1929
160 Title Deeds of 44,46,48,50,52 Goldsmith Road. 18 November 1930
161 Bishop of Kingston. Sermon at Southwark Cathedral. 3 June 1947
162 Extract taken from 'What's Happened at the UGS?' John Lane. Volume 1 1975. Source unknown.
163 Jessica Broomhall, Warden. UGS Record. Autumn 1955
164 Schoolgirl. Report on Social Service Day. CLGS magazine. July 1947
165 Jill Andrews (nee Fairclough). Personal Reminiscence of 1955
166 Phyllis Hughes. Personal Reminiscence of 1929
167 Jill Andrews (nee Fairclough). Personal Reminiscence of 1955
168 Phyllis Hughes. Personal Reminiscence of 1929
169 UGS Annual Report. 1947
170 Joyce Baxter. Report in 'The Gazette' Wycombe Abbey. March 1956
171 Rev Canon Lloyd of Winchester. Annual Service Sermon. 13 May 1958
172 Susan Waggitt. Personal Reminiscence of 1963
173 Anne McFayden. Schoolgirl report on visit. UGS Review. No. 6. Summer 1967
174 Patty Paice. UGS Summer News. June 1970
175 Annual Report. 1971
176 UGS Settlement News. 1961
177 Mary Welsh. Personal Reminiscence of late 1950s
178 Peckham Mirror Supplement. 1973
179 John Lane. Publicity Brochure. 1973
180 Susan Waggitt. Personal Reminiscence of 1963
181 George Smith. Personal Reminiscence of 1980s
182 Angela Davies. UGS Review. No. 6. Summer 1967
183 E Allen. Schoolgirl report on a visit to the UGS. CLGS magazine. December 1956
184 Remark attributed to John Lane. Peckham Mirror Supplement. 1973
185 Tania McPherson. Personal Reminiscence of 1999
186 George Smith. Personal Reminiscence of 1980s and 1990s
187 Angela Davies. UGS Review. No. 6. Summer 1967
188 C Havergal. Diary of Wartime Visit to Settlement. 26 August 1941
189 Joyce Baxter. Letter to Wycombe Abbey Seniors. 5 October 1953
190 Joyce Baxter. Letter to Wycombe Abbey Seniors. 21 November 1956
191 Geoffrey Heal. UGS Report. 1964
192 Martin Pickstone. Appeals Brochure. 1977
193 Document referring to draft proposals at start of Martin Pickstone's term of directorship. 1978
194 Kitty Leek. Personal Reminiscence of 1987
195 Florrie Whale. Personal Reminiscence of 1961
196 UGS Record. Autumn 1947
197 Kitty Leek. Personal Reminiscence of 1988
198 Barbara Hill. Peckham Settlement Newsletter. No.4. Spring 1982
199 Elsie Bowerman. Report to Wycombe Abbey Seniors. December 1951
200 Settlement Newsletter. Issue No. 5 February 1955
201 'The Milestone' BSG magazine. 1961
202 Gill Fletcher-Watson. Report to Wycombe Abbey Seniors. 1996
203 George Smith. Personal Reminiscence.
204 David Kitchen. Report on Peckham Settlement. 1998

Chapter 6

205 C. Rouse. 'Fulfilling its Mission'. South London Press. 17 August 1976
206 M. Williamson in a letter to Wycombe Abbey. 27 May 1899 [Wycombe Abbey archives]
207 Marion Gain (nee Hamilton). Wycombe Abbey Senior. Personal Reminiscence of 1925
208 Mrs Gamble. In a letter to Mickelfield School. 1968
209 Peggy Weller. Friday Club leader. July 1999
210 Canon Barnett. Quote from 'History of the Settlement Movement' by John Matthews and James Kimmis. Manuscript. 1997
211 Jessica Broomhall. Annual Report. 1953
212 Joan Kirby. Personal Reminiscence of late 1950s
213 Marion Gain (nee Hamilton). Wycombe Abbey Senior. Personal Reminiscence reported in the Centenary Edition of 'The Gazette' 1996
214 Morwenna Hocking (nee Crawshaw), Wycombe Abbey Senior. Personal Reminiscence reported in the Centenary Edition of 'The Gazette' 1996
215 Hilary Pincott. Personal Reminiscence of late 1950s
216 Report in James Allen's School magazine. 1965
217 UGS Settlement News. December 1962
218 Report in 'The Gazette' Wycombe Abbey. 1974
219 UGS Record. Autumn 1947
220 Joan Serle. Head Teacher of Nursery School. UGS Peckham Summer News. 1970
221 Jill Andrews (nee Fairclough). Personal Reminiscence of 1955
222 Florrie Whale. Personal Reminiscence of the late 1950s
223 Jill Andrews (nee Fairclough). Personal Reminiscence of 1955
224 J Oakes. Report in CLGS Magazine. December 1954
225 Florrie Whale. Personal Reminiscence of the 1950s
226 ibid.
227 UGS Record. Autumn 1947
228 J Oakes. Report in CLGS Magazine. December 1955

229 Report in 'The Gazette' Wycombe Abbey. November 1972
230 Jennie Weldon (nee Fisher). Personal Reminiscence of the late 1960s
231 Report from Winceby House School in UGS Record 1947
232 Enid Binstead. Report in James Allen's School magazine. 1959
233 Joan Kirby. Personal Reminiscence of late 1950s and early 1960s
234 Report on 'Royalty at Camberwell' South London Press. 25 October 1902
235 Susan Wright (nee Ruegg). Personal Reminiscence of mid 1950s
236 Theo Waite. Organising Secretary. Letter to Wycombe Abbey Seniors. 7 October 1958
237 Susan Waggitt. Personal Reminiscence of 1963
238 '66 Girls take Action' UGS Review. Spring 1966
239 'What on earth does visiting mean?' UGS Review. Summer 1967
240 '66 Girls take Action' UGS Review. Spring 1966
241 ibid.
242 'The Schoolgirl Visiting Scheme' UGS Review. Autumn 1965
243 Jennie Weldon (nee Fisher). Personal Reminiscence of the late 1960s
244 Susan Waggitt. Personal Reminiscence of 1963
245 Geoffrey Heal. New Life in Peckham. 1973
246 Julia Beredznay. Bellerby's College. 1998
247 Harry Veasey. 'The History of the UGS. 1897-1945'
248 Canon Elliot of St. Paul's Cathedral. Report in 'The Times,' 23 May 1929
249 Annual Report. 1962-63
250 G Tuffnell and H Weinberg. Report in CLGS Magazine. 1964
251 'What's happened at the UGS?' John Lane. 1975
252 E Duncan and C Lancaster. Report in Wycombe Abbey Gazette. 1975
253 L Pickup and V Hinks. Bruton School. Report in 'News from the Peckham Settlement" Spring 1976
254 Kitty Leek. Personal Reminiscence of 1990s
255 ibid.
256 The Peckham Settlement. Publicity leaflet. 1992
257 Joan Kirby. Personal Reminiscence of late 1950s and early 1960s
258 'Wycombe Abbey School 1896-1996.' Lorna Flint. 1996
259 UGSM School Sheet. 1924
260 City of London Girls' School Magazine. 1946
261 Elsie Bowerman. Report to Wycombe Abbey Seniors. December 1951
262 A. MacGregor Lewis. Report in 'The Gazette' Wycombe Abbey. December 1952
263 The Story of Mary Datchelor School. 1877-1977
264 Miss Wilson. In a letter to Harry Veasey. 19 November 1905 [Wycombe Abbey archives]
265 AR Burne Secretary to Miss Dove. In a letter to Harry Veasey. 12 September 1907 [Wycombe Abbey archives]
266 Miss Dove. In a letter to Harry Veasey. 1 February 1906 [Wycombe Abbey archives]
267 Miss Dove. In a letter to Mrs Talbot. 10 February 1906 [Wycombe Abbey archives]
268 ibid.
269 AR Burne Secretary to Miss Dove. In a letter to Harry Veasey. 2 November 1908 [Wycombe Abbey archives]
270 Miss Dove's Suggestions. Undated. Circa 1938.
271 ibid.
272 ibid.
273 John Lane. Personal Reminiscence of 1972 to 1978
274 The Story of Mary Datchelor School. 1877-1977
275 'The Milestone.' BSG Magazine. 1918
276 Miss M C Alsop. 'The UGSM Early Days' 1939
277 ibid.
278 Lorna Flint. 'Wycombe Abbey School 1896-1996'
279 Lady Howe. Report to Wycombe Abbey Seniors. Spring 1971
280 Mary Welsh. Personal Reminiscence of early 1970s
281 John Lane. Personal Reminiscence of 1972 to 1978
282 Peckham Schools' Liaison Committee Minutes. 7 October 1981
283 Director's Report. January 1987
284 'The Milestone' BSG Magazine 1990
285 Miss Dove. To Executive Council. 1914 [Wycombe Abbey archives]
286 Harry Veasey. Letter to Miss Baird, Head Teacher of Malvern. 5 December 1911 [Wycombe Abbey archives]
287 'The Milestone' BSG Magazine. 1954-1960
288 Joan Kirby. Personal Reminiscence of late 1950s and early 1960s
289 Social Service 1969-1970. Report in James Allen's School Magazine. 1970
290 Report in CLGS Magazine. 1964
291 Joan Kirby. Personal Reminiscence of late 1950s and early 1960s
292 'The Milestone' BSG Magazine 1979
293 JY. Report in 'The Gazette'. Wycombe Abbey. November 1980
294 ibid.
295 Mary Rose Farley (nee Bateman) Personal Reminiscence of 1980s
296 Susan Wright (nee Ruegg). Personal Reminiscence of 1980s
297 Reply to EFT Cribb after appeal sent to Harrogate College. 20 June 1986
298 Executive Committee Minutes. 19 March 1991
299 Executive Committee Minutes. 18 November 1992
300 Malcolm Johnson. Personal Reminiscence of 1980s and 1990s
301 Ruth Plant. Report in Wycombe Abbey Centenary Edition of 'The Gazette.' 1996
302 Elizabeth Grace. Personal Reminiscence of early 1950s
303 Susan Waggitt. Personal Reminiscence of 1963
304 Jill Andrews (nee Fairclough). Personal Reminiscence of 1955

305 Ruth Muffett. Personal Reminiscence of 1959
306 Gill Fletcher-Watson. Personal Conversation. 1999
307 Maureen Marshall. Personal Reminiscence of 1958
308 Two schoolgirls from Malvern College on work placement. Personal Conversation. 1999
309 Report in ' The Times' 24 October 1929

Chapter 7

310 Peckham Settlement Newsletter. Spring 1981
311 Jane Dove. In a postcard to Harry Veasey. 6 January 1898 [Wycombe Abbey archives]
312 Jane Dove. In a letter to Harry Veasey. 27 January 1908 [Wycombe Abbey archives]
313 Miss Connolly. Head Teacher of Haberdashers' Aske's School. In a letter to Harry Veasey. 20 December 1901 [Wycombe Abbey archives]
314 Jane Dove. In a letter to Harry Veasey. 23 October 1901 [Wycombe Abbey archives]
315 Jane Dove. In a letter to Harry Veasey. 15 February 1909 [Wycombe Abbey archives]
316 ibid.
317 Jane Dove. In a letter to Harry Veasey. 18 December 1927 [Wycombe Abbey archives]
318 AR Burne Secretary to Miss Dove. In a letter to unknown receiver. 3 December 1900 [Wycombe Abbey archives]
319 Executive Committee Minutes. 11 June 1990
320 Bishop of Southwark. In a letter to Harry Veasey. 4 June 1918
321 The Settlement 1906 to 1927 'The History of the UGS 1897-1945'
322 Declaration of Trust. Gooch Memorial Fund. 17 November 1908
323 Articles of Association. 1931
324 Elsie Bowerman. Report to Wycombe Abbey Seniors. December 1958
325 Theo Waite. In a letter to Wycombe Abbey Seniors. 1951
326 Elsie Bowerman. Report to Wycombe Abbey Seniors. December 1951
327 Commentary in Diamond Jubilee film 'In the Service of Life' 1956
328 'A Fire Officer backs the UGS' UGS Record. 1961
329 Dr D Groves. From 'Negotiating the Glass Ceiling' 1998
330 Theo Waite. Organising Secretary. Letter to Wycombe Abbey Seniors. 14 June 1950
331 ibid.
332 Margaret Cousins. 'A day in the life of the Settlement' UGS Record. May 1961
333 Eve Keatley. Personal Conversation. 2000
334 John Lane. Personal Reminiscence of 1972 to 1978
335 Lady Howe. Personal Conversation. 2000
336 John Lane. Personal Reminiscence of 1972 to 1978
337 ibid.
338 Deeds of Pitt Street Settlement. Recorded in Executive Minutes. 1998
339 Trust deeds of Camberwell Relief in Need Charity. Recorded in Executive Minutes. 1998
340 Christine Richards. Personal Conservation. 1999
341 Gill Fletcher-Watson. Personal Conversation. 2000
342 Sheila Robertson in 'The Gazette.' Wycombe Abbey. 1998
343 Lady Howe. Personal Conversation. 2000
344 Kitty Leek. Director's Report. May 1989

Photographs and Illustrations

Every effort has been made to trace the people or organisations whose photographs are displayed. I thank them all and hope this acknowledgement will serve as recognition of the value of their photographs towards this history.

1 Ronald Stephens
2 Settlement Archives
3 Settlement Archives
4 Wycombe Abbey
5 Settlement Archives
6 Settlement Archives
7 Settlement Archives
8 Settlement Archives
9 Tony Sleep
10 Settlement Archives
11 Shelagh Collingwood, Wycombe Abbey Senior
12 Tariq Chaudry
13 Settlement Archives. Reprinted in Annual Report, 1967/68
14 Settlement Archives
15 Tony Sleep
16 M Pictures, London
17 Daily Mirror. Reprinted in Annual Report, 1971
18 Settlement Archives
19 Freddie Read, Daily Mirror and Tony Sleep
20 Keystone View. Settlement Archives
21 Settlement Archives
22 Settlement Archives
23 Harold King. Settlement Archives
24 Settlement Archives
25 Possibly from The South London Mercury
26 Settlement Archives
27 Ronald Stephens
28 Ronald Stephens
29 Settlement Archives
30 M Pictures and Harold King. Settlement Archives
31 Settlement Archives
32 Settlement Archives REprinted in UGS Record, 1960
33 Freddie Read, Daily Mirror. Reprinted in New life at Peckham.
34 M Pictures. Settlement Archives
35 Possibly from The South London Mercury
36 M Pictures. Settlement Archives
37 Jan Photo Series. Reprinted in UGS Review, 1967
38 Harold King. Settlement Archives
39 Settlement Archives
40 M Pictures. Settlement Archives
41 Photograph lent by Jennie Weldon (nee Fisher)
42 Settlement Archives.
43 Harold King. Settlement Archives
44 M Pictures. Settlement Archives
45 Tony Sleep
46 LCC for LFB. Reprinted in UGS Record, 1963
47 Possibly from The South London Observer
48 Settlement Archives. Reprinted in Annual Report, 1971
49 Settlement Archives
50 Settlement Archives
51 South East London Mercury
52 Settlement Archives. Reprinted in the Peckham Mirror
53 Settlement Archives
54 Settlement Archives
55 Settlement Archives
56 Settlement Archives
57 Associated Newspapers
58 Ronald Stephens
59 Ronald Stephens
60 Newspaper photographs. Settlement Archives
61 Settlement Archives
62 Settlement Archives
63 Ronald Stephens
64 Harold King.
65 Photograph lent by George Smith
66 Settlement Archives
67 Ronald Stephens
68 Settlement Archives
69 Settlement Archives
70 Ronald Stephens
71 Ronald Stephens
72 Settlement Archives
73 Settlement Archives
74 Ronald Stephens
75 Photograph lent by John Beasley
76 Photograph lent by George Smith
77 Planet News and Julia Morgan. Settlement Archives
78 Wycombe Abbey Archives

79 Settlement Archives
80 Jennifer Stephens
81 Jennifer Stephens
82 Wycombe Abbey Archives
83 Settlement Archives
84 Photograph lent by Jennie Weldon (nee Fisher)
85 Settlement Archives
86 Settlement Archives
87 Wycombe Abbey Archives
88 Photograph lent by Jennie Weldon (nee Fisher)
89 Settlement Archives
90 Photograph lent by Paddy Cribb
91 Ronald Stephens
92 Settlement Archives
93 Settlement Archives
94 Settlement Archives
95 Settlement Archives
96 Freddie Read, Daily Mirror. Reprinted in New life at Peckham
97 Julia Morgan
98 Settlement Archives
99 Settlement Archives
100 Settlement Archives
101 Settlement Archives
102 Settlement Archives
103 Reprinted in UGS Record 1947
104 M Pictures. Settlement Archives
105 Cecil Beaton. Reprinted in Diamond Jubilee Service Sheet, 1956
106 Daily Sketch
107 Mirror Pics.
108 Central Press Photos
109 South London Press
110 Settlement Archives
111 Ronald Stephens

Appendix: Acronyms

AGM	Annual General Meeting
BAS	British Association of Settlements
BASSAC	British Association of Settlements and Social Action Centres
BBC	British Broadcasting Corporation
BSG	Bournemouth School for Girls
CCHF	Children's Country Holiday Fund
CLGS	City of London Girls' School
COS	Charity Organisation Society
CV	Curricula Vitae
DES	Department of Education and Science
DFE	Department for Education and Employment
GLC	Greater London Council
ILEA	Inner London Education Authority
ICAA	Invalid Children's Aid Association
JAGS	James Allen's Girls' School
LBS	London Borough of Southwark
LCC	London County Council
LSE	London School of Economics
NALGO	National And Local Government Officers Association
NNEB	National Nursing Examination Board
NSPCC	National Society for the Prevention of Cruelty to Children
NVQ	National Vocational Qualification
OGA	Old Girls' Association
PDCCA	Peckham and Dulwich Caribbean Community Association
PT	Physical Training
RNLI	Royal National Lifeboat Institution
RSPCA	Royal Society for the Prevention of Cruelty to Animals
TB	Tuberculosis
TEC	Training Enterprise Council
UGS	United Girls' Settlement
UGSSS	United Girls' Schools for Social Service
UGSM	United Girls' Service Mission
VAT	Value Added Tax
WAG	Wycombe Abbey Gazette
WUS	Women's University Settlement

Acknowledgements

Peckham Settlement

Lady Howe	President
David Kitchen	Present Director 1997- present
John Lane	Director of Peckham Settlement 1972-1978
Kitty Leek	Director of Peckham Settlement 1986-1997
Paddy Cribb	Chairman of Executive Committee 1982 to date
Derek Lowman	Member of the present Executive Committee
Joan Kirby	Member of the present Executive Committee
Hilary Pincott	Member of the present Executive Committee
Reverend Malcolm Johnson	One-time member of the present Executive Committee and Vicar of St John's Church, Peckham
Michael Fowke	Member of the present Executive Committee
Nicki Brown	Manager of All Nations Nursery
Sharon McNeill	Nursery officer - All Nations Nursery
Tania McPherson	Nursery officer - All Nations Nursery
Kate Lindsay	One-time Deputy of All Nations Nursery
Femi Mafoh	Leader of the Latch Key Project
Babs Sohna	Leader of the Friary Open Learning Centre
Jennie Weldon (nee Fisher)	One-time social worker
George and Ann Smith	One-time caretakers
Chris Richards	One-time community worker
Dr Dulcie Groves	Warden of Peckham Settlement 1964

Users of Peckham Settlement

Florrie Whale	Thursday Club
Peggy Weller	Friday Club
Louie Slough	Friday Club and one-time member of the Executive Council
Other members	Friday Club.
Doris Munday	One-time helper at Black Eagles Club
Pamela Roach	Trainee at Friary Open Learning Centre
Two schoolgirls	On work experience from Malvern College for Girls
Lucinda Atobatele	Rise and Shine
James Kigiri	Agape Foundation

Friends or Residents of Peckham

Winifred Jordan	
Phyllis Hughes	
Sheila Neville	One-time volunteer at Cambridge Union Mission and on staff of Mary Datchelor School for Girls.

Voluntary Officers

Mary Rose Farley (nee Bateman)	One-time Schools Liaison Officer and Executive Committee Member. One-time Head of Berkhamstead School and of Perse School, Cambridge
Mary Welsh	One-time Executive Committee Member and Chair of the Nursery School Committee
Maureen Marshall	One-time member of staff at Peckham and an Old Girl of James Allen's Girls' School, Dulwich.
Eve Keatley	Wycombe Abbey Senior. One-time Organising Secretary and Executive Committee Member
Gill Fletcher-Watson	Wycombe Abbey Senior and Peckham Representative for Schools. One-time member of the Executive Committee

Schools

Mrs Alison Heath	Archivist at Wycombe Abbey School
Mrs Van Hanell	Head of History, Streatham High and Clapham High School
Mrs Margaret Smith	Librarian at City of London Girls' School
Mrs Marion Gibbs	Head teacher of James Allen's Girls' School
Mrs Cynthia Pullin	Librarian at James Allen's Girls' School
Mrs Emma McKendrick	Head teacher of Downe House, Berkshire.
Judy Hardy	OGA Secretary of Malvern College for Girls
Sue Ginger	Senior teacher at Bellerby's College, East Sussex
Jenny Holmes	OGA Representative at Sydenham High School for Girls
Rev Richard Warden	Wycombe Abbey School Liaison with Peckham Settlement

Old Girls

Helen Braund	One time Head and Chair of Bournemouth School for Girls OGA
Winifred Bray	One time secretary of Bournemouth School for Girls and member of OGA. [died 16.04.01, aged 89]
Susan Waggitt	James Allen's OGA
Elizabeth Grace	James Allen's OGA
Fiona Mather	General Secretary of Wycombe Abbey Seniors
Susan Wright (nee Ruegg)	Wycombe Abbey Senior
Jill Andrews (nee Fairclough)	Wycombe Abbey Senior
Marion Gain (nee Hamilton)	Wycombe Abbey Senior
Elizabeth Carling	Peckham Representative at St Swithun's School, Winchester
Ruth Muffett	St Swithun's OGA

Other Contributors

Viscount Ullswater	Private Secretary to HRH The Princess Margaret
Paul McGoldrick	British Association of Settlements and Social Action Centres [BASSAC]
John Beasley	Local Historian
The Librarians	Southwark Local Studies Library, Borough High Street
The Librarians	London Metropolitan Archives
The Librarians	The Newspaper Library, The British Library, Colindale
Richard Cook	Church of England Record Centre, Bermondsey
Susie Strachan	Librarian at the Fawcett Library in London Guildhall University
The Librarian	Peckham Library
The Librarian	New Cross Library
The staff	Southwark Cathedral
The South London Film Society	
Mary Gardiner	Blackfriars Settlement
Sue Youthed	Education Centred Manager, Bede House, Bermondsey
David Raines	Amateur historian
Jonathan Glasby	Researcher and Author, Birmingham University
Bob Smyth	One-time Executive Committee Member and Local Councillor

Books and Documents

A History of the United Girl's Schools Mission, 1897-1945. Various Authors

Wycombe Abbey School, 1896-1996. A partial history by Lorna Flint. Privately Printed.

The Story of Mary Datchelor School, 1877-1977. Various authors. Hodder and Stoughton, London

The Story of St Mary's, Abbots Bromley, Shrewsbury. 1947. M Rice. Wilding & Son

What Happened at the UGS. Change in a voluntary social work agency-from Public School Mission to Community Resource. May 1975. Manuscript in two volumes submitted as a final year project for the Diploma in Management Studies. John Lane

Ye Parish of Camerwell. 1875. W H Blanch. E W Allen, London

The Regional Distribution of the Unemployed 1929-1936. Interim paper. Dr H W Singer. Pilgrim Trust (William Ebor)

The Story of Peckham. 1983. 2nd Edition. J D Beasley. LBS.

The Story of Peckham and Nunhead, J D Beasley. Neighbourhood Histories No. 3. Published by LBS

The Peckham Settlement. (Circa 1986) George Nicholson, Treasurer of Willowbrook, Southwark Community Planning and Education Centre. Unpublished manuscript.

The History of Peckham Park School. 1989. Vera Conway. LPL Services

Toynbee Hall and Social Reform 1880-1914-The Search for Community. 1987 Standish Meacham. Yale University Press, New Haven

The History of the English Settlement Movement. 1997. John Matthews and James Kimmis. Manuscript version.

Cambridge House, the first 100 years. Colin Rochester. 1996.

The Cambridge Mission to South London. A Twenty Years Survey. Ed. A Amos and W W Hough. Macmillan and Bower, Cambridge. 1904

By Peaceful Means-The Story of Time and Talents. 1887-1987. 1989. M. Daunt. Time and Talents Association. Rotherhithe

Negotiating the Glass Ceiling. Careers of Senior Women in the Academic World. 1998. Ed, M David & D Woodward. Falmer Press

Bede House Association. Fifty years 1938-1988. Susanna Watson. The Print Place, Bede House

Blackfriars Settlement-a short history. 1887-1987. Gladys Barrett. Blackfriars Settlement, Nelson Square.

Origins of the Diocese of Southwark. 1877-1905. Mrs Jas A Heaton the Shirley Press Ltd. 1949

The Southwark Story. Florence Higham. Hodder and Stoughton. 1955

Peckham and Nunhead Churches. 1995. J D Beasley. Published by South Riding Press.

Origin of Names in Peckham and Nunhead. 1993. J D Beasley. South Riding Press.

St. John Chrysostom. A biography. Undated. Les Mole. Printed by the Additional Curates Society.

St John's Church, Peckham and its Inheritance. Undated. Les Mole. Printed by the Additional Curates Society.

St. Chrysostom's and St. Jude's Church Magazines. 1950-1965

The Southwark Poverty Profile. Planning and Regeneration Division. February 1996. Southwark Council.

Living in Consort and Friary Wards. A Community Survey - Wave 2. Southwark Council. July 1999. Office for Public Management
Information leaflets from BASSAC

School Magazines. Various dates from 1896-present day. From City of London Girl's School, James Allen's Girls' School, Wycombe Abbey, Haberdashers' Aske's School, Bournemouth School for Girls, Mickelfield School.

Archive material from Wycombe Abbey School and Mickelfield School. Specified in references.

Executive Committee Reports, Directors Reports and Financial Committee Reports of the Peckham Settlement. Various dates from 1896 to present.
The UGS, later named the Peckham Settlement, Annual Reports. From 1908 to present day.

The UGSS Review, sometime named The UGSM School Sheet or the UGS Record. Various editions from 1906 to 1986.

Settlement newsletters, variously named UGS News or Peckham Settlement Newsletters from 1947-2000

Handwritten account of a wartime visit to the UGS Settlement. C Havergal. Representative of Swithun's School, Winchester. August 26, 1941

Appeal brochures, letters and other documents. Specified in references.

Maps, deeds, plans concerning The Settlement. Specified in references.

The Bridge. Newspaper of the Anglican Diocese of Southwark. Various dates.

The Peckham Mirror. 1972-1973 and 1978.

Articles from the South London Press and the South London Advertiser. Specified in references.

Index

A

Abel Smith, Lady May...10, 17, 20, 70, 138
ACCESS...27
Acorn Estate...10, 39, 72
    Tenants Association...25
Acorns Youth Club...49, 50, 53, 54
Advice Centre...11, 49-50, 56, 57, 124
    legal...9, 12
Agape Foundation...56
Albany Institute...118, 125
All Nations Nursery...11, 40-42, 56, 80, 136
All Saints Church...49
    Mission...17
Alsop, Miss...17, 18, 59, 101
Amott Road...111
Anderson Consultants...81
Andrews, Jill...44, 71, 72, 87, 108
Annual General Meeting...9, 10, 54, 62, 104, 109, 113, 122, 129
Annual Report...13, 28, 29, 30, 36, 37, 39, 43, 49, 56, 57, 62, 72, 73, 77, 94, 124, 130, 133
Annual Service...9, 11, 54, 59, 61, 62, 71, 93, 103, 115
Appleton Rev...17
Archbishop of Canterbury...11, 12, 63, 64
Archer Jeffrey...11, 124
Articles of Association...113, 129
Association of Friends...10, 55
Astor Lady...10, 20, 34,
Asylum Seekers...12, 50
Atlee, Clement...16

B

Badminton School...100
Bailey Mrs...17, 18, 138
    Rev C R...10, 17, 65, 138
Baker, Wing Commander Ben...11, 61, 66, 103, 118, 119, 138
Baldwin, Sir Stanley...9
Band of Hope...23, 91
Barclay's Bank...124
Baring's Bank...124
Barnes, Hetty...45
Barnett, Samuel...16, 84
    Dame Henrietta...16
Barry Richards Charitable Settlement...129
BARS...113, 119
basement...26, 28, 39, 48, 78, 126
BAS...31
BASSAC...11, 24, 33, 40, 96, 97, 113, 126
Bateman, Mary Rose...96, 104, 105, 107
Baxter, Joyce...10, 68, 72, 76, 86, 114, 138
BBC...117
Beasley, John...14
Bede House...46, 124
Bedford College...92
Bellerby's College...89, 92
Bells Garden Estate...25, 41
Benenden School...20, 97, 98, 104
Berkhamstead School...96, 107, 115
Bernstein, Dr...95
Beveridge, Lord...16
Bexhill School...80, 98, 133
Black Eagles Club...90
Blackfriars Settlement...46, 94, 118, 124, 129
Blackheath High School...62, 102, 104
Blackmore, Lady Pamela...122, 124, 127
Board of Education...34, 35, 36
Booth, Charles...74
Boston House School...99
Bouckley, Daisy...117
Bournemouth School for Girls...14, 60, 80, 84, 85, 87, 101, 104, 105, 106, 115, 133, 134
Bovis Court...124
Bowerman, Elsie...11, 36, 38, 47, 65, 66, 78, 80, 92, 98, 101, 114, 116, 138
Braund, Helen...14
Bray, Winifred...85
British Caribbean Society...23
Brittan, Sir Leon...11, 97
Brockwell Park...31
Broomhall, Jessica...10, 71, 85, 138
Brown, Nicki...41
Brownies...90, 91
Bruton School...103, 104
Buchanan, Rt Rev C...67
Burge, Rt Rev, Dr...9, 111, 138
    Mrs...138
Burne, Miss A R...99, 111
Building Fund...110, 111
    The Settlement...75-83, 111, 118, 124, 128, 129
Business in the Community...12, 27
Butler, Rt Rev T...67

C

Calmington Road...9, 19, 69, 110, 112
Camberwell...9, 10, 17, 18, 25, 29, 44, 49, 51
    Borough Council...10, 22, 43, 69, 117
    Costers' Benevolent Association...127
    Health Society...23
    Holiday and Welfare...117
    Housing Society...23
    Mayor...69, 78, 133
    Old Age Pensioners Welfare Association 117
    Relief in Need...12, 127
    Settlements Enquiry...11, 24, 25, 119
Cambridge House...17, 46, 120, 124
Camelot School...87
Canada Insurance Stock...112

Capital Cares…12, 81
Care Committee…23, 30-31, 47, 49
Centenary…12, 63, 67, 84, 107, 128
chapel…65, 66, 78, 80
Charity Commissioners…126, 127
Charity Organisation Society…15, 23
Charrington, Mrs…116, 132
Charterhouse Settlement…17, 124
Children's Country Holiday Fund…23, 31, 45, 110, 115
Children in Need…128
Christopher H Reeves Trust…129
Christ's Hospital…87
Christ's College, Cambridge…124
Church of England…27, 58, 92, 95
church services…59-64
Citizens' Advice Bureau…23, 49, 50
City of London Girls' School…91, 98, 102, 106, 115
City Parochial Foundation…24, 54, 124, 127
Clapham High School…18
Clayton, Hazel…129
Coburg Road…19
Collett, David…94, 118, 119, 122, 129
Community Affairs Committee…124
    Centre…50
    Development…16, 24-25, 47, 126, 128
    Work…24, 32, 47
    Worker…24, 25, 39, 41, 46, 49, 50, 56
Computer Insight…27
Consort Ward…42, 75, 130
Constitution…9, 12, 99, 104, 107, 113, 129
Corless, Carole…41
Corteen, Miss…138
Costa…74, 82
country holidays…44
Courcier, Annie…47
Cousins, Miss Margaret…10, 55, 117, 133, 138
Cribb, Paddy…11, 27, 83, 124, 125, 136, 138
Croydon, Bishop of…60
Crystal Prospect…54, 79, 124

D

Davy, Honor…49
day nursery…10, 21, 36, 40-42, 80
de Burgho-Hodge, Miss…9, 138
Department of Education and Science…42, 124
Department of the Environment…75
Diamond Jubilee…10, 13, 22, 60, 61, 78, 115, 132
    Film…13, 36, 45, 58, 116
Dinner Club…10, 43, 117
Docklands Mission…17
Douglas, Mary…18, 76, 102, 112, 138
Dove, Jane Francis…9, 10, 18, 58, 59, 67, 82, 99, 100, 105, 110, 111
Dove-Bowerman Trust…11, 101, 127, 128
Downe House…20, 92
Downs School…80, 88, 133
drama activities…49, 51, 54, 57, 78, 92
Duke of Edinburgh Scheme…23, 50
Dulwich College…85, 108, 127
Dyke, Rev John…17
Dynamo Football Club…54

E

East Dulwich Road…71
East Peckham Consortium…12, 130
Edinburgh Settlement…12, 64
education…15, 16, 17, 21, 23, 26, 27, 31-42 , 49, 56, 85, 92
    Board of…34, 35, 36, 113
    Home Visiting Scheme…41
    Institute of…95
    Ministry of…36
Eliot, Lady Althea…94
Ellis, Miss…10, 75, 138
Employment Action Service…27
Eton College…85
Evans, Dame Edith…71
Executive Board…102
    Committee…13, 14, 15, 23, 27, 30, 37, 38, 52, 55, 56, 64, 65, 66, 67, 69, 76, 82, 83, 85, 86, 90, 94, 97, 98, 100, 101, 102, 103, 105, 107, 111, 113, 116, 120, 122, 124, 125, 127, 128, 129, 130, 135
    Council…9
Expenditure…110-130
Extension Guides…94

F

Face to Face…50
Family Welfare…23
Federation of Settlements…118, 119
Fire Brigade…52, 133
    Officer…55, 116
    Station…55, 68, 78, 87, 116
Fisher, Jennie…45, 46, 90, 91, 93, 118
Fletcher-Watson, Gill…56, 82, 108, 109, 128
Flint, Lorna…101
Foot Clinic…10, 43, 117
Friary Neighbourhood Youth Development Project…48
    Open Learning Centre…27, 54, 56, 80, 136
    Ward…42, 75, 130
Friday Club…53, 89
Friends of the Settlement…11, 36, 45, 54-56, 98, 102, 116, 122, 134
    Association…11, 55

G

Gain, Marion…84, 85
Garbutt, Rt Rev Dr…138
garden…31, 34, 37, 41, 80-81
General Fund…99, 111
gifts…15, 28, 29, 31, 39, 45, 85-87
GLC, Greater London Council…11, 48, 123, 124, 125, 126

Gluck, Graham...79
Glyndebourne...10, 35
Godolphin School...18, 98, 102, 112
Godolphin and Latimer School...104
Godstowe School...104
Goldsmith Mansions...45, 72, 73
Goldsmith Road...10, 11, 22, 70, 71, 72, 75, 76, 81
Goldsmiths College...24, 31
    Hall...62, 122
Gooch, Georgina...9, 99, 138
    Memorial Fund...12, 112, 118
    Scholarship...10, 112
Gordon Jones, Miss...10, 138
Grace, Elizabeth...108
Graham Street School...18
Granger, Isobel...100, 103
Green, Miss...9, 138
    School ...106
Greenwich...11, 31
Griffiths, Grace...11, 45, 102
Groves, Dr Dulcie...10, 46, 77, 80, 100, 117, 138
Guide Movement...23
Guildhall...11, 124
Gulbenkian Foundation...24, 119
Guthrie, Robin...47
Guy's Hospital...11, 124

H

Haberdashers' Aske's School...90, 91, 102, 106, 110
Hale, George...45, 55
hall...25, 26, 51, 53, 57, 66, 78-79
Harkness, Edward...112
Harrogate College...105
Havergal, Miss...75
Havil Street...22
Hawkes, Rt Rev F.O.T...17, 138
Headstart...11, 22, 57
Heal, Rev Geoffrey...46, 67, 77, 120, 134, 138
health...21, 31, 35, 36, 42-45, 57
Heard, Mr...69, 72
Heath, Alison...14
Heinz Food Company...124
Herbert, Rt Rev Dr...138
Hilden Trust...127, 128
Hill, Barbara...39, 40, 62, 79, 95, 122, 124
    Octavia...15
Hitchin Grammar School...80, 133
holidays...21, 44
holiday play scheme...9, 12, 21, 31, 56, 107, 123, 128
homelessness...25-26, 80
Honorary Secretary...20, 35, 80, 99, 101, 116
Honorary Treasurer...10, 66, 100, 101, 111, 112, 113, 116
Honor Oak School...91, 102
Hospital Savings Association...23
hospital teachers...22
Hour Bank...12, 56, 57
housing...15, 21, 25-26, 49, 50, 72-75, 95, 96, 126
Howe, Baronesss...11, 12, 29, 62, 63, 95, 101, 109, 122, 124, 128, 136, 138
Hughes, Phyllis...72, 102

I

ICAA, Invalid Children's Aid Association...9, 10, 23,70, 110, 114
ILEA, Inner London Education Authority...11, 24, 39, 48, 95, 96, 123, 124, 125, 126
income...110-130
Index of Local Conditions...74
Infant Welfare Clinic...9, 10, 22, 35, 42, 111
Infirmary...22
Irons, Constance...56, 102

J

James Allen's Girls' School...11, 38, 47, 62, 86, 88, 90, 91, 98, 102, 104, 106, 109, 110, 115, 121, 131
Job Club...11, 21, 25, 26-27, 49, 50
Johnson, Jane...12, 30, 52, 53, 127
    Marjorie...112
    Rev Malcolm...64, 107
Jordan, Win...134
jumble sales...87, 88
Junior Advisory Committee...22

K

Karib Association...25, 54, 123
Keatley, Eve...14, 46, 77, 93, 94, 101, 118, 120
Keefe, Jane...39
Kempshead Road...9, 19, 69, 111
King Edward Grammar School...107
King George VI Club...44
King George VI Fund...117
King's College Hospital...94
King's Messengers...23
Kingston, Bishop of...17, 20, 21, 60, 65, 67, 69, 70, 71, 76, 113, 120
Kirby, Joan...85, 90, 98, 102, 106
Kitchen, David...12, 13, 14, 46, 83, 129, 130, 136, 137, 138
kitchens...10, 79, 128

L

Lady Florence Institute...118
Lady Margaret Hall...17
Lambert, Miss...34, 36
Lambeth Palace...11, 124
Lane, Rev John...11, 12, 14, 22, 24, 25, 31, 62, 66, 74, 75, 95, 100, 103, 117, 120, 121, 122, 123, 134, 138
Latch Key Project...11, 12, 33, 56, 80, 136
Lausanne Road...71
Lawrence, Lady...70

LCC, London County Council…9, 29, 31, 34, 35, 36, 69, 76, 80, 98, 113, 114, 117
League of Health and Beauty…52
Lee, May…37, 38, 102
Leek, Kitty…11, 12, 26, 27, 31, 32, 40, 41, 64, 77, 78, 97, 125, 128, 138
legacies…112, 116, 124, 127
Leicester University…92
library…31
Library Fund…117, 127, 129
Liddle Ward…75
Lindon Grove…126
Lindsay, Kate…40, 41, 68
Lloyd, Canon of Winchester…60, 72
London Bible and Domestic Female Mission…111
London Child Care Organisation…31
London Marathon…12, 130
London School for the Blind…94
London School of Economics…23, 91, 92, 108, 112
London Zoo…11, 124
Longcroft Road…9
Lord Robert's Workshop…94
Low, Miss…111, 112
Lowman, Derek…13, 15, 126, 130

M

Mafoh, Femi…33
Make do and Mend Club…52
Malvern College for Girls…80, 92, 95, 98, 105, 109
Management Committee…12
    Council…67, 113, 114, 120, 125, 128
Manchester Guardian…17
Manchester High School…101
Marks and Spencer…11, 124
Marmont Road…72, 81
Marshall, Maureen…31, 44, 52, 108
    Rt Rev Michael…63, 138
Martin, Rev Edward…62
Mary Datchelor School…59, 60, 91, 98, 100, 102
McArthur, Henrietta…9, 17, 112, 117, 127, 129
McNeil, Sharon…40
McPherson, Tania…30, 40, 75
Meals on Wheels…10, 21, 22, 43-44, 45, 87, 91, 116, 117, 133
Meeting House Lane…12, 41, 62, 80
Melanesian Mission…9, 59, 106, 111
Mercer's Company…127
Mickelfield School…80, 84, 89, 104, 107
Miller, Miss…18
Mission Work…16, 17, 19, 23, 47, 58, 59, 60, 64-67, 98, 100, 110, 111
    Children…84, 90
Monday Club…51, 134
Montgomery Campbell, Elizabeth…119, 122
moral welfare…29
Morrison, Miss…18
Mother and Toddler Club…34, 41, 73, 80, 135
Muffett, Ruth…68, 108
Munday, Doris…28
Mum's Club…23, 31, 50, 51, 88, 91, 92, 116, 134
Museum of London…11, 124

N

National Gallery…124
    Lottery Board…130
    War Savings Scheme…22
Nell Gwyn Nursery School…11, 39, 41, 126
New Cross…24
New Theatre Programme…54
New Zealand…85
Newbury School…86, 87, 97, 116
Newsletters, Peckham Settlement…11, 44, 45, 46, 68, 73, 80, 86, 104, 110, 132, 133, 136, 137
Nicholson, George…14, 96
Norland Nurses…36, 92
Northampton High School…103
Nottingham University…92
Nursery, All Nations Day…11, 40-42, 56, 80, 127, 128 136
    day…21, 36, 40-42
    education…34-42, 95
    School…21, 22, 31, 34-40, 47, 56, 75, 76, 77, 81, 87, 91, 92, 113, 116, 124, 126, 127, 134
    Committee…34, 35, 37, 38, 44, 102, 103
    Nell Gwyn…11, 12, 39, 41, 126
Nutt, Miss…99, 111

O

Ofsted…42, 136
Ogilvie, Lady Anne…22, 61
Old Girls…20, 23, 55, 56, 98, 99, 100, 103
Old Girls Association…9, 60, 84, 85, 91, 97-98, 100, 103, 104, 105, 107, 110, 113, 114, 115, 122, 124, 127, 132
Oldham, Miss…18
Old Kent Road…71
Oliver Goldsmith Estate…25
open days…92, 104, 105
Open Door Housing Trust…12, 57
    Mental Health…23
O'Reilly, Deirdre…25
Organising Secretary…29, 36, 37, 45, 85, 91, 94, 98, 100, 101, 103, 113, 114, 117, 120
outings…44-45, 51, 88-90

P

Paice, Patty…48,72
Pankhurst, Louise…125
parties…88-90
Patron…10, 61, 114, 122, 131, 133
Patten, Chris…12
PDCCA, Peckham and Dulwich Caribbean Community Association…11, 39, 78, 126
Peckham Dramatic and Opera Society…117

Manor School...86
Mirror...11, 62, 74, 122
Park School...23, 30, 79, 85, 94
Project...11, 26, 48
Properties...96
Road...9, 19, 20, 65, 69, 110, 113
Varieties...54
Youth Project...11, 32, 33, 56
Pembroke House...17
Pentacostal churches...67
pensioners...10, 29, 30, 45, 52, 54, 56, 77, 78, 84, 87, 88, 89, 91, 93, 97, 105, 126, 133, 134, 135, 136
Perse School...96
Phillips, Mike...39
pickle factory...71, 72, 82
Pickstone, Dr Martin...11, 77, 123, 124, 135, 138
Pilgrim Trust...58, 112
Pincott, Hilary...86
Pitt Street...12, 17, 20, 124, 127-128
Pittard, Mary...11, 28-30, 78, 128
Plant, Ruth...108
Playing in the Park Scheme...11, 31, 32
play schemes...12, 31-33
Plough Redemption Foundation Trust...12, 33, 67
Plowden Report...39, 119
police...12, 32, 48, 49, 52, 56, 57, 105, 127, 128, 130
Poor Man's Lawyer...49
Pop in Centre...12, 54
Potter, Canon George...10
poverty...21, 24, 28-31, 42, 58, 66, 84, 127
prayer...58, 59, 60, 66
Pre-school education...33-42, 95
President...10, 17, 20, 29, 76, 95, 101, 113, 122, 128
Prince of Wales Fund...23
Princess Alice...71
Princess Christian...9, 20
Princess Elizabeth Flag Day...38
Princess Helena College...18, 104, 110
Princess Margaret...10, 11, 12, 28, 38, 40, 48, 56, 61, 79, 102, 109, 114, 122, 131-137
Provident Collecting Scheme...22
Public Health Department...29
Putney High School...52

Q

Queen Alexandra Day Fund...117
Queen Mary...10, 20, 68, 69, 134
Quesnal...9, 111

R

Ramsgate...44, 45, 55
Rank Organisation...124
Ranyard Nurses...111
Religion...58-67
residents...28, 35, 40, 42, 45, 55, 56, 58-67, 70, 72, 74, 80, 90, 91, 92, 95, 112, 116, 120, 123
Rest Room...10, 66, 77, 132
Richards, Christine...11, 25, 49, 50, 128
Right to Read Campaign...31
Roan School...112
Robinson, Archibald...70
Rochester, Bishop of...17
Rochester and Southwark Diocese Church Trust...112
Roedean School...20, 95, 97
Roffen, Rt Rev Randall Davidson...17
Rotherhithe Settlement...17
Royal College of Nursing...92
Royal Commonwealth Society...11, 97
Royal Festival Hall...10, 13, 60, 61, 115, 132
Runcie, Rt Rev Robert...63
Ruri-Decanal Conference...9, 59
Rye Annexe...41

S

Safety Valve Group...49
St Alban's School...95
St Andrew's Church...9, 57, 59, 72, 111
St Bartholomew's School...89
St Batholomew's Hospital...94
St Bernard's School...18
St Chrysostom's Church...9, 10, 45, 59, 62, 72, 78, 115
St George's Church...17
St Hilda's Settlement...83, 129
St John's Ambulance...44, 45
St John's Church...11, 12, 57, 62, 63, 64, 67, 78, 134
St John's College...16
St Jude's Church...16 , 62
St Mark's Church...9, 10, 17, 19, 22, 59, 61, 72, 98, 99, 100, 111, 115
St Martin's in the Fields...59
St Mary's and St Anne's School...93, 105, 112
St Mungo's Charity...23
St Saviour and St. Olave's School...133
St Swithun's School...55, 75, 98, 104, 115
Samaritan Outreach...56
Schools Council...96
Schools Liaison Committee...11
Group...104, 105
Officer...85, 96, 100, 101, 122
Scout Movement...23
Sembal Trust...46, 119
Serle, Joan...36, 87, 134
Settlement Development Working Party....24
Sexeys School...104
Sexual Abuse Support Association...56
Sheppard, The Very Reverend David...122, 138
shop, second-hand...11, 28-30, 78, 116, 123, 128
travelling...29
Shove, Miss Dorothy...20, 66
Silverthorne School...91
Simpson, Rev Bertram...66, 115, 133, 138
Singer, Dr H...58
Singerman, Gladys...119
Skinner, Bettie...38, 39, 102
Smith, Ann...83

George…12, 30, 74, 75, 83
Smith's Charity…117, 124, 128
Smyth, Bob…22
Snowden, Mrs…109
social action centre…16, 20, 24
activities…48, 50-54, 55, 58, 65, 80, 83, 93
needs…21, 45-50, 94
service…23, 24, 57, 60, 85, 93, 100, 105
work…23, 24, 66, 93, 94, 95, 108
worker…24, 80, 90, 93, 97, 108, 118
Social Service Conferences…9, 23, 46, 64, 93, 94-95, 105, 120, 122
Sohna, Babs…56, 136
Sojourner Truth Youth Association…54
Soldiers and Sailors Families Association…23
Soldiers and Sailors Help Society…23
South London Church Fund…18
South London Film Society…13
South London Home for Donkeys and Ponies…127
South London Press…133, 134, 135
Southwark, Asylum Seeker's Project…57
Bishop of…9, 17, 20, 58, 60, 67, 69, 112, 113, 114, 120, 125
Cathedral…10, 11, 59, 60, 61, 62
Childminding Assocaition…56
Civic Award…12
Community Affairs…128
Community Survey…42
Councillor…96
Infotech Centre…96
Institute…41
Leisure and Recreation Fund…128
London Borough of …10, 25, 26, 32, 40, 41, 42, 74, 81, 82, 118, 123, 124, 125, 126, 127, 128
Mayor of…11, 40, 128, 135, 136
Police and Community Consultative Group…56
Race Equality Unit…126
Residents Group…25
Service Scheme…11, 24, 41, 46-47, 66, 106, 123, 129
Summer Holiday Project…12, 21, 128
Travellers Action Group…12, 57
Wildlife Group…22
Youth Project…32, 50
S-W London Institute of Social Work Training…95
Squirrels Youth Club…52, 53
Stacey, Meg…93
Staffordshire Street…9, 10, 11, 13, 31, 58, 65, 68, 69, 74, 75, 82, 113
Stannard, Rt Rev…138
Stockwood, Rt Rev Mervyn…62, 63, 134, 138
Stones…116
Streatham Hill School…18
Street, Miss…138
Sunday Cinema Grant…117
Sunday Club…54
Supporting Schools…9, 39, 56, 59, 60, 62, 67, 77, 84-90, 111-115, 117, 121, 124, 127, 129
Surbiton School…18
Sure Start…57
Sydenham High School…80, 87, 89, 95, 103, 104, 127, 134

T

Talbot, Bishop…9, 17, 22, 58, 59, 64, 99, 110, 138
House Mission…17, 20, 118, 120
Mrs…111, 138
Task Force…26, 74
tenants associations…21, 25, 57
The Times Newspaper…22, 34, 69, 70, 93, 109
Thompson, Helen…48
Thursday Club…77, 87, 88, 89, 90, 136
Tiffin's Girls' School…100
Time and Talents Mission…17
Tower of London…11, 122
Townsend, Mrs Ursula…10, 70
Toynbee Hall…16
training, for work…20, 26-27, 50, 97
social service…21, 92-97
social work…23-24, 92-97
teacher and nursery…36, 38, 40, 92-97
spiritual…21, 58, 59, 64-67, 92
TEC, Training Enterprise Council…27
Triple S Scheme…11, 24, 41, 46-47, 66, 106, 123, 129
Tuesday Club…52
Turner, Isobel…35, 124
Turning Point Apprentice…11, 24

U

UGS, United Girls Schools…11, 20, 42, 58, 59, 60, 64, 65, 70, 76, 78, 92, 98, 100, 101, 102, 103, 106, 108, 113, 114, 119
History of…18
Minibus…31, 115
Mission…9, 10, 64-67
Record…9, 17, 23, 37, 45, 55, 69, 71, 77, 78, 85, 86, 88, 91, 103, 115, 116, 131, 132, 134
Review…11, 29, 38, 46, 47, 56, 77, 87, 91, 92, 94, 103, 119, 120
UGSM, United Girls Schools Mission…9, 14, 19, 22, 59, 64, 84, 98, 100, 102, 105, 113
UGSS United Girls Schools Settlement…14, 98, 104, 112, 114
UGSSS, United Girls Schools for Social Service…9, 10, 19, 71, 108, 113, 131
unemployment…15, 21, 22, 25, 26-27, 49, 50, 57, 58
Unemployment Insurance Scheme…22
Urban Studies Centre…11,14, 80, 95-96, 103, 104, 122, 124
US, United Settlement…108

V

Veasey, Rev Harry…9, 10, 18, 19, 21, 22, 23, 28, 42, 58, 59, 71, 91, 92, 99, 100, 105, 106, 110, 112, 113, 138

Vickery, Ann...95
Victoria and Albert Museum...11, 124
Vietnemese Elder Persons Group...54
Vietnamese Employment Bureau...27
Visions Youth Club...49
visiting...21, 45-47, 74, 80, 84, 85, 91-92
Voluntary Work...23, 26, 29, 46, 48, 52, 55, 58, 101, 102, 108, 109, 119, 123, 126
Volunteers...13, 15, 24, 29, 30, 31, 32, 40, 43, 44, 45, 46, 47, 49, 50, 56, 57, 65, 74, 80, 81, 85, 91, 92, 116, 117, 125, 127, 128

W

Waggitt, Susan...44, 52, 72, 74, 91, 92, 108
Waite, Theo...29, 37, 45, 60, 91, 103, 115, 117
Walthamstow Hall School...80, 89, 104
Walworth...17
Ward, Mr Heaton...43
Warden, Rev Richard...109
Warwick Park School...85
Watson, Charles Lisle...20, 127
Wednesday Club...11, 30, 52, 53, 127
welfare work...94
Weller, Peggy...84
Welsh, Mary...38, 44, 66, 74, 103
Weslyan Chapel...68, 70, 78
Wesleyan Day School...9, 70, 82
Westminster Abbey...61, 122
Whale, Florrie...38, 51, 52, 77, 87, 88, 130, 137, 138
Whinney, Rev Michael...138
Whitelaw, Miss...22, 85, 98
Wildlife Area...22
    Garden...72
    London Trust...22
Williamson, Miss...18, 84, 99, 110
Willoughby, Dr Gertrude...10, 28, 69, 71, 113, 138
Willowbrook...11, 96
Wilson, Des...61
Wilson, Mrs...99
Wilson's School...85
Wimbledon School...18
Winceby House School...90
Windsor Great Park...104, 127
Wolfson Foundation...124
Women, Chruch Work for...94, 103
Women's Committee Support Unit...40, 125
Women's Voluntary Service...23
Woodford School...85
Woolwich, Bishop of...20, 62, 67, 78, 99
Work and School Project...26
Wraight, Peggy...51, 54
Wright, Susan...53, 91, 107
Wycombe Abbey Gazette...42, 56, 82, 86, 89, 102, 107, 114
Wycombe Abbey School...9, 14, 18, 22, 29, 36, 45, 56, 59, 70, 75, 76, 80, 84, 85, 86, 89, 90, 93, 95 98, 99, 101, 104, 106, 109, 110, 111, 115, 117, 122, 127, 132
Wycombe Abbey Seniors...29, 36, 45, 51, 53, 56, 66, 70, 80, 82, 84, 85, 86, 97, 98, 99, 102, 106, 107, 111, 114, 122, 128

Y

Youth, Acorn Youth Club...49
    Bird in the Bush Club...49
    British Council...96
    club...9, 21, 23, 39, 40, 47, 48-50, 51, 54, 77, 78, 80, 91, 135
    Drama...51
    Project...11, 32, 33, 50
    Travellers' Group...57
    Work...26, 48-49, 125